D1549851

BLOCKADE

BLOCKADE

BERLIN AND THE COLD WAR

BY

ERIC MORRIS

VICTORIAN (& MODERN HISTORY)
BOOK CLUB
Newton Abbot 1974

To my father

CONTENTS

LIST OF ILLUSTRATIONS

between pages 54 & 55

MAPS

(drawn by Patrick Leeson)

ACKNOWLEDGEMENTS

This book owes much to many people: to Professor Michael Howard for his help and advice in the formative stages; to Murray Forsythe and the Department of European Politics at Leicester University; to John Garnett and the Department of International Politics, University College, Aberystwyth; and to David Chandler and my colleagues in the Department of War Studies at the Royal Military Academy, Sandhurst.

The manuscript was typed intelligently and accurately by Sue Gordon, whose husband Allan played no small part in deciphering my writing. Colonel Allan Shepperd and the library staff at Sandhurst have been especially helpful, as has the library at the International Institute for Strategic Studies in London. My gratitude also to the Press Department of the Embassy of the Federal Republic of Germany for making available so many documents.

The photographs have been provided by the British Army Public Relations Staff in West Berlin and by two Army friends, Captains Don Gordon and Peter Ashton-Wickett.

Christopher Sinclair-Stevenson and Alan Dingle read the manuscript in whole; their constructive comments and advice have improved the text considerably.

Finally, a special thank you to my wife Pamela for all her patience and spiritual sustenance during the writing of this book.

C.E.M.

Sandhurst, July 1972

Part One

I

A CHRONICLE OF WAR

THE AUTUMN of 1942 marked the turn of the tide for the Allies in the war against Nazi Germany. During October and November the German Army reached the limits of its advance, and from that time on would be fighting in defence, a role in which it had hitherto had little experience. No longer would the crushing Goliath of the Panzer divisions move forward supported by an all-powerful Luftwaffe; the German forces were now generally suffering from extended lines of communication, a lack of air support and insufficient fuel to allow them to deploy tactically in their usual manner.

The Allied counter-offensive began on the night of 23 October 1942, as 884 pieces of artillery hurled their shells on the German positions at El Alamein. For ten days the two armies fought a vicious but conventional infantry battle, with all the characteristics of a Flanders. But by 4 November the breakthrough had been achieved, and the Eighth Army rolled forward slowly; even so, Rommel reacted quickly and saved as much as he could from the wreckage. Indeed, the long battle had so exhausted the victors that a complete triumph eluded them. However, within a few days of El Alamein, the whole German position in North Africa was made strategically untenable by the successful landings of American and British troops along the coastline of French North Africa, the object being to trap Rommel between the Eighth Army and the forces advancing from the West. Once North Africa had been liberated it was to be used as the springboard for the assault into Europe.

November 1942 was indeed a black month for the Wehrmacht; trapped in North Africa by a great pincer movement, it was also to suffer grievous losses on the Eastern Front. For by the 21st of the month, General Von Paulus's Sixth Army had been crushed at Stalingrad. The Russians, however, argue that Stalingrad was not the real turning point of their war against Germany; for them, possibly, their great winter offensive of 1942 had a deeper significance. That offensive, in the Ukraine, had proved tactically indecisive; it had begun well but with the onset of the spring thaw it had lost momentum, and the Germans had recovered much of the lost ground. However, its real importance lay in its impact on the morale of the Russian people. These early successes proved that a victory was indeed possible against the hitherto infallible German military juggernaut. This conviction, now firmly imprinted on Russian minds, certainly prepared the way for the stout resistance of the people and the army at Stalingrad. The battle for that city, at least in its early stages, had been fought defensively by the Russians. The Red Army had been in retreat since the summer of 1941; Smolensk, Leningrad, Moscow, the Caucasus and Kursk had been milestones along the path that led to the great last stand at Stalingrad. In spite of the unfavourable outcome for them of this initial period of the war, the Russian High Command had at last begun to recognize the fundamental error of military strategy that it was making, namely an overestimation of the capabilities of its own troops coupled with an underestimation of enemy potential, particularly the mobility of the Panzer divisions.

By the autumn of 1942, however, the High Command was well on the way to mastering the fundamentals of a successful strategic defensive. Stubborn resistance along the fortified perimeter on the outskirts of Stalingrad exhausted the spearhead Panzers of Von Paulus's Sixth Army by the end of October. Then in early November, as the temperature dropped and ice began to appear on the Volga, the Russians counter-attacked on three fronts, and twenty-two German divisions were encircled.

The remaining weeks of the fierce Russian winter of 1942 saw the death throes of the Sixth Army. Denied their only salvation, a concerted breakout on a short front, the beleaguered garrison were ordered by OKW[1] to dig in and await the relieving force of Field Marshal Von Manstein's Fourth Panzer

[1] German Supreme Command.

Army, with the 57th Panzer Corps (commanded by General Hoth) as vanguard.

The Russians resisted superbly; their tactical exploitation of German weaknesses was of a high standard. When General Hoth was within forty miles of Stalingrad, the Russians counter-attacked: Marshal Zhukov launched a massive offensive along the middle Don and tore a sixty-mile gap in the front held by the Italian Eighth Army. To stem this Russian flood Von Manstein had no alternative but to use the Sixth Panzer division, an essential part of the Corps commanded by Hoth. The final stages of the German thrust for Stalingrad witnessed a brilliant deployment of Russian armour. The speed and concentration of the Russian tanks decimated the German Panzers and by the end of December all hope for Von Paulus's Sixth Army was lost. On 21 January 1943, Von Paulus, who had been promoted to Field Marshal only the day before, surrendered. The Germans lost 60,000 vehicles, 1,500 tanks and 6,000 guns. Of the 280,000 men originally encircled, only 42,000 were air-lifted out: 91,000 surrendered.

The year 1943 saw a gathering of momentum in the assault against Germany itself. In the air, the great bombing offensive against the heart of German industry began to assume an ordered pattern, of destruction and disruption of the enemy economy. In the early spring and summer, the Ruhr was constantly attacked by the Royal Air Force, and in May the Mohne and Eder Dams were destroyed in a daring raid by 613 Squadron. The first attack on Berlin came as early as January 1943—thus all the boastings of Goering were revealed at their true value to the unimpressed Berliners. The air offensive assumed even greater intensity when the US Eighth Air Force began its regular daylight precision bombing. However, all this proved but a foretaste of what was to come. In July, Hamburg was devastated by Allied strategic bombers, which kept up a day and night attack; 40,000 people were killed, the vast majority in the 'fire storm' of 28 July, and a million fled the city. Economically speaking, Hamburg was knocked out of the war. For the first time in the war the spectre of possible defeat was brought home to the German people. Stalingrad had been a major disaster, and the Germans had solemnly observed state mourning. But Stalingrad was on the Volga, hundreds of miles away, while Hamburg was on the Elbe, in the heart of Germany.

The lesson was further brought home to the Germans when the so-called 'Battle for Berlin' got under way in the late summer. Three fierce raids were mounted against the city, resulting in heavy damage and a wholesale exodus of the populace. Once again this was only the dress rehearsal. Despite appalling weather conditions, the main bombing offensive against the capital was mounted in the winter of 1943. Berlin suffered heavily; 74,000 people were killed and 3,000,000 made homeless, with 5,000 acres of the city completely devastated. Only the redirection of Bomber Command's energies, against the strategic targets of Operation Overlord, gave the city of Berlin time to make good its losses and prepare for the next onslaught.

The strategic situation and balance of forces which emerged at the end of the war in Europe was the direct result of the decisions taken before Operation Overlord on the deployment of Western armies in the reconquest of Europe. For, as the war in North Africa came to its end, a bitter debate began to develop between the three war leaders on future strategy. Churchill and the British military chiefs saw the logical next step to be a major offensive against Sicily and the Italian mainland. Besides the military convenience of an onslaught against the Mediterranean littoral, there were very attractive political advantages in the possible demise of Italian Fascism. Churchill developed his grandiose schemes for Southern Europe by talking in terms of operations in the Adriatic and Yugoslavia. Despite the highly inhospitable terrain of the Dalmatian coast it was felt at the time that there would be the advantage of the active co-operation of the Yugoslav Resistance Movement. In addition, it was known that the Fascist forces of occupation in Yugoslavia were of inferior quality. The goal for major operations in Southern Europe would be the Ljubljana Gap, leading to an advance of Allied forces into the plains of Southern Austria. Whether Churchill foresaw the likely *status quo* in 1945, and the accompanying hostile attitude of Stalin, is very much open to debate. Certainly hindsight reveals more positive advantages than would have been apparent at the time in initiating such operations in the Adriatic; in terms of later developments there would also have been considerable political wisdom in mounting attacks against some of the German satellites, particularly Hungary.

However, such discussion is merely hypothetical, since Allied operations in Southern Europe, particularly after the fall of Sicily, were destined to become very much subsidiary to Operation Overlord. The Americans were influenced in their strategic thinking by a number of factors: the first was their desire to finish the war in Europe as quickly as possible, so that all their resources could be diverted to the effort against Japan. They saw this aim as being best achieved by the landing of major forces on the western coast of Europe and by marching eastwards across terrain favourable to the full exploitation of Allied supremacy in air power and armour. The close proximity of England would give the Allies an ideal base for the mounting of such operations; a short sea voyage to the invasion zone and subsequently short lines of communication to a base area, from which could be effected the necessary build-up before exploiting the initial bridgeheads. To say that the Americans failed to appreciate the potentialities of a major operation in Italy would, however, be unfair. In their case, it was purely a question of priorities. The Allies did not have sufficient resources to maintain major amphibious operations in two European theatres simultaneously, as well as maintain the momentum of advance in the Pacific and support the build-up of forces in south-east Asia. The American leaders believed that, given the forces available, a solution could best and most quickly be achieved by major operations in western Europe.

The campaign against the Germans in Italy was not totally without influence upon the major theatre of war, however. The assault began in 1943 and marked a significant occasion, the return of Allied forces to the mainland of Europe. The operations in Sicily took longer than expected, since the German reaction was swift. Consequently, when the invasion of the mainland was launched, powerful enemy resistance was encountered, whilst Allied mishandling of the details of the Italian surrender allowed the Germans to disarm the Italian divisions and at the same time retain effective control of the country.

Thus, despite the able leadership of Alexander and the military efficiency of the veteran Allied forces, the Italian campaign inevitably became a sideshow. At best, the heavy casualties and ponderous advance can be vindicated as a holding operation of significant proportions, tying down two German Armies (involving some twenty-four divisions). The two Allied Armies, the American Fifth and the British Eighth, themselves amounting to only twenty-three divisions at the end, slogged valiantly up the Italian peninsula. They were at times completely frustrated by the harshness of weather and terrain, which gave the Germans so many advantages in their defensive retreats. Other factors, such as the withdrawal of troops for Operation Overlord and later the campaign in southern France, and high casualty figures, especially among the infantry, meant that at times the offensive ground to a halt. Costly battles such as Cassino and Anzio, along with a pedantic application of the cherished doctrines of armoured warfare, which meant a ratio of armour to infantry far too high for the terrain involved, resulted in a campaign which was unimaginative and conventional, yet politically necessary. In no other campaign did the German soldier acquit himself so well in defence, and the fighting has been recognized as some of the most fierce of the war. Unfortunately, the fact that this campaign became so much a secondary one to Operation Overlord must deny it further treatment in this account. Had Churchill's strategy been adopted in the Adriatic, then the events surrounding Berlin in the post-war period would have turned out rather differently. As it was, the major Allied campaigns, involving the American and British forces advancing from the west and the Russian juggernaut from the east, had the greatest influence on the future of the city.

The Germans still held vast areas of Russia, but Stalingrad had weakened them. The reasons for their failure there were many and complex. Hitler had invaded Russia with a fine flourish of optimistic ignorance. He had allowed his armament industries to languish, rather than attempt to equip his troops properly. Anticipating a quick victory, he had not prepared for the Russian winter. He had attacked without a definite plan and when one more major offensive towards Moscow might have given him decisive victory he had turned aside for a quick, cheap success in the Ukraine. In 1942 he had ignored the advice of his leading generals to chase the undefeated Russian armies and had preferred the illusory rewards of economic conquest. Also to be reckoned with was the Communist governmental machine; all-powerful, highly centralised and utterly unscrupulous, it ruled a tough and numerous people. Most daunting of all, Russia was an apparently limitless country, with few and primitive roads.

Hitler's military mistakes were compounded by his political errors. There were many regions under Russian control which had welcomed the Germans as deliverers, not only the Baltic States but also White Russia, the Ukraine and the Caucasus. But as the Wehrmacht moved on to fresh conquests they handed effective government of the subjugated territories over to the puppets of the Nazi Party machine. Hence many a potentially friendly Russian citizen was misgoverned into joining partisan groups.

Large-scale guerrilla activity was a notable characteristic of the Russian campaign. Initially these were nothing more than substantial by-passed bands of Russian infantry and as such were easily located and destroyed by the Germans. But by the end of 1942 the guerrillas had developed a high degree of professionalism. They operated in small, highly-skilled bands against the German communications system, with great success. From 1942 the Russian government took energetic measures to co-ordinate guerrilla activity with army offensives, and frequently supplied them by air.

The German army was also seriously handicapped by Hitler's policy of 'divide and rule'. The Wehrmacht generals were never trusted to the full by Hitler and their degree of control was consequently severely limited. In addition, the so-called 'élite' units of the SS and Luftwaffe field forces, besides being singled out for the best and first of everything, also had the right of direct appeal to their respective chiefs, Himmler and Goering, when they were dissatisfied. Hence a Wehrmacht general often found that a united, fully-integrated command became impossible, since it might threaten the happiness of these two private armies. The Luftwaffe in general was also open to criticism. Like the Wehrmacht, it had not been intelligently equipped or organized for this campaign. It lacked a powerful strategic counter-force capable of attacking Russian munition

centres far behind the front line. There was also a shortage of
large and fast transport aircraft capable of neutralizing the vast
communications problem posed by the wastes of the Steppes.

All these factors taken together, plus the decisive drawback
that the war was being fought on two fronts, would seem to
suggest that, once the Russians began their major offensive
along the five hundred miles of the Don front and Anglo-
American forces struck eastwards across occupied Europe, the
end was surely in sight for Nazi Germany.

During the autumn of 1943 the Russians stepped up the
momentum of their general offensive. Stalingrad had given
them heart and hope, and the Germans never really made up
for what they had lost. Though the Russians did not always
have unalloyed success, their great numerical superiority enabled them to deliver a succession of massive offensives against
widely-separated sectors of the German front. When successful,
these enveloped and destroyed considerable enemy forces;
when repulsed, the Russians merely attacked elsewhere. They
used masses of tanks and men, backed by enormous concentrations of artillery. Generally, Soviet equipment was inferior to
that of the Germans. The Russian T34 tank was fast, manoeuv-
rable and well suited to offensive armoured warfare, but compared with most modern German designs it was undergunned
and often needed superior numbers to outmatch opposition.
The Russians quickly appreciated that sheer quantity of tanks,
through standardization of this simple design, was the only way
to balance the firepower and quality of the German Panzer.
Also, in the human battering-rams of the Russian divisions,
appalling losses were accepted stoically. The open terrain of the
Russian Steppes afforded few natural defensive positions, and
though the great Panzer generals such as Manstein and Kluge
handled their dwindling forces superbly, the very fact that they
were forced to shift rapidly from one crisis to the next soon wore
down the armoured units. With the storm gathering in the
west, the eastern forces were always hard put to make good
their losses.

In the late autumn the German forces fell back in an orderly
manner to the line of the Dnieper River. The west bank of the
river was unfortified and ungarrisoned. (Hitler opposed the
construction of rear defence positions, claiming that it made his

generals less aggressive.) Consequently, Russian spearheads were able to seize and consolidate small bridgeheads in the area of Kiev. The Germans contained these but were unable to liquidate them, the Russian skill in defending such positions being legendary.

The closing weeks of 1943 saw the Russians trying to emulate previous successes by capitalizing on winter conditions with new offensives. At first their attempts to break out of their Dnieper bridgeheads were bloody failures, but their huge predominance in armour and artillery and their brutal 'human wave' tactics eventually wore down German resistance. By the end of the year Kiev and Smolensk were once more in Russian hands and the central offensive was within 150 miles of the Polish frontier. In the north, although Leningrad was still in Russian hands, the front remained fairly static, whilst in the far south a German salient stubbornly denied the Russians the Crimea.

The Russians now abruptly shifted their attention to the Leningrad sector. In the spring of 1943 the Russians had finally lifted the siege of that city. They had traded 270,000 casualties for a corridor six miles wide along Lake Ladoga into Leningrad. For the remainder of 1943 things had been static; the German Eighteenth Army had become complacent, and most of its reserves had been stationed elsewhere. Now, in January 1944, the Baltic front exploded into action as eight Russian armies backed by vast quantities of artillery poured across the ice of the frozen Gulf of Finland. Surprise was total and the German lines were quickly penetrated. Nonetheless, they rallied quickly and, aided by an unexpected thaw, held the Russians fifty miles south of the city.

It was now that the colossal dimensions of the Russian war machine became manifest. For as the German Army Group North concentrated their reserves for what they believed would be a continuation of the Russian offensive along the Baltic Front, the major Russian effort was in fact concentrated on the south. Late in January the four Ukrainian and Russian armies attacked simultaneously in a giant pincer movement, and trapped two German Corps. Weather and exhaustion prevented German counter-attacks from relieving their hard-pressed troops in the salient. As the thaws of March set in, the beleaguered German Corps broke out, but they left a quarter of their number and all their precious artillery as a prize for the Russians.

With only a short break in order to re-form, the Russians continued the pressure on the weakening Ukrainian front, where despite the rapid thaw, the greater flotation of their broad-tracked tanks and American-built trucks enabled them to keep up a furious pursuit of the Germans. The First Panzer Army was isolated and Hitler ordered it to stand its ground and fight; Manstein remonstrated against such futile instructions and was dismissed. Nevertheless, the Panzers, under their one-armed commander, General Hube, remained concentrated and moved at will behind the Russian front, causing havoc to the communications networks. A local offensive by the Fourth Panzer Army drove eastwards in an attempt to extricate the weakening First Army. Hube attacked westwards, fighting front, flank and rear, and brought his command out with practically all its equipment intact. From mid-April on the central Front stabilized.

The tremendous advantage that the Russians had in artillery and their increased skill in its deployment and use is aptly illustrated by their April offensive in the Crimea. The Russians fought a holding action against the Wehrmacht divisions in the front, whilst throwing the main weight of their offensive against the weaker Rumanian forces of the Seventeenth Army. Within a week the Germans, outflanked, were forced back within the Sevastopol fortifications. On 7 May they were attacked by the Russians, who were supported by 300 guns for every mile of front. Against such crushing weight of artillery, the German defence crumbled and the town was quickly abandoned. Sevastopol was completely in Russian hands by 9 May 1944.

At this point it is as well to examine the events in the west. The succession of stunning triumphs, from the invasion of Poland in 1939 to the victorious summer of 1942, which made Germany practically the masters of Europe, is beyond the scope of this book. But, as has been stated, by August 1942 the high tide of German aggression had been reached. With the United States in the war, her vast military and industrial resources had already provided substantial aid to Russia and Britain. Mention has already been made of the inexorable Russian resurgence and the succession of Allied victories in the Mediterranean.

Now, in the high summer of 1944, a large Allied force stood poised in England ready to invade France, while fleets of bombers rained destruction on the German homeland.

An essential prerequisite to the build-up of Allied forces for the invasion of Europe was the mastery of the sea routes of the Atlantic. The Battle of the Atlantic was one of the war's most critical battles, and statistics reveal by how narrow a margin the Allies won. For it was not until 1943 that the Allied navies succeeded in countering the German submarine menace, to the extent that new ship construction tonnage exceeded the tonnage of ships sunk. From that date onward, Allied superiority was maintained, in spite of German efforts to reverse the tide by increased production of improved submarines. Ultimately, the battle was won by such measures as the employment of escort carriers with convoys, air–sea co-operation, improved radar, and the bombing or capture of submarine bases.

Whilst this battle was still at its height, an invasion force was being gathered in England. As far back as June 1942 the United States had established the European Theatre of Operations and had sent a little-known general, Dwight D. Eisenhower, to London to command it. Originally it was planned to mount an invasion along the Atlantic seaboard of France in 1943, but events in the Mediterranean caused its delay. Disagreements over strategy were hammered out in the series of Allied conferences at Casablanca, Quebec, Cairo and Teheran. Finally in February 1944 the original planning group was absorbed into Supreme Headquarters Allied Expeditionary Force (SHAEF) and Eisenhower was recalled from his relatively successful command in the Mediterranean to assume control in Europe; Montgomery was to lead the ground forces. During the next three months the operation, given the code name 'Overlord', was planned. When it emerged in its final form, Operation Overlord involved a five-division amphibious assault supported by airborne landings. The landing zones were to be the beaches on the bay of the Seine at the base of the Contentin Peninsula. More than 2,750,000 men, divided into forty-five divisions, were assembled in England. The task of equipping and supplying this tremendous force was staggering, and it was only achieved by practically converting the United Kingdom into a huge military base.

In the months leading up to the invasion date of June 1944, the combined bomber offensive was intensified and tactical air forces struck at German defences and communications in France. The weight of strategic air power was added for strikes at bridges, roads and railways leading to lodgement areas. By the time of the invasion, Normandy was virtually isolated.

For the Germans, this period seemed full of foreboding. There was little doubt in the minds of the Wehrmacht that the Allies would mount a major landing somewhere in Western Europe. However, the question was where along the vast Atlantic wall of Fortress Europe this blow would fall. Rommel believed that the Pas de Calais was the obvious target, but conceded that this might well be followed up by supplementary landings elsewhere. Many in OKW feared the Dutch or Belgian coastline, whilst Hitler was constantly looking over his shoulder at the mountain expanses of Norway, or even Denmark.

This much-vaunted Fortress Europe boasted fifty-eight divisions in France and the Low Countries, six in Denmark and, to add greater emphasis to the Führer's belief, twelve crack Wehrmacht divisions were concentrated in the bleak wastes of Norway. Yet all was not as it should be with the German forces in Western Europe. They were suffering from the effects of the malpractice which bedevilled the German forces in Russia, the tripartite fragmentation of Wehrmacht, SS, and Luftwaffe. In addition, the divisions of the Wehrmacht were in considerable confusion; many were below strength and inadequately equipped and at best could only be considered as second-line troops.

The strategy of defence caused much contention. Von Rundstedt, who commanded OB West, believed in tightly-held coastal areas with mobile striking forces of armour held in readiness further back. Rommel, fearful of Allied air attack, wanted a powerful coastal defence backed up by strong local reserves. Hitler vacillated between the two and came down on the side of neither. This conflict was especially relevant to the deployment of the élite Panzer divisions. Rommel knew that if the Allied beachheads were to be smashed before they could be built into secure bridgeheads from which offensives might be launched, the Panzers would have to be stationed near the beaches. OKW were given the final authority as to their positioning, and came down on the side of Von Runstedt's doctrine of a mobile reserve; but, as Rommel well knew, their use in battle from these positions demanded as a pre-condition German air superiority.

Nor was the famed 'Atlantic Wall' particularly strong. Since December 1943 Rommel had made tremendous progress towards its improvement, yet by the late spring of 1944, according to Von Runstedt, these coastal fortifications were 'sheer humbug'. Some of the coastal cities like Cherbourg were garrisoned by fanatically loyal troops under orders to resist to the last—an utter waste of valuable resources. In short, Von Rundstedt was ill-prepared to resist the massive Allied assault. The Allies did not know this, but had wisely prepared to meet a typically professional defence.

The major factors influencing the selection of the date and hour of the landings in Normandy were tidal conditions (this was important because of possible German beach obstacles), the necessity of moonlight for airborne drops, and acceptable weather. After much deliberation the period from 5 to 7 June was selected. The troops were already embarked and preparations initiated for a landing on the 5th when unfavourable weather forecasts forced Eisenhower to postpone the operation. As the weather continued to deteriorate, the general was faced with the agonising choice between a second postponement or going ahead, in the hope that a slight moderation in the gales would allow the landings to take place. The loneliness of command must now have struck Eisenhower with full force, for the final decision was his alone to make. Still unhappy with the weather prospects, but aware of the even greater disadvantages of postponement, he made that decision in the early hours of 5 June, and designated D-Day as the following day.

Shortly before midnight on the 5th, airborne units began taking off for their assaults, which had been timed for the early hours of 6 June. Elements of three airborne divisions formed the vanguard of the assault on Western Europe. The US 82nd Airborne, now recovered from the disasters of Sicily, were to establish a bridgehead across the Merderet River; the 101st Airborne were to secure the exits to the beach code-named 'Utah', in order to support the landings of the 4th Division. The British 6th Airborne had the task of capturing the crossing of the Orne River, to protect the Allied flank.

Troops from five divisions, British, American and Canadian, made the amphibious assault, swarming ashore after heavy air bombardment and naval gunfire. The landings came as a complete surprise to the Germans. Aerial attacks and subterfuge had neutralized their radar screen, whilst the beach garrisons considered the weather too rough for a landing. The German chain of command was caught completely off guard and this initial confusion was exacerbated by the stubborn refusal of OKW to believe the reports of the local commanders, that these were the *main* landings. The full fury of the Allied assault fell upon the divisions of the German LXXXIV Corps, and by the end of D-Day the Allies had established their beachheads. Only one counter-attack was made by the harassed Germans: the 21st Panzer Division struck against British forces north of Caen, but this assault was broken up by Allied air attacks and supporting artillery fire.

By the end of the first day the Allies had in fact nowhere reached their planned objectives. But except for Omaha Beach, where the Americans were pinned down by the enemy, who covered the two beach exits for many hours, they had firm footholds. The greatest initial success was achieved in the British zone where, landing in great force and against moderate opposition, their troops had made sizeable gains.

Between 6 and 12 June the Allies built up their beachhead strength to sixteen divisions and feverishly poured supplies ashore. Intensive Allied air attacks caused heavy enemy losses and severely restricted the movement of German reinforcements as they tried to concentrate.

The initial logistic support of the invasion was to be across the beaches. The Allies had constructed an extremely efficient type of artificial harbour called 'Mulberry'. There were two such installations, one for the British, the other for the Americans, each with an unloading capacity of 6,000 tons a day. But as the Allied beachheads expanded inland it became essential for a major port to be captured and its installations utilized. Such a port was Cherbourg, and the need to capture it became even more urgent when the Mulberry being used by the Americans was destroyed in a particularly heavy storm less than four days after the first landings.

General Montgomery says in his memoirs that 'Caen was the

key to Cherbourg'. Certainly operations in the two areas were very closely related. The capture of Caen would reduce the movement of Germans into the peninsula, free British forces for a move westwards and release more Americans for action in the Cotentin Peninsula. A spirited British offensive in the direction of Caen soon became bogged down in the infamous *bocage* country of that region. Normandy could have been specially constructed for defensive operations—its ditches and sunken roads, together with its numerous hedgerows, were natural obstacles to mechanised warfare. Montgomery called a halt to the offensive and intended instead to institute 'active static warfare', whereby he would attract the bulk of the Germans into his front and so ease the situation for the Americans. But the latter had by now succeeded in finding the formula for effective action in the *bocage*, by driving forward on narrow fronts with reserves in depth. In response to adverse American comment Montgomery re-instituted a major offensive, this time backed by heavy air support, in the direction of Caen; but again he was bogged down by the German defence. Along the thirty-one miles of the German front the British were opposed by seven Panzer and two infantry divisions, whilst the Americans along a fifty-mile front faced the equivalent of seven infantry divisions.

The American VII Corps struck viciously at the disintegrating German defences in the Cotentin Peninsula. They reached the coast on 18 June and sealed off the peninsula. Turning north, their forces closed with the outer defences of Cherbourg ten days later. The German garrison refused the American surrender ultimatum and the city held out for five days before eventually capitulating. Unfortunately the port installations had been so thoroughly demolished that they could not be used again until 7 August. However, beach unloading at Cherbourg began on 16 July.

Whilst the Americans developed operations into the far west of France, Montgomery's attention was concentrated on the eastern flank of the Allied bridgehead. He anticipated that the Germans would develop their main defensive moves against the Allied left. The position of the Allied landing point meant that sooner or later the enemy would have to attack their flank, forming a front parallel with their own lines of communication, which ran eastward through Paris. Thus an Allied break-through at Caen could lead straight on to the German line of retreat and supply. Rommel therefore had to hold this hinge or risk annihilation.

By the beginning of July the scene was set for the Allied break-out. In the sectors against which the Americans intended to put the full weight of their armoured thrust there was only weak German infantry. It was Montgomery's task to ensure that the enemy did not transfer armour to these areas. Hence the ensuing American delay meant increased demands on the British sectors, where British and Canadian divisions stormed in against the Caen defences. Two German Corps were dug into a massive five-layered system of defences, backed by three armoured divisions and two battalions of tanks. The British, cramped by a narrow bridgehead, failed to develop their attack in its final stages. However, strategically it was successful, for the Germans were now more convinced than ever that the major offensive was still to come, with the British trying a second time to break through at Caen. So that when the Americans finally launched their offensive in late July, the enemy were caught off balance, with twenty-one American divisions set against their two Panzer and six exhausted infantry divisions in a static defensive position. Immediately before the attack the American forces in the front line were drawn back and nearly 3,000 aircraft plastered the German defences; two-thirds of the German defending division were knocked out. When the Americans at last began their push, it took them only three days to punch their way through the last of the *bocage* country. On 30 July the American First Army swept into the Avranches; beyond, lay open country stretching all the way to the Loire.

The offensive was now taken up by General Patton's newly-committed Third Army, with three fresh Corps advancing at a fast rate. The Battle of Normandy had become the Battle for France. The British broke through at Caen and moved towards Falaise. For five awful days the German Fifth Panzer and the Seventh Armies tried desperately to get out of the 'sack' they had thus found themselves in. The battle of the Falaise Gap cost the Germans 10,000 dead and 50,000 prisoners. On 15 August the Allies landed ten divisions near Cannes. The German evacuated the South of France and retreated up the Rhône Valley at speed.

Once the momentum of the Allied advance had got under way there seemed to be little the Germans could do to prevent it. They never recovered from their losses in Normandy and Western France and were not even able to hold the Allies at the Seine. The whole campaign in the West cost the Germans 500,000 casualties; 200,000 of these were incurred in the coastal fortresses. Their losses in equipment were immense.

By 19 August, the US XV Corps had seized a bridgehead across the Seine. On the same day Paris itself rose in revolt, with the Gendarmerie seizing the Île de la Cité and the Resistance fighting a pitched battle against the German garrison. By 25 August the Americans had reached the capital, the honour of the triumphal entry being given to the French Second Armoured Division. On 11 September the Allied forces from southern France linked up with the Northern Landing Groups at the Sombernon, while in northern France the British and Canadians, flushed with victory, drove hard for the Low Countries and the German frontier.

The Allied commanders had given much thought to the correct strategy to adopt for the advance against the west wall of Germany and on into the Reich itself. A massive single thrust had been ruled out, as being subject to canalization and concentrated counter-attack. The main advance, on a broad front, was to be along the Amiens–Liège–Ruhr axis, supported by a secondary effort in the direction of Verdun and Metz. However, Montgomery and Bradley considered that the Germans had been so decisively defeated in France that two single thrusts in each Army Group sector would suffice.

The British and Canadian assault on the Low Countries achieved spectacular results. General Dempsey's XXX Corps advanced with remarkable speed through Amiens and captured Brussels on 3 September. The Canadians had already been given the dubious task of driving up the coast and securing the Channel ports. German reaction to this combined attack was initially slow; Dempsey was able to capture Antwerp on 4 September. The speed of his advance was such that all the harbour installations were captured intact. At this point, however, the Germans acted: the First Parachute Army and the Fifteenth

Army raced to block the Albert Canal and the Scheldt estuary. Without access to the sea, Dempsey's victory was for the present a hollow one.

It was Patton's advance in the south that the Germans really feared and against him they concentrated the bulk of their remaining forces. Nevertheless, the American First Army under Hodges reached the German frontier on 24 September.

Montgomery still hoped to bring the war in Europe to a swift conclusion. It was to this end that Operation Market Garden was planned. The three divisions of the First Allied Airborne Army were to capture the key bridges of Holland and thus open the way for the British army to outflank the Siegfried Line. The Allied parachute drops at Eindhoven and Nijmegen secured the passage of the Maas and the Waal. It was at the third drop, that of the British Airborne at Arnhem, that this ambitious plan went astray. German response to the landing of these British paratroops, with their light equipment, was immediate and decisive. The Ninth SS Panzer Division had been re-grouping and re-equipping in the area. Within a week it was all over for the gallant British forces. They had few anti-tank weapons and were forced to break out of the German encircle-ment on the night of 25–26 September. 2,163 survivors escaped, out of the 10,000 who had originally landed; 1,130 had been killed and 6,450 captured.

Logistically the Allies were unprepared for the rapid advance to and beyond the Seine. The hampering effect of the lack of seaports and the long supply hauls slowed down their progress. The British effort to reduce the Scheldt estuary thus became even more essential for the future conduct of the war: the first ship to reach Antwerp arrived on 26 November.

Whilst the Allies tried to solve their supply problems, Von Rundstedt drew his shattered armies together and stabilized a defensive line along the western frontier of the Reich—the so-called 'West Wall'.

Allied strategy for the winter of 1944 was aimed at maintain-ing the offensive. Montgomery in the north was to make a thrust towards the Rhine; this would be supported by Bradley's First Army drive towards Cologne. By the middle of October 1944 Eisenhower realized that Montgomery, burdened with the Scheldt operation, was too weak to maintain the main Allied offensive against the Rhine as well. Bradley's northern armies were thus given the main task of the November offensive; Montgomery, Patton and Devers (in the far south) were to make secondary efforts. All armies were to close on the Rhine and seize bridgeheads. Ultimately Eisenhower hoped to shift the main effort back north to Montgomery's section in order to use the better avenue of approach into Germany.

In the event the November offensive proved disappointing. German resistance had stiffened, especially against the Americans in and around Aachen, whilst the early onset of a hard winter created additional logistical problems for the Allies. At the same time some rather disturbing tendencies were emerging among the Allied troops. They were becoming complacent, believing the war to be nearly over, and for this understandable reason began to adopt a more relaxed approach to what they thought was to be the final stage of the conflict.

Consequently, a massive German counter-offensive on 16 December fell with devastating effect on the unprepared Allies. The attack was intended to thrust through the Ardennes and swing north-west toward Antwerp, destroying in its path Allied forces north of the line from Bastogne to Brussels and Antwerp. The Germans scored their initial success against the US VIII Corps which, strung out on a long front, was routed. However, Eisenhower took a strong grip on the situation and, very much like Joffre in 1914, gave ground rather than let his line break; the Allies thus rode the German punch like a 'seasoned prizefighter', while Eisenhower gathered together reserves. Allied resistance soon stiffened and all attention was focused on the defence of Bastogne by the 101st US Airborne. Bad weather had hitherto denied the Allies full air supremacy, but by Christmas Day this had cleared, and 5,000 aircraft took to the air against the ample target of the German armies caught in the open without air cover of their own. The Allied armies returned to the offensive and the front was stabilized.

In the last days of 1944 both sides paused a little to regroup. Then, in the New Year, the armies met head-on, as each returned to the offensive. The battle raged through the forests of the Ardennes, but the Allied assault had more substance and within a week the German armies were exhausted. By the end of the second week in January they had conceded defeat and were in general retreat towards the Ardennes. Allied casualties had been heavy, nearly 80,000, but the last reserves of the Wehrmacht had been destroyed. The twenty-six divisions in the Ardennes had bought six weeks more life in the west for the Nazi régime, but there were insufficient resources to beat the perfectly-timed Russian winter offensive in the east, which clearly caught the Germans off balance.

While the Americans and British had worked on the final preparations for Operation Overlord, the Soviet armies were poised along Russia's 1939 western frontier. The summer offensive was designed to take the Russian forces into the tiny Baltic States and Poland in the north, while in the south advances were planned into Rumania and Hungary.

At the Teheran Conference of November 1943 it had been agreed that the Russians would attack on the eastern front at about the same time as the Americans and English landed in northern France, so that the two offensives would be mutually supporting. So throughout the month of June, while the Allies in the west tried to expand their Normandy bridgehead, the Russian Army bludgeoned a 250-mile gap in the German front. Russian artillery stood hub to hub and poured thousands of shells into the German defences of Fortress Europe, while their air force gained mastery of the skies above the battlefield. During this battle the Russians advanced into the Carpathian Mountains, inflicting on the Germans their worst-ever defeat; twenty-five enemy divisions were overrun. Eventually, however, as logistic problems grew, the Russian advance lost its momentum.

In July the Russians advanced in the north along the shores of the Baltic, and by August advance elements had reached the Vistula south of Warsaw. With their usual agressive spirit, these advance forces established bridgeheads on the west bank of the Vistula, and it was only at the cost of enormous casualties that the Germans were able to neutralize or contain them.

The arrival of the Russians on the Vistula was the signal for the Polish Resistance, led by General Bor Komorowski, to seize control of most of Warsaw. The ill-fated uprising of these underground forces is one of the most controversial episodes of the whole war in the east. There has been no lack of Polish, British and American writers to put a sinister interpretation on the out-

come of the incident. Immediately after the war, and throughout the Cold War, it was generally believed that the Russians,
having nominated their own Polish Communist government,
stood by cold-bloodedly as hastily-assembled SS units put down
the uprising, in a brutal house-to-house battle which lasted
more than two months. However, in recent years there has been
a more balanced attitude to the question. The Polish underground forces undoubtedly attempted to liberate their city
without prior consultation with the Russian forces. The Germans in the area were not merely second-line troops and Police
SS units (although the latter were indeed used to put down the
insurgency); they were in fact crack Panzer units. These had
been concentrated at Warsaw by Guderian, not because of any
fear of a popular uprising, but rather because the road through
Warsaw was Russia's shortest route to Germany.

The Polish Resistance began their attack when the Russians
were still twenty miles from Warsaw. It is important here to
appreciate the condition of the Russian forces at that time.
They had been continually on the offensive for two months and
had sustained more than a quarter of a million casualties during
that period. A German counter-attack, mounted by four Panzer divisions, drove the main body of Russian troops back at
least sixty miles from Warsaw, at the same time isolating the
few bridgeheads which the vanguard of the Russian advance
had seized. So even if the Russians had reacted to German
counter-pressure, it is highly unlikely that they would have
reached the Vistula in any strength before the middle of
August. At the time the Russians were bitterly criticized for
refusing the Western Allies the opportunity to send supplies
through to the beleaguered Poles. This would have necessitated
Allied aircraft landing on Russian airfields to refuel before they
could return to Western Europe.

The official Russian military answer to this request rested on
two premises. First, they doubted whether an air-drop would
have any real chance of success; the Poles held no sizeable part
of the city in any real strength and most of the supplies were
thus bound to have fallen into German hands. Secondly, with
their own front in a state of flux and their resources stretched
beyond the limit, the Russians did not, as the Russian
commander General Rokossovsky later put it, 'want any

British and American planes mucking around here at the moment'.

Also, the German Panzer general Guderian noted at the time his impression that the Russian failure to enter Warsaw was due primarily to energetic German counter-attack rather than to a desire to cripple the Polish revolt.

What is relevant to this book, though, is that the Allies in the West fervently believed that the Russians were guilty of sabotaging the Warsaw Uprising. Certainly inter-Allied co-operation received a pronounced set-back as a result of this incident, and the image of the Russians became rather more ominous in the eyes of Western public opinion.

Meanwhile, the Russian advance further south had resulted in the complete disintegration of the German flank. On 5 September 1944 the Rumanians turned their coats and went over to the Russians, and sixteen German divisions were trapped. The Russians drove south of the Carpathians towards the twin city of Budapest. The Germans frantically fortified Buda, the portion of the city on the high west bank of the Danube, since it was a natural fortress; Pest, on the flat east bank, was of little military value. German and Hungarian resistance was fanatical and the city held out until 13 February 1945.

The new year of 1945 saw the German troops on the eastern front outnumbered by a ratio of eleven to one in infantry, seven to one in tanks, and twenty to one in both artillery and aircraft. The cream of the remaining Panzers had been sent to the abortive Ardennes offensive. Meanwhile, the Anglo-American bomber offensive, by steadily wrecking the German communications and petroleum industry, had created a serious fuel shortage in the east.

Late in January Marshal Zhukov and the First White Russian Army broke out of their Baltic bridgehead east of Danzig. The Russians met fanatical resistance but nevertheless maintained the momentum of their advance until they had outrun their supply lines. On 1 February they seized bridgeheads across the Oder and paused to regroup; they were just forty-five miles from Berlin.

The German defence of East Prussia had been fierce, especially around key fortresses such as Danzig and Königsberg, but there could be no Tannenberg to restore the situation.

Thousands of Germans were successfully evacuated by sea, for the Russian Navy remained largely inoperative.

To the south, the Second and Third Ukrainian armies over-ran most of south-eastern Germany—the last major industrial area still functioning. Despite an energetic counter-attack by the Sixth Panzer Army in Hungary, the Russians retained the initiative and captured Vienna on 13 April.

II

THE BATTLE OF BERLIN

IN THE early days of 1945 all attention on the eastern front was focused on the Oder-Neisse sectors, where the Russian Army had initially followed its by now traditional procedure of securing a number of sizeable bridgeheads on the west bank of the Oder. In March, with the spring thaw, German Panzers, by now shadows of their former selves, were able to knock out a few of these bridgeheads, in some of the most frenzied fighting of the war, but did nothing materially to alter the strategic balance.

In the south the Russian advance into Austria and Czechoslovakia had been slowed down by a combination of adverse weather[1] and terrain. The mountains of south-east Europe were a major obstacle to the Russian soldier, since they demanded a technique of fighting for which he displayed neither talent or enthusiasm. In Yugoslavia, after successfully holding a combined onslaught by the Russians and their new-found allies the Bulgarians, and continually defeating the amateurish and half-hearted tactics of Tito and his partisans, the Wehrmacht in early April were forced to retreat, to conform with the strategic line of the German front in the east.

Meanwhile, back on the Oder front, the centre of gravity for the final battle, the Russians consolidated their units along the whole length of its 250 miles and made good use of the bitter winter weather to prepare for the final attack. Their main problem during this period was their long lines of communications and the need to regroup their forces. Although now only seventy kilometres from Berlin, the Russians were grateful for this opportunity to haul thousands of tons of much-needed equipment and war stores across what were now the bleak and

[1] The German winter of 1944–5 was one of the worst on record.

devastated wastelands of Eastern Europe up to the front line. At the same time, special shock-troop units were being hastily trained in street fighting; new training manuals were produced and tactics practised time and time again, in preparation for the Battle of Berlin. The Red Army had in fact improved considerably during its ponderous advance westwards. Most of its junior officers and senior NCO's were by now hardened veterans in contrast to their German opposite numbers, many of whom were hastily-promoted youths who possessed only a fanatical devotion to National Socialism, rather than the essential military skills which can only be learnt in actual combat. Indeed, desperately few German NCO's had survived the Russian campaign long enough to be of any positive value in the coming encounter.

For the final assault on Berlin, the Soviet Supreme Command was able to draw on troops from three fronts. The Second White Russian Front under Marshal Rokossovsky was to force the Oder, smash through German defences and destroy the Nazi *Festung*[1] at Stettin. The First White Russian Front under the great Zhukov, containing five infantry armies and two tank armies, was to advance directly on Berlin and beyond to reach the inter-Allied demarcation line on the Elbe on the twelfth to fifteenth day. Finally, the First Ukrainian Front, similarly composed to Zhukov's forces, was to cross the Neisse, capture Dresden, and advance further west to the Elbe.

Even at this stage of the war German defences were still formidable, and together with climate and terrain made the hastily-prepared Russian plan hopelessly optimistic. For the Russians to maintain momentum in accordance with their timetable, they would have to advance through defensive positions of great strength and depth at a rate of a kilometre an hour and keep this up for ten days.

On 15 April 1945, the eve of the final battle, the balance of forces was as shown on page 29.

Hitler in the meantime had left the 'Wolf's Lair' in East Prussia and taken up residence in his battered capital. The Führer's bunker, in the very centre of the city, was a labyrinth

---

[1] *Festung* or fortress: the military term dreamed up by Hitler for a town or village which had been hastily given all-round defences and from which there was to be no retreat.

FINAL RUSSIAN OFFENSIVE
16 April–7 May 1945

NORTH
SEA

Gulf of
Finland

BALTIC SEA

2nd Baltic

Riga

3rd White Russian

Rostock
Hamburg •Wismar

21
MONTGOMERY

Elbe

2nd White Russian
ROKOSSOVSKI

Stettin

POLAND

Berlin

Oder

1st White Russian
SOKOLOVSKI

Vistula

12
BRADLEY

Neisse

ZHUKOV •Warsaw

Dresden

1st Ukrainian
KONIEV

Prague

4th Ukrainian
YEREMENKO

Danube

6
DEVERS

2nd Ukrainian
MALINOVSKI

Budapest

15
CLARK

•Graz

3rd Ukrainian
TOLBUKHIN

RUMANIA

Trieste

ITALY

YUGOSLAVIA

0   50   100   200
mi

	Russian	*German*
Divisions	193	85
Men	2,500,000	1,000,000
Guns/Mortars	41,000	10,000
Tanks/S.P.	6,250	1,500
Aircraft	7,500	3,300

of ferroconcrete corridors, off which were dim, spartan conference rooms, forty feet beneath the Chancery. In January 1945 he had celebrated, in his macabre manner, the twelfth anniversary of his coming to power. Now in March 1945, along with his subordinates and his people, he knew that the war was lost. So, whilst Berliners froze in sub-zero temperatures and their city burned around them, Hitler appeared to retreat into the dark recesses of his paranoia, a physical and psychological wreck. There are many accounts on record of his appearance at this time, none more poignant than that of Captain Gerhardt Baldt, then Guderian's A.D.C.:

> His head swings slightly. His left arm hangs down as if paralysed, the hand trembling all the while. His eyes shine in an indescribable way, suggesting almost inhuman anguish. His face and the pockets under the eyes emphasise his exhaustion. He moves like an old man.

If Hitler did know that the war was lost, he did not seem to care; the one thing he was certain of was that he had long before outlawed himself beyond all hope of mercy. Like all dictators in the final hours of their power, he was bent on only one thing, taking as much of the world as he could with him to final destruction. Most of the city also went underground in the final months of the war. In the dives off Friedrichstrasse and the Kurfürstendam those that remained in the city[1] spent the nights in a frenzied attempt to live for the moment. By day, thousands of refugees—the mass of human misery from Eastern Europe—fled through the city westwards. The hospitals of the city, those that had survived the bombing, were packed, whilst the barracks were denuded of troops as the remnants of what was once the most proud and all-conquering army in the history

---

[1] It is estimated that more than a million people left the city in the last six weeks of February and March alone.

of Europe moved into their final defence positions. The quality of these troops varied enormously. There were hardened SS and Waffen SS men, some the survivors of the once-for-midable contingents from the conquered territories; men who, now that the tide of war had turned against them, had no country to return to, and who were to fight with the desperation of the damned. There were the Volkssturm, the German Home Guard, composed of tired old men and frightened children, ill-armed, poorly clothed and completely without training. There were too few troops who were seasoned veterans of Wehrmacht campaigns. All these huddled in misery and fear, manning suicidal defence positions, whilst behind the lines roamed the SS, carrying out summary executions of would-be falterers and deserters.

At 0400 hours on the morning of 16 April 1945, 40,000 guns, lined up wheel to wheel, opened fire on the first Russian objective, the Seelow Heights. At the same time Hitler published his last order of the day:

> Soldiers of the German front in the east!
>
> The hordes of our Judeo-Bolshevist foe have rallied for the last assault. They want to destroy Germany and to extinguish our people. You, soldiers of the east, have seen with your own eyes what fate awaits German women and children: the aged, the men, the infants, are murdered, German women and girls defiled and made into barrack whores. The rest are marched to Siberia.
>
> We have been waiting for this assault. Since January every step has been taken to raise a strong eastern front. Colossal artillery forces are welcoming the enemy. Countless new units are replacing our losses. Troops of every kind hold our front.[1]
>
> Once again, Bolshevism will suffer Asia's old fate—it will founder on the capital of the German Reich.
>
> He who at this moment does not do his duty is a traitor to

---

[1] Russian sources claim that Berlin alone was defended by forty-eight infantry divisions, ten motorized divisions, four Panzer, thirty-seven infantry regiments and ninety-eight independent battalions, although many of these units were probably unidentifiable, their size and composition seriously deteriorated.

the German nation. The regiments or divisions that relinquish their posts are acting so disgracefully that they must hang their heads in shame before the women and children who here in our cities are braving the terror bombing.

If during these next days and weeks every soldier in the east does his duty, Asia's final onslaught will come to nought —just as the invasion of our western enemies will in the end fail.

Berlin stays German. Vienna will be German again. And Europe will never be Russian!

Rise up to defend your homes, your women, your children —rise up to defend your own future! At this hour the eyes of the German nation are upon you, you my fighters in the east, hoping that your steadfastness, your ardour and your arms will smother the Bolshevist attack in a sea of blood!

This moment, which has removed from the face of the earth the greatest war criminal of all ages,[1] will decide the turn in the fortunes of war.

The reality of war was somewhat different from Hitler's jingoistic ranting. Russian storm troopers, fresh and rested, well-equipped and by Russian standards well-trained, pressed forward to their objectives. The Seelow Heights fell on 18 April, only twenty-four hours after the planned Russian deadline, and although the attack now lost some of its strategic cohesion, units of the First White Russian front soon surged out of the basin of the Oder towards Berlin.

The early stages of this final offensive involved infantry and combat engineers storming cunningly-sited German defensive positions, further hampered by the flooded countryside and the numerous water obstacles. The great Russian advantage, overwhelming superiority in armour, had thus been neutralized by the terrain. So the final march on Berlin was not, as it is often depicted, an armoured thrust, but for much of the time close hand-to-hand combat between infantry. Wave upon wave of Russian troops broke the German defence lines and hurled the

---

[1] Hitler is referring to the death of Roosevelt, an event which seemed to suggest to his followers that the great Allied coalition might now break asunder under the problems of co-operation. It certainly gave fresh heart to many Nazis at this time.

defenders back into Berlin. The Germans fought with fanatical
devotion to a lost cause; notions of long-term national security
were forgotten in the heat of battle. Indeed, they fought with
the desperation of animals, since survival was the keynote in
this combat where no quarter was asked or given. By 20 April
all thought of a German counter-attack had been forgotten, as
the battered remnants of the German Army fell back into the
very suburbs of Berlin. On 21 April the Russian spearheads
crossed the autobahn that ringed the eastern suburbs and on
that day began the death agony of the Third Reich.

The battle for Berlin proper began badly for the Russians.
In many ways the city was ideally suited for defence. The
numerous lakes, linked by concentric lines of rivers and canals,
acted as natural tank obstacles. The actual German defences,
such as they were, were built on the concentric rings of the
Teltow, Hamel and Tegel Canals and the elevated railways

which curved around the inner suburbs. And where the walls of old Berlin rose up there stood the Nazis' most powerful defence line of all, the Landwehr Canal and the sharp bend of the river Spree, its high banks clad in concrete. This inner zone guarded all the government offices, the Imperial Chancery and the final objective, the Reichstag. Into this claustrophobic network of streets the over-optimistic Russian commanders hurled the T-34s and the new Joseph Stalin tanks of the First Tank Army, only to suffer heavy losses at the hands of fanatical defenders equipped with the superb Panzerfaust anti-tank bazookas. From 21 to 25 April, Russian units worked around the outer ring of the city and linked up, thus completely surrounding it. The juncture of the 8th Guards Army (1st White Russian Front) and the 3rd Tank Army (1st Ukrainian Front) on the Teltow Canal completed the first phase of the Berlin operation.

On 25 April 1945 the final stage of the 'Great Patriotic War' began, the actual storming of Berlin; 1,900,000 shells were fired into the inner suburbs of Berlin alone. The leaders of the Third Reich, who cowered in the cellars of the Imperial Chancery on the Voss Strasse, knew that the city was surrounded, but none the less demanded of their soldiers that they fight to the last cartridge. By so doing they condemned to annihilation both the garrison and the civilian population of the capital. Hitler apparently felt no compassion for the agony of his people and he still commanded the loyalty of enough faithful fanatics to make opposition by any other leader almost suicidal. For he believed that the German people had betrayed both him and National Socialism; hence, in terms of a political creed which measured war as an indicator of national survival, the people must be condemned to perish in the final holocaust.

The regular forces of the Reich had largely disappeared; the other were encircled and in the process of being annihilated piecemeal. Thus the battle for Berlin soon became isolated from the equally catastrophic events on other fronts and in other theatres. This was particularly the case after 26 April, when units of the First Ukrainian Front captured the operations complex of the German General Staff in the suburb of Zossen. This meant that the control system for the entire forces of the Third Reich was destroyed amd co-ordination on a national level became impossible.

As the fighting for Berlin reached its grisly climax, Soviet and American units joined up at Torgau on 26 April. This meeting of the armies of the two super-powers on European soil symbolised both the end of Germany's bid to be the greatest power in the world and also the end of Europe's greatness.

By 29 April all that was left of *Gross Deutschland* was the territory of the Tiergarten, an elongated ellipse eight kilometres long and two kilometres wide; an island encircled by an inexorably tightening ring of fire. The main defence of the Tiergarten consisted of two mighty six-storied bunkers (ZOO Bunkers) situated in the centre of the park. These had walls six feet thick, with three levels below ground and three above. Since 1942 they had operated as the brain of the anti-aircraft defence of the city; now they were to serve their final function as the scene of the last stand of organized resistance. The Imperial Chancery, the Reichstag, the open theatres, palaces and museums, for the most part empty bomb-scarred shells, had also been turned into strongpoints and powerful defence complexes by the Nazis.

On 22 April Hitler himself had decided to remain in Berlin to the bitter end. His determination not to surrender endured throughout and so too did his determination to destroy. His megalomania was such that he could not conceive of a Germany which could survive without him. On 28 April Hitler learned of Himmler's attempt to reach peace terms through the Swedish Count Bernadotte. For Hitler this seemed the final betrayal, and on 30 April he committed suicide. Not before, however, first marrying his long-time mistress Eva Braun.[1] While the wedding party in the bunker were drinking champagne Hitler withdrew with his secretary to dictate a political testament and his personal will. The circumstances surrounding the death of Hitler have been a source of controversy ever since the event.[2] That day, Hitler took his lunch quietly, much as usual. Then he said goodbye to Goebbels and Bormann, and soon after three p.m. he went to his rooms with Eva. The

---

[1] It seems strange that amidst scenes of catastrophe Hitler's middle-class ideas of respectability should compel him to this action.

[2] The events and atmosphere of the period are beyond the scope of this book. There are many excellent accounts of the last days of Hitler, of which those of Alan Bullock and Professor Jarman must be considered the finest.

sound of a revolver was heard and aides found Hitler shot through the mouth, with Eva by his side; she had taken poison. The bodies were burned, as instructed by Hitler in his will. Admiral Doenitz was named as Hitler's successor.

In the early hours of 1 May, General Krebs, Chief of Staff of the 56th Panzer Corps, was received at the command post in the city by General Vasili Chuikov, Commander of the 8th Guards Army of the 1st White Russian Front. Krebs was an experienced diplomat: he had been German Military attaché in Moscow before the war and spoke fluent Russian. At this first meeting Krebs did not attempt to negotiate a surrender, but rather to make a deal. He brought news of Hitler's death,[1] and proposed an armistice with the government which had succeeded him. Whilst talks dragged on into another day, the fighting continued unabated. By daylight there was no longer solid resistance anywhere along the front of encircled forces. Only a few isolated garrisons and detachments of SS troops, still fairly strong, were willing to continue the fight.

In the early afternoon Krebs returned to Goebbels at the Chancery with the Russian conditions for a cease-fire. They were, briefly, the unconditional surrender of Berlin, all those surrendering to give up their arms; the lives of officers and soldiers would be spared and assistance to the wounded was assured.

Whilst the Germans deliberated and argued over these conditions, the defenders of Berlin reached the limit of their endurance. Covered by a massive artillery bombardment the Russians advanced through the Tiergarten. The Gestapo headquarters fell, and the vanguard of the Red Army shock troops secured the Swedish Embassy[2] and moved into the Charlottenburg.

At 0400 hours on 2 May, the radio operators of the 79th Guards Division intercepted a message in Russian asking for a cease-fire; envoys would be sent to the Potsdamer Brücke. At six o'clock on that fateful morning the Berlin garrison commander, General Weidings, and his staff crossed the bridge and surrendered.

---

[1] It must have been something of a shock to Chuikov who nevertheless, in a masterly fashion, shrugged off the news as if he already knew it.

[2] Observing strick protocol and courtesy to the Embassy staff.

The Battle for Berlin was practically over, and the ceasefire was generally observed. However, a battle group composed of elements of the Müncheburg Division and the XVIII Panzer Grenadiers tried to break out to the west. The tanks and trucks of the division stormed across the Hamel Bridge, ploughing through crowds of refugees and the flotsam of an army all headed in the same direction. Heavy Russian fire broke up the cohesion of this group, and its survivors disappeared amongst the debris of war; few could have reached the western outskirts of the city, let alone make any contact with the Americans in the west.

On 2 May Doenitz moved the seat of his government to Flensburg near the Danish frontier and formed what he regarded as a non-party government. On 4 May German forces in north-west Europe surrendered at Montgomery's headquarters on Lüneburg Heath. Finally, at Rheims on 7 May 1945 General Jodl signed the unconditional surrender of all German forces, in the presence of representatives of the United States of America, Britain, France and Russia. The war in the west was ended, and with it the Third Reich.

III

THE RAPE OF BERLIN

IN MAY 1945 the city of Berlin lay in ruins. For over four years it had been systematically destroyed by the Western strategic bomber force. One-tenth of all the bombs dropped on Germany fell on Berlin, and now its devastation had been made virtually complete by a week of vicious street fighting. The level of destruction in the centre of the capital was ninety-five per cent, and in the city as a whole more than seventy per cent. Only about a quarter of the houses in the city were in a habitable condition, and the pre-war population had been reduced by more than a million. The normal services of a municipal authority, such as gas, electricity, water and transport were either non-existent or operating at a vastly reduced level; all were totally inadequate to meet the needs of the survivors of the war. In the main water network alone there were more than 3,000 breaks.

The unfortunate position in which Berlin found itself at the end of the war was a result of the Allied decision to occupy the whole of Germany after the collapse of the Nazi régime. This policy can be traced back to the Casablanca Conference in January 1943, which demanded the unconditional surrender of Germany as the main war aim of the Allies. This persistent refusal to negotiate an armistice with the enemy created major problems for the Allies. First, it meant that the war would be prolonged and more violent. The German nation no longer fought for Hitler and his particular creed, but for the defence of the homeland and preservation of their whole social fabric. Secondly, the responsibility for administering Germany would devolve on the Allies themselves, pending the conclusion of a peace treaty with a new German government.

The post-war settlement of the German question in general, and Berlin in particular, has come to be regarded as one of the most complex problems of modern international relations. The end of the war in Europe had removed the overriding reason for inter-Allied co-operation between East and West, that is, the need to win the war. It also brought to an end one of the most unnatural alliances the world has ever seen and, with the end of hostilities, the members of that alliance simply began to behave in a more characteristic manner. Added to this was the fact that in immediately post-war Europe the whole German question was made even more complex by the dropping of the atomic bomb on Japan. On the one hand, of course, this event did mark the end of the Second World War in the Pacific in military terms; but to leave it at that is far too simple an interpretation, since it had a far-reaching influence on the Russian attitude towards Europe and the rest of the world. Japan was a defeated nation before the atomic bomb was dropped. Her industrial capacity had been almost totally disrupted by the strategic bombing, her armed forces were crippled and ineffective, her merchant marine driven from the seas. Food supplies for civilian consumption were fast running out. All the Americans needed to do was to wait patiently for formal surrender. But instead, the atomic bombs were used. Why? Probably no really comprehensive answer will ever be found to this question; however, certain factors seem to suggest a partial solution. Russia entered the war against Japan on 8 August, with an invasion of Japanese Manchuria, and the Americans seemed desperately anxious to ensure that the Soviet Union would not figure in any settlement of the war in Asia. Therefore, that war had to be brought to a speedy conclusion before the Russians could make any significant contribution. So it seems that the State Department could not afford the luxury of waiting for Japan to surrender. Furthermore, American scientists in the Manhattan Project[1] had spent vast sums of money[2] on the development of this atomic weapon—they feared a public outcry if it were not used. Ironically, the bombs had little influence on the eventual Japanese decision to ask for terms. Indeed, few Japanese knew that they had been dropped

---

[1] Code name for the Atomic Weapons Development Programme.
[2] $200 million.

until after the war. A power struggle within the Japanese cabinet, coupled with a realization of the implications of the Soviet declaration, was enough, in the context of the Japanese military and economic position, to lead to a surrender. But the effect on the Soviet Union of the atomic bomb and its use was both complex and profound. Hiroshima and Nagasaki opened up vast new problems in the sphere of international relations.

The nuclear additive had particularly far-reaching effect in terms of the new power structure in Europe. The war had thrown up an unprecedented phenomenon in the form of two 'super-states', Russia and the United States of America; occupy-the no-man's-land between these two great blocs was a weak, divided and devastated Europe. The possession of a nuclear device by one super-state completely upset the military balance, giving the other an immediate awareness of inferiority. Thus nuclear capability confronted the United States with an awesome problem. Should the secrets of atomic weapons be shared with the other nations, in the interests of world peace? Should the USA attempt to keep the secret to herself? Or should the fearsome power of the new weapon be used to coerce the Russians into accepting the American design for the post-war international order?

The United States, having fought to liberate Europe from German domination, could not tolerate a renewed subjugation of the continent (including Germany), this time by Moscow. On the other hand, a Germany reconstructed on the basis of democratic and capitalist principles was incompatible with Soviet objectives. The Americans were aware of Russian intransigence over this question; the latter's obvious desire to take advantage of the newly-created political vacuum in central Europe did not come as a surprise to the USA, a sudden revelation of their past misunderstandings, nor was it considered to be a result of the death of Roosevelt. True, American foreign policy throughout the Second World War had been essentially the policy of Roosevelt. In the same way, Anglo-American relations throughout the war were in effect the relationship between Churchill and Roosevelt (and were usually harmonious, despite Roosevelt's mistrust of British colonial ambitions). Under Roosevelt, American foreign policy had become open-ended, outgoing; in 1945 there could be no turning back into isolationism. In 1941 Roosevelt had written to his trusted friend and adviser, Averill Harriman: 'You naturally understand that in this global war there is literally no question, political or military, in which the United States is not interested.' Roosevelt, contrary to the popular conception, was by no means a naïve politician when it came to dealing with Communism; rather, his policies were based on a prescient vision of the appalling consequences of a failure to secure Russian co-operation.

Throughout the war years, various schemes for the structure of a future German state were produced by the Allies. They varied from the relatively mild terms of Churchill's suggestion for a Danubian Confederation to the extremism of Henry Morgenthau's plan, for a future German economy based on an agrarian infrastructure. On 14 May 1945, Directive JCS 1067, a top-secret document, was issued to Eisenhower; it was intended as the final policy guideline for the American occupation forces in Germany. According to this document, which was to operate for a maximum period of two years, the American military government in Germany was 'to decentralize the structure and administration of the German economy to the maximum possible extent'.[1] The influence of the Morgenthau Plan could also be seen in the directive to 'require the Germans to use all means at their disposal to maximize agricultural output and establish as rapidly as possible effective machinery for the collection and distribution of agricultural output'.

However, the most immediate problem that faced the Western Allied commanders in Europe in May 1945, besides the obvious one of the redeployment of men and materials to the Pacific, was firstly, to gain access to Berlin, and secondly, to secure their own zones and introduce efficient military administration. Meanwhile, their political masters, amidst the turmoil of governmental changes, were preparing for the forthcoming Allied summit meeting at Potsdam.

Winston Churchill had become increasingly alarmed at the attitudes adopted by the Soviet Union to the newly 'liberated' areas of Eastern Europe. Much of what the Russians did in this period was, in Churchill's view, completely contrary to both the spirit and even the letter of the Yalta Agreements. He was

[1] Department of State Bulletin, July 1945, pp. 601–2.

particularly distressed by the Russians' unilateral decision to hand over to Poland large tracts of Prussia east of the Oder and Neisse rivers, in return for a sizeable portion of Eastern Poland.[1] Another example of Soviet inflexibility to which he reacted strongly was the problems the Western Allies were experiencing in gaining access to Vienna, and later the severe restrictions put on the movements of the Western contribution to the Allied Control Commission in Austria.

Accordingly, Churchill asked the new American President, Harry Truman, to maintain both the force-level of American units in Europe (rather than return them either to the USA or the Pacific), and at the same time to maintain those forces in their armistice positions, pending the meeting with Stalin at Potsdam in June 1945. However, Truman believed that there could be no hope of establishing four-power government in occupied Germany until each national force had withdrawn to the agreed zones of occupation. He also believed that failure to do this would result in positive harm to inter-Allied relations, and that the conference at Potsdam would begin on the wrong foot unless everybody was in the agreed areas.[2]

Churchill and Truman did, however, agree to bring pressure to bear to ensure Western forces could advance from their demarcation lines into Berlin. Russian obstruction in this area was becoming an increasingly vexed question for the two leaders. Accordingly, both wrote to Stalin on the subject in early June 1945. Churchill stressed the need for: 'The simultaneous movement of Allied garrisons into greater Berlin and for the provision of free movement for British forces by air, rail and road, to and from the British Zone to Berlin'.[3] Stalin's somewhat ambiguous reply suggested that the Western Allies might move into the city on 1 July. He explained that the reason for the delay was that Russian commanders were required for a high-level conference in Moscow for most of the latter part of June, and that his forces were having great difficulty in clearing mines from the city.

[1] See map, page 28.
[2] It is important at this stage to understand the difference between 'a zone' (which refers to the areas of occupation in Germany) and 'a sector' (which refers to those suburbs of Berlin occupied by the Allied Forces).
[3] Quoted from *Triumph and Tragedy*.

The whole question of zones of occupation in post-war Germany, and the subdivision of the city of Berlin, is a complex one. It was first raised after the Moscow conference of Foreign Ministers in the summer of 1943, and discussed formally in Teheran by the Allied leaders in October 1943. They agreed to create a tripartite organisation called the European Advisory Commission (EAC), composed of a representative from each of the main Allied powers, Britain, the United States of America and Russia, and that it should meet in London under the chairmanship of the British deputy premier, Clement Attlee. The task of this negotiating body was to consider the problem of the ultimate fate of enemy countries in greater detail (presumably thereby allowing the Allied leaders to concentrate on the major priority of winning the war). Although the EAC later became the scene of a bitter dispute over jurisdiction, it was this organization which drew up the final zonal arrangements for the approval of the Allied leaders. Nothing illustrates more clearly the political vacuum in which the Allies pursued their war aims than the workings of this Commission. To the Allied leaders, it was very low on the list of priorities, and many of its decisions were made by default. Also, there was a very uneven balance between the military and political requirements of the Commission's work. For although the organization was backed up by each country creating an inter-service committee, each individual committee operated in its own country, and in the case of the United States it was chaired by a naval officer with the rank of lieutenant!

The eventual geophysical division of Germany by the Allies represents, even in the most charitable view, a quite extraordinary solution and only by appreciating this low priority given to the Commission by the Western politicians can one understand how Germany came to be subdivided into these four particular zones, with a further subdivision of Berlin, situated 115 miles inside Russian-occupied territory. The obvious solution would have been to divide Germany into four zones which radiated out of Berlin like the spokes of a wheel. This indeed had been Roosevelt's initial suggestion, as he toyed with a National Geographical Society map of Europe on his way to the Teheran Conference. Had this solution been adopted its effect on the post-war world would have been far-reaching.

There would have been no blockade of Berlin by the Russians and therefore no need of an airlift by the Allies. Even more important for the recent history of Europe, the emergence of the two Germanys as political entities would have been geophysically almost impossible and so politically unlikely. So how did this odd division come about? The answer lies partly in the fact that Roosevelt, poorly supported by his advisers, both military and political, soon became involved in what were then regarded as more urgent priorities. The President was already a desperately sick man, and his advisers, in trying to ease the physical burden of government, tended (out of the most humane motives, but with disastrous political consequences) to tell him the things they thought he wanted to hear. Even then, discord did arise between Roosevelt and the State Department, in particular with Secretary of State Cordell Hull, because the President believed that the definition of the zones was essentially a military solution. The relationship between the State Department and the Pentagon was never harmonious and often strained. A subdivision of prize territory between East and West, on a river line running north to south, seemed the best solution to the military, and their recommendations were embodied in the proposals of the EAC; the State Department, unable to gain any recognition from the President for their viewpoint, agreed almost by default—in fact, they had no clearly-defined and valid alternative to offer, even as a negotiating point. The fact that the solution so obviously met with the approval of the Russians was another factor in its favour from Roosevelt's point of view. For both he, and to a lesser extent Churchill, believed that there was a very real chance that the Russian advance westwards might well end at Poland's western frontier, or even the old Russo-Polish border, with no invasion of Germany and possibly even a Russian deal with the Nazis, thus isolating the Western Allies to pursue the war as best they could. Therefore, much of Western policy towards the Russians was based on the premise of a need not to upset their temperamental ally from the east; it was believed that a division of territorial spoils favourable to the Russians would be sufficient to ensure the continued advance of the Red Army into the German homeland. Another important factor was that Roosevelt was interested in securing Russian co-operation and military participation in the war against Japan. Two-thirds of the Imperial Japanese Army were tied down on the Asian mainland,[1] and a Russian military contribution was regarded as absolutely essential to American plans for the final offensive of the Pacific war. Lastly, Roosevelt had an idealistic vision of a New Order in the post-war world and was anxious to secure Russian support for his schemes; Russian military and political presence in Europe proper would offer a greater chance for his plan to become reality.

None of these solutions taken in isolation provides a really satisfactory explanation of why the Western Allies agreed to a partition of Germany so much biased in favour of the Soviet Union, but at least they suggest something of the background to the Allied, and in particular the American, position.

What is perhaps even harder to understand is that, right from the very beginning, there was no mention of access routes into Berlin. This was primarily because the West naïvely believed that a zone of occupation in the city of Berlin automatically assumed right of access. The Americans felt that to have raised this question in any of the conferences, especially in the increasingly fragile political climate, would only result in confusing the issue. On 12 September 1944 the first *Protocol on Zones of Occupation* was agreed in London by the Allied representatives. This document did not mention access routes. However, it did establish the inter-Allied governing body for the administration of the Greater Berlin area, the Kommandatura. The subdivision of German territory into the zones of occupation was agreed to be carried out according to the 1937 frontiers.

Even the letters written by Churchill and Truman to Stalin in June 1945 made no mention of the question of Allied access into Berlin. Indeed, the first time that it was raised was at a meeting in Berlin between Eisenhower's representative, General Lucius Clay, his British colleague, General Sir Ronald Weeks, and General Zhukov.

Initially, the Anglo-Americans asked for the use of three railways lines, two roads and as much air space as was necessary to open and maintain contacts between the western zones

[1] Either in fighting the Chinese or as forces of occupation in conquered territories of China and Manchuria.

and their sectors in Berlin. Zhukov would not agree that these routes were essential to the Allies; he further attempted to obstruct British and American wishes by stating that the existing communications facilities were so badly damaged after the fighting that no repairs could be carried out for the present, as the Russians needed what facilities there were to demobilize their own forces.

General Clay says in his book *Decision Germany*:

General Weeks supported my contention strongly. We both knew there was no provision covering access to Berlin in the agreement reached by the European Advisory Commission. We did not wish to accept specific routes which might be interpreted as a denial of our right of access over all routes. Therefore, Weeks and I accepted, as a temporary arrangement, the allocation of a main highway, a rail line and two air corridors.

A number of interesting points arise from this meeting. Firstly, no record was kept of the proceedings and the words of General Clay represent his own notes taken at the meeting and dictated to one of his staff in the evening. Furthermore, both Clay and Weeks had fully intended to reopen the question of Allied access to Berlin at the later sessions of the Allied Control Council. However, neither realized that all decisions in the Council required a unanimous vote. This left the way wide open for future Russian application of their veto.

In this first meeting with Zhukov both the Western commanders also stressed that all Allied traffic into Berlin must be free from any form of border search, whether by a civil or military customs control.

Clay, when writing the memoirs of his tour in Germany, some time after the events of the Berlin Blockade, pointed out that the Western Allies made a serious error in not making free access to Berlin a condition of American withdrawal from their demarcation line to their occupation zone. This was essentially a military problem and Eisenhower, and Clay for that matter, both had the requisite authority to force this condition on the Russians. Yet neither chose to do so. Another possible reason why the vital question of access was not given greater priority in the West is that Truman had hardly had time to assume the full responsibilities of office (indeed, the constitutional limitations of the position of Vice-President would have denied him the opportunity to assume power with a full knowledge of world problems); meanwhile, in Britain the nation was preparing for a General Election.

So, on 1 July 1945, with as yet no clear agreement on access, the first British and American military formations, each the strength of an armoured brigade, moved rapidly behind their advance parties into the mounds of war-scarred rubble which were all that remained of what had once been the capital of the most powerful political system in Europe since the days of Rome.

The four great powers now occupied a city divided into twenty boroughs, with a total population of 3,300,000. The Russians occupied the largest section, the eastern third consisting of eight boroughs. In the north was the small French sector of two boroughs.[1] The British took over four boroughs in the west and the Americans the remaining six boroughs, in the south-western sector of the city.

The Allies found a Berlin that had not only suffered from five years of aerial bombardment and a week of bitter street fighting, but also from the violence of the recent Russian occupation. On the one hand this had taken the form of a systematic looting of the surviving industrial capacity of the city, as the Russians dismantled machinery and plant for shipment home as reparations. Such was their maltreatment of this equipment while taking it apart that much of it was reduced to scrap metal long before it began its long journey in flat cars to the war-damaged industrial areas of Russia.[2]

On the other hand, the occupation involved a less systematic but far more brutal pillage of the people of Berlin, by a Soviet soldiery let loose in the traditional style of the Mongol and Tartar hordes. The Russian cry of '*Uti, uti!*' ('Watch!') or '*Frau, komm*' became commonplace in a city which now suffered a period of degradation difficult to parallel in recent history. As the Allied troops tried to restore order to a city which had thus been subjected to the atrocities of an eighteenth-century siege, the Allied leaders gathered to confer at Potsdam,

[1] Arbitrarily carved out of the British and American Sectors.
[2] 90 per cent of iron and steel; 75 per cent of printing; 70 per cent of vehicle plant; 85 per cent of electrical and optical producing machinery.

a suburb to the east of Berlin. It had not been originally intended that a peace conference should follow immediately after the ending of the war. All were aware that this was a mistake which had been made at the conclusion of the Great War. Even so, the conference, which represented both the last great war meeting and the first 'Summit' of peace-time, might have been expected to produce more significant conclusions than in fact it did. Just as at the Versailles Conference of 1919, most of the decisions reached either gave tacit recognition to an existing state of affairs, or parcelled out territories which were disputed between the principal protagonists and their respective foreign ministers.

Since the last great conference at Yalta at the end of 1944, Allied leadership had undergone a significant change and, by the end of the Potsdam Conference, of the great wartime leaders only Stalin remained in office. On 12 April 1945, Roosevelt had died and had been succeeded by his Vice-President, Harry S. Truman. The American system of government, coupled with Roosevelt's thinly-veiled dislike of his political running-mate, had excluded the Vice-President from any really intimate knowledge of events, and the men who could now best advise Truman were themselves divided in their counsels.

Of somewhat less significance was the change in government that occurred at this time in Britain, the result of the first General Election held in post-war Europe. A Labour Government was brought to power with an overwhelming majority for the first time in its history. Clement Attlee became Prime Minister, and Ernest Bevin succeeded Eden at the Foreign Office. Important though this election was to the British people, the transition from a Conservative caretaker government to a Labour administration was in fact, in the context of foreign policy, a smoother transition than the rapid succession from Roosevelt to Truman. For Britain, her most powerful trade union leader was now her Foreign Minister. Bevin had enjoyed considerable success in the wartime Cabinet as Minister of Labour and poignantly, considering his new rôle, he had had long experience in combating Communism in the pre-war trade union movement. By modern standards, Bevin[1] was an uncouth,

[1] It was George VI who initially suggested Bevin for the post of Foreign Secretary.

even illiterate, man, but recognized by his contemporaries
as an awesome House of Commons figure. His power and
influence lay in his tremendous gifts of oratory, his acute
political awareness, and his native shrewdness when dealing
with people. Nevertheless, the transition from the suave and
polished Eden to the 'working man's' Bevin must have been a
disturbing experience for the old school at the Foreign Office.

The Potsdam Conference lasted from 17 July 1945 to early
August. For a venture of such importance the extent of effective
agreement was small, and even this agreement was concerned
primarily with questions of German disarmament, de-Nazification and the Nuremberg War Trials. The successful solution of
those questions was mainly due to the deal arranged by
Truman's Secretary of State, Byrnes,[1] who was desperately
anxious to reach agreement with the Soviet Foreign Minister,
Molotov. The Western leaders operated under considerable
disadvantages at the conference. Truman at this stage was still
feeling his way in the new surroundings in which he now found
himself. Attlee (who had had considerable diplomatic experience by this time, because Churchill had always kept him fully
briefed throughout the war) operated under different liabilities.
Stalin and the Soviet delegation were deeply suspicious of the
new left-wing British administration and this proved a definite
obstacle in the negotiations. The breakdown in discussion at
Potsdam occurred because the threat of war had been removed,
and also because in the previous conference everything had
depended on the interplay of personalities amongst the great
war leaders. The overriding impression that emerges from
Potsdam is that Stalin simply lost interest in the proceedings;
under these circumstances agreement became virtually impossible. Therefore, on the wider questions of the reconstruction of Germany, the re-education of the German people and
the decentralization of government, no solution could be
reached simply because these terms had different interpretations for the different powers.

Parallels have already been drawn between Potsdam and
Versailles, and another similarity between these two great
conferences was the concern over the question of reparations.
Like France in 1919, Russia in 1945 adopted an extreme posture

[1] He was later dismissed by Truman for 'overstepping his brief'.

in this matter, wishing to draw to the maximum extent on the economic resources of the whole of Germany without sacrificing any loss of influence over the affairs of her own zone. As they had been in 1919, the Americans, and to a lesser extent the British, were in 1945 desperately anxious to ensure that Germany should not be so heavily milked of her resources as to make it impossible for her to stand on her own and survive economically. At the same time, the West were politically motivated in their attitude by the need to avoid a situation in which they would have no say in the eastern zone, yet have to provide reparations for the Soviet Union from their own areas of occupation.

The solution that emerged from the Potsdam Conference was the worst form of compromise. It solved nothing and left too many gaps and loopholes which could cause misunderstanding in the future. It gave neither side what it regarded as even minimum requirements. The eventual decision was incompatible with the political realities of the post-war world, since it left the Soviet Union dependent on the good will of the West for twenty-five per cent of her reparations, which in any case was twenty-five per cent of an unspecified amount. In one area only was agreement possible: the Russians secured unqualified agreement from the West on the position of the new Polish frontiers, and in particular on the vexed question of the Oder-Neisse territories.

Failure to reach agreement at Potsdam meant the beginning of a disintegrating process which was to result in a Cold War situation; it meant a rapid divergence between East and West which within three years was to culminate in the Berlin Blockade, the formation of NATO, and the division of Europe into mutually antagonistic power blocs.

IV

THE ORIGINS OF THE COLD WAR

IT WOULD now be helpful to examine in detail the objectives of the developing foreign policies of the victorious powers, in terms of their attitude towards one another, to the post-war world in general and to Germany and Berlin in particular. Without such analysis it is difficult to appreciate the growing international tension which provoked the transition from immediate post-war calm to the turbulence of the Cold War.

One of the most volatile controversies amongst contemporary historians since 1945 has concerned the exact origins of the Cold War and, more specifically, which nation's national policy has been principally responsible for it. Some suggest that the beginnings of the crisis are to be found in the spring and summer of 1945, when the failure of the Allies at Potsdam to agree on the future of Central Europe marks the point where the schism in East–West relations first becomes evident. On the other hand, others maintain that the Cold War really began in 1917, with the birth of Bolshevik power. Both views are extreme; the facts seem to point more to a period lying between the two dates. However, East–West relations were never a vital issue in the inter-war years, when almost every sophisticated industrial power was deeply involved in its own problems.[1] During the Second World War, East and West were thrown together in a unique alliance; war always tends to create strange bedfellows and the Grand Alliance against Nazism was no exception. What the war did achieve was to create an aware-

[1] The list of domestic crises of a political and social nature would include the constant political upheavals in France, the malaise of the Weimar Republic and the frequent changes of government in the United Kingdom, not to mention large-scale crime resulting from Prohibition in the USA, the international economic crisis arising from a world slump in trade which provoked the Wall Street Crash, and the General Strike in Britain.

ness of the potential of 'super-power' status, a potential which, although always present in both the USSR and the USA, had lain dormant until the advent of a world war had stimulated their growth-rates to an unparalleled extent. The Western democracies had never understood the nature of Russian society, even under the Tsars; the war brought this mighty Asiatic enigma into Central Europe, and hence into Western experience and culture, in an unprecedented manner. In the same way, the United States, though she had always drawn her new citizens from the cosmopolitan reservoir of Central Europe, had never enjoyed the security of a long-lasting relationship with Europe[1] until the war brought her into that continent in a similarly unprecedented position of strength. Areas of discord had existed from the very earliest days of this Grand Alliance in 1941, but these had been smoothed over in the interests of the mutual need for victory.

Contrasted with this new manifestation of power was the decline in status of the nations of Western Europe who, weakened by mutually antagonistic nationalism and the concomitant loss of their imperial possessions, compared unfavourably in the post-war world with the new super-states. Hence one might seek the origins of the Cold War in the failure by the super-powers to accommodate to one another's needs; the repercussions of such failure being over-reaction to a security-conscious environment, resulting in warlike postures of threat and counter-threat. Coupled with this situation, new to the world political scene, was the fact that neither super-power had come of age in terms of international politics. Each had for different reasons previously existed in isolation, not only of each other but of world trends in general; this isolation had been particularly watertight in the 1920s and 1930s. The transition from such isolation to the limelight of international affairs had been too sudden to allow them sufficient time to adapt to their new environment. The result was an often crude use of intimidation when what was required was a more subtle manipulation of power in keeping with the new political situation.

[1] A rather nebulous political connection between the USA and the English-Speaking Union has always resulted in politicians of every generation extolling the virtues of a 'special relationship' which has really never existed.

Even more controversial than the question of the origin of
the Cold War has been the attempt to establish which particular action by which super power initially provoked it. Commentators of the Cold War generation such as Chester Wilmot,[1]
and even Churchill, suggest that the prime responsibility rests
with the 'opportunist' Soviet Union, who duped the relatively
innocent and idealistic United States. On the other hand, the
historians of the New Left, who have entered the debate during
the last five years, lay the blame squarely on the shoulders of
the US administration under Truman, which they maintain
initiated the conflict by brandishing the atomic bomb, a
weapons system unprecedented in destructive power, thus
attempting to thwart the Soviet Union's legitimate efforts to
safeguard its national security. Unfortunately, this controversy
will never really be satisfactorily concluded, since there exists
no actual documentary evidence to confirm positively one
interpretation or the other.

The period 1945-7 was one of uncertainty for the decision-
makers of American foreign policy, a situation made all the
more complex by the fact that the United States, owing to her
unilateral possession of the atomic bomb and the military
presence of still-significant remnants of its Expeditionary
Forces in continental Europe, was automatically a major force
in European affairs.

This uncertainty over foreign affairs soon affected US
domestic politics. The question of the direction of US foreign
policy was openly debated in the presidential election of 1948
and degenerated into a bitter and divisive battle. The (by contemporary standards) modest left-wing opposition led by
Henry Wallace, ironically a former Vice-President in an earlier
Roosevelt administration, voiced the fears of that section of
American public opinion which saw the United States as
becoming too militarist, too willing to use its power. The
extreme form of this opposition advocated a return to the days
of isolationism and 'Fortress America'. Wallace, whilst not
wholly subscribing to these views, nevertheless saw the true rôle
of the United States as working through the channels of the
fledgling United Nations. However, his platform lacked any
real political fire and polled only a fragment of the total vote.

[1] In his *Struggle for Europe*.

This defeat of the political Left in 1948 resulted in its virtual demise, until the 'New Left' emerged from the escalating opposition to American foreign policy of the late 1960s, in particular Vietnam.

The US foreign policy-makers also suffered from the lack of a clear understanding of the implications of nuclear capability. Every weapons system has a political significance and it is reasonable enough to assume that the more destructive the weapon, the greater that significance. Logically, therefore, a weapon which is so destructive that it becomes almost too frightful to use has supreme political importance. For Truman, however, the question was never one of whether or not to make political capital out of this new weapon, but rather to what particular political end it should be used. This shift in the balance of power was increasingly felt in Germany, and especially Berlin.

Truman was very much a representative of the post-war mood of the United States. He was as different from Roosevelt as was the pre-war American from his post-war counterpart; a simple, uncomplicated and direct man, Truman possessed few of the subtleties of his predecessor. He was a politician well known in his own country but little heard of in the outside world; a man who believed in political courage and the value of ideologies and principles. In this sense he stands in sharp contrast to the pragmatic Roosevelt. As an idealist, Truman was less interested in the subtle developments in relations between the super-powers than in what he regarded as the more clearly-defined conflict between Communism and the non-Communist world. Like the majority of the American people at that period, he saw Berlin and a divided Germany as the meeting-point of alien systems and even civilizations, rather than merely the confrontation of potentially antagonistic political entities.

Therefore, in so far as the United States had any clearly defined policy towards Europe, it was to use her military force and her democratic example to obstruct Soviet encroachment into the West. The task of the military presence was to counter the physical menace of Russian arms, whilst the generous distribution of money and aid, in the name of the preservation of 'democracy', would help to contain the ideological menace of Communism.

Throughout 1946 the United States moved towards a more clearly-defined foreign policy and in the following year this took shape and substance in the Vandenburg Declaration and Marshall Aid. In the meanwhile, specific agencies of the embryonic United Nations, such as the United Nations Relief and Rehabilitation Agency, received massive American financial support. The problem of refugees and communications was becoming desperate, in the shambles that was post-war Europe, and US assistance was particularly generous in rehabilitating this drifting multitude of displaced persons.

The United Nations Organisation was something on which there had been a fair measure of American–Soviet co-operation. The name 'United Nations' had been devised by President Roosevelt and was first used in the Declaration of United Nations of 1 January 1942, when representatives of twenty-six nations pledged their governments to continue fighting together against the Axis powers. This organization, which thus had as its foundation a vast alliance of collaborating countries, was intended by Roosevelt and Churchill to be the instrument for settling post-war international disputes. In this respect it had the support of Russia, who hoped that it might prove a useful forum for the propagation of the Communist gospel. A charter was drawn up at the San Francisco Conference, which met from April to June 1945; at these meetings there was a measure of agreement between the great powers, but this was as usual limited.

Stalin's attitude towards the West at that time is difficult to fathom; however, two points can be isolated as the basic premises upon which Soviet foreign policy was apparently based. Firstly, Stalin sought to recover the maximum possible amount of war reparations in the shortest possible time. Secondly, he was determined to guard against the threat of a revitalized and remilitarized Germany emerging in future years.

Russian foreign policy was also shaped to a significant degree by the immediate demands of national security. Soviet concern over this question has only recently come to be appreciated in the West. Russia's western frontiers have always been her area of maximum weakness; their vulnerability is demonstrated by the fact that they have always been the path of the invader,

Soviet troops march into Berlin, May 1945

The effect of the Allied bombing offensive on Berlin

Keystone

Attlee, Truman and Stalin at Potsdam 1945

Keystone

General Clay

Keystone

General Sokolovsky

George Marshall

Marshall aid helps
rebuild Berlin

Keystone

Anti-Communist demonstration at the Reichstag,
11 September 1948

Keystone

British military police keep order during
the September 1948 demonstration

A Communist mob storms the Berlin
City Hall, September 1948

Ernst Reuter, Mayor of Berlin

Airlift, 1948—an Avro York in bad weather

An R.A.F. Hastings in Berlin

Airlifted coal
arrives in Berlin

Keystone

Robert Schuman announces his plan for
European coal and steel, Paris, June 1950

Keystone

Molotov (second from left) and Bulganin (centre)
at the signing of the Warsaw pact, May 1955

Keystone

A Soviet tank pursues rioters during
the East Berlin uprising of June 1953

Early on 13 August 1961 the East Germans
seal off East Berlin with barbed wire

23 August, 1961—the barbed wire becomes the Wall

The Wall today

from the Teutonic hordes of the thirteenth century, who Christianised the Slavs at the point of the sword, to Napoleon and the burning of Moscow in 1812. Russia had already suffered two disastrous incursions from the west in the twentieth century, each following more or less the same route; Hitler's invasion alone cost the Russians twenty-five million casualties. It would be difficult for a nation to forget such a traumatic experience. There is no clearly-defined natural frontier to the west of Russia, no mountain range, coast or river line which could present a physical barrier to any would-be invader. Coupled to this is the fact that some of Russia's richest provinces, in particular the Ukraine, lie immediately in the path of the attacker from the west. The solution to this problem throughout Russian history has always been the acquisition of more land, the possession of 'sponge' territories which can be used to absorb the impetus of an invader before he can reach the vital areas. As a result of this policy, for centuries Russia has represented a gigantic menace to her immediate neighbours; 'the Tartar horde' and 'the Russian steam-roller' have been enduring concepts throughout the history of East–West relations. (She is after all the largest condominium in the world, with a population of two hundred and forty millions, made up of one hundred and fifty different ethnic groups.) Since 1945 the West has frequently experienced the acquisitiveness of this mighty power bloc; of the twelve states that bordered the west and south frontiers of the Soviet Union in 1939, only one, Afghanistan, has not since been forced either to cede territory or indeed disappear altogether. This Soviet obsession with the security of her western territories does much to explain her attitude towards Europe and the Western world. A further weakness is that Russia can be outflanked from the sea[1] and so since 1945 there has been an increasing emphasis within the Soviet Union on the need for a powerful maritime presence as a further safeguard for her vital interests, both to protect her narrow sea exits from the Baltic and the Black Sea, as well as the defence of actual Russian territory, in particular the naval bases at Leningrad and Odessa.

[1] The Soviet Navy had been aware of this particular weakness since the early 1920s, and a massive naval construction programme was well under way when war broke out in 1941.

By 1945 the Soviet Union under Stalin no longer saw her prime function as the ideological base for the spread of Communism; the new power-politics and its implications had come to exert more pressing demands. That this was so can be demonstrated by the fact that the satellite states of the Eastern bloc, created (admittedly with puppet governments) in the years after 1945, all maintained a separate identity rather than becoming part of the Soviet Union, as they would have done had Stalin scrupulously followed the Marxist-Leninist line on the function of international Communism.

Stalin in 1945 believed that the only way in which the Russia's western frontiers could be made inviolate was for her to control events in the whole of Germany through the mechanisms of a satellite Communist state. He thought this objective could best be achieved by a policy of opportunism, capitalising on the declaration by Roosevelt at the Yalta Conference that the Americans would withdraw from Europe within two years of the cessation of hostilities. Coupled to this was the somewhat unrealistic Russian conviction of the inevitable economic collapse of the Western capitalist system. For Russia to make the most of the opportunities presented, it was necessary for her to ensure absolute control over the Eastern Zone as a secure base from which to operate, from there to work for the maximum possible influence over events in other parts of Europe. As an immediate political necessity the Russians sought to undermine the Western position in Berlin, if possible to make it untenable, or at least to secure a position whereby the integrity of the Western presence in the city was recognized as being dependent on the goodwill of the Soviet authorities.

There is no reason to believe that events would have been any different if America had decided in 1945 to share her twin secrets of death and prosperity with Russia. But it is clear that the refusal to share this knowledge gave encouragement to those behind the Iron Curtain who were ideologically convinced that the capitalist and Communist systems were irreconcilable and that an armed conflict was inevitable. There was a marked contrast between the Soviet Union, who had come out of the turmoil of war with twenty-five million casualties, entire provinces laid waste and her industrial capacity cut by forty-two per cent, and the United States, where casualties were less than 0·2 per cent of the population, where in four years of war the economy had blossomed and the national income had doubled. It would certainly have taken many years for the development of the peaceful uses of atomic energy to have advanced sufficiently to make any substantial difference to the Russian economy, but the mere offer of disinterested co-operation in working for the future might have caused such a psychological shock within Russia as to sweep away many an objection to the U.S.A., and possibly even lead to a complete reappraisal of Soviet policy.

Instead, Washington chose to refuse even the slightest technical assistance at the very time when the end of the war put a stop to Lend–Lease. Truman had the opportunity to offer a devastated world a vast programme for the international development of the peaceful uses of atomic energy. Even if Russia had then chosen to spurn this offer, world opinion would at least have been mobilized in support of the United States. This American decision to wrap her brand-new power in a cloak of secrecy was doubly futile, since many of its secrets had already been leaked by spies such as Fuchs, even before Hiroshima and Nagasaki.

The United States compounded the error by choosing to share the secrets only with Britain and Canada, a course of action which in Soviet eyes seemed a stark contradiction of the promise of co-operation made in the Yalta Declaration only nine months before.[1] At the same time, the composition of the new United Nations—despite the seats granted to the Ukraine and Byelorussia as a favour to Stalin—assured the United States of a majority, a situation limited only by the power of veto which each of the five permanent members of the Security Council possessed. In the meanwhile, as the two super-powers sought to reach out to new positions in the early days of peace, the once-powerful nations of Western Europe, in particular Britain, found the problems of readjustment equally complex.

In Britain the after-effects of war were felt almost immediately; both at home and abroad her circumstances had altered

[1] When the Big Three had pledged their 'common determination to maintain and strengthen in the peace to come that unity of purpose and of action which has made victory possible and certain for the United Nations in this war'.

drastically. The cost of the conflict had been enormous and the strain it had imposed on British industry meant a continuation of restrictions and rationing; food and fuel shortages were to become an integral feature of the New Age. A Labour administration tried manfully to honour their election pledge of a Welfare State. The resulting nationalisation of industries and communications did little to solve the economic crisis which the country had inherited. Churchill, who had lost the election because he had had nothing to offer a post-war electorate, many of whom could themselves remember with distaste the great man's record in past peacetime administrations, travelled the globe, receiving honours and making speeches on the future problems of world politics. To the world at large he was still a great symbol of defiance in the face of tyranny, but the truth of the matter was that he had stood for the defence of an Imperial past. The war had not been responsible for the radical transition from Empire to Commonwealth; this had begun as far back as 1921, with the British declaration of her intention to vacate India. For the Attlee administration, Britain's rôle had changed because her position, influence and wealth had changed. Before the war the frontiers of Britain had been the Himalayas, and the Imperial possessions had been built up around the nucleus of India. After 1946 the independence of partitioned India challenged the whole *raison d'être* of the British Empire. A chain of outposts had been established across the Mediterranean, Africa and the Middle East purely to safeguard the Imperial lines of communication to India. The independence of India in 1948 meant that Imperial possessions elsewhere ceased to have a function, except as outposts of colonialism *per se*, and so they became symbols of reaction, of retrenchment. Wherever Britain offered them an evolutionary development towards the satisfaction of nationalist aspirations, their demand was usually for revolutionary change. Defence of these areas thus became a major preoccupation and placed further burdens on an already weakened economy.

Ironically, only in Europe was Britain's prestige high. Indeed it had never been higher, since Britain alone of the European democracies had not succumbed to Nazi tyranny. Governments in exile had lived out the war in London, and when they returned home their feeling of gratitude towards Britain was immense. Also, Britain had been the springboard from which the liberation of Europe had been launched; she had progressed from a beleaguered fortress to an island bastion for the offensive. This European respect and gratitude was a political asset of such dimensions that leadership of a new Europe could have been Britain's for the taking. A positive foreign policy in this direction might well have resulted in Europe emerging as a power bloc of unprecedented influence. The actual physical resources of Europe in the immediate post-war years were admittedly at a low ebb, but the potential of two hundred and fifty million of the most sophisticated peoples of the world was ignored by Britain. In the same way that the United States let slip the golden opportunity of a new age of atomic co-operation with the Soviet Union, so Britain failed to take advantage of her position in Europe. Since 1945 this European sense of gratitude has been a declining asset; the real irony of the situation has been seen in recent years, with Britain's frequent cap-in-hand requests to sit at the rich men of the EEC's table.

British foreign policy entered the post-war period with an apparent lack of firm direction. The world was now subdivided into three 'circles';[1] Europe, the Commonwealth, and the Atlantic Alliance. Britain's approach to each area has been governed ever since by the prerequisite that a policy towards one must not be such as to jeopardise relations with the other two; this principle also had bedevilled her various attempts to join the European Economic Community.

The United States, on the other hand, envisaged Britain as the new leader of post-war Western Europe, ushering it along the path to recovery. But Britain's failure to sponsor the future of democracy in Turkey and Greece and her impotence in putting her own house in order forced the United States radically to reappraise her own foreign policy. The result, the Vandenburg Declaration and Marshall Aid, will be discussed more fully in the next chapter.

Meanwhile, in Germany, as 1945 drew to a close the Allied Military Government began to function more smoothly. One of its first major problems was that of 'de-Nazification'. This involved re-establishing German local administration on a

[1] Called 'the three circles concept' in the sphere of British international relations.

democratic basis. The difficulty was to find German officials who were reasonably competent yet had not been associated in some way with the Nazi régime. The priorities of de-Nazification were thus to locate and intern dangerous Nazis, to repeal Nazi law, to seize Nazi property and to block Nazi bank accounts; and finally to disband organizations and societies which were Nazi in origin.

The Nazi régime, following the usual practice of police states, maintained rigid documentation and a comprehensive filing system right up to the last days of the war. The Americans captured the Party records almost intact when their forces entered Munich in April 1945. As in many totalitarian states based on an élitist system, it was found to be extraordinarily difficult to be a party member, and the German love of thoroughness demanded careful and fully documented research into an applicant's ancestry before he was allowed to join. Here at least was final proof that few people were *forced* to join the Nazi Party.

All this placed the Allies in a difficult position. It was their earnest desire to have Germany return to a position of normality as soon as possible and yet the twelve million or more Germans who had been identified in varying degrees with past Nazi activities could not be kept apart for ever from the political and economic life of the new German state. The result was the classification of these ex-Nazis into various categories, depending on the extent of their commitment to the party. In the American Zone alone there were 120,000 Nazis who were classified as 'extremely dangerous' under the new system and they were interned to await the application of the processing law.

Berlin had survived the reign of terror from 2 to 9 May and the period of systematic looting which followed, and a gradual return to life soon became evident. Restaurants and cabarets, the last places to close down during the final days of the city's siege, were the first to open again, on 2 May. On 3 May the Russians introduced an arbitrary and highly inefficient form of food rationing. On the following day Radio Berlin, under total Russian direction, began to broadcast once again. In the less devastated areas of the outer suburbs, some public transport operated, on a much reduced scale, from 13 May. On the fourteenth the overhead railway, the *U-Bahn*, began to function again.

To all intents Berlin had become a prize of war to the Russians, who now intended to press home their advantage by creating a working system of government throughout the boroughs before the Western Allies arrived. Such plans were an attempt to capitalise on their incontrovertible possession of a moral mortgage on the future of the city, which had been achieved behind the façade of delaying tactics before the Allied arrival.

The Russians were also fortunate in that the people of Berlin remained subservient and amenable during their occupation. Historians have often asked why there was no positive reaction to the Soviet presence by the citizens of Berlin, in the form of protests or even a popular uprising. An examination of the situation at that time reveals the utter implausibility of any such action; two-thirds of the remaining Berliners were women and children, who were so dependent on the Russians for food that it became relatively easy for their new masters to make obedience the price for survival. At the same time, the only way in which resistance, and in particular armed revolt, could conceivably break out was through the survival of some militant organization capable of carrying it out. In the Berlin of 1945 only the SS could have provided such a basis for rebellion, but the diehards were dead and their camp-followers had denied previous loyalties in order to merge with the people and survive. The Berliner has always been a realist in terms of his philosophy of life, and since he had never been an uncritical admirer of Hitler and his creed, he saw no reason to die for a cause which was now obviously best forgotten. He also recognized that the devastation inflicted by his own country's invasion of Russia in 1941, and the horrors perpetrated during the subsequent occupation of large tracts of Soviet territory, were bound to be reciprocated in kind. For those in Berlin in 1945 the dictum 'to the victor belongs the spoils' came to have a very real significance. They survived simply by tightening their belts, 'suffering the indignation of the Slav' and hoping for a better future with the arrival of the Americans.

The Russian approach to the administration of Berlin was both confused and complex. In the very early stages of their occupation they had abolished political parties as a means of ruling the city. Instead they created what became known as the Anti-Fascist Coalition, which was intended as an all-embracing organization which would not only meet the needs of local politics but also administer the city. This coalition was the machinery through which the first crude forms of rationing were introduced in Berlin. The Russians arbitrarily divided the streets and houses up into blocks and issued the rations to their appointed House or Street Master. Sometimes these people, men or women, were Communists, but more often just some dazed citizen who was picked on the spur of the moment. However, in June 1945, the Russians suddenly allowed the rebirth of four political parties. It is interesting to speculate on their motives for such an apparent *volte face*. Some historians have detected behind this action the recognition by Stalin that the future lay in two distinct Germanys, this being just the first step towards the creation of new state machinery. Yet at the same time Ulbricht, the chief Communist sympathiser, was talking of the future of 'the German Republic', obviously thinking in terms of a single united Germany. The real reason was probably that the Russians recognized, very soon after its creation, the severe limitations of the Anti-Fascist Coalition, the main one being that, in the absence of political parties, it might be too closely identified with the Red Army and thereby possibly produce a reaction amongst the people against the government. And so, on 10 June 1945, a month after the surrender, the Russians allowed the creation of the Christian Democrats (CDU), the Liberal Democrats (LPD), the Social Democrats (SPD) and the Communists (KPS). At the same time social and economic groupings such as trade unions, professional associations and the like were created, to serve the same functions as the political parties. This attempted mobilisation of mass support for the Communist régime was obviously aimed at producing a chain of command and control between the occupiers and the citizens of Berlin. The key figures in the new set-up were the German Communists who had lived in exile in Moscow since 1934, such as Ulbricht. In each district figureheads were placed in nominal control as mayors, but whatever their political hue a Moscow Communist was their deputy and the real wielder of power. Thus by the time the

Allies from the West entered Berlin the Russians had already created a city administration (the *Magistrat*) which was in operation. A new mayor of Berlin (*Oberburgmeister*) was appointed at the end of May, Professor Arthur Werner, a sixty-seven-year-old retired architect who had had no previous political experience. A new system of law and order[1] was established by Paul Markgraf, the new Chief of Police, an ex-Wehrmacht officer who had been captured at Stalingrad and had thereafter seen 'the error of his ways'. The senior posts in education and radio, and the central organization for trade unions,[2] were all controlled by the Communists. On 30 May private enterprise, from shopkeepers to large companies was abolished and its function assumed by commercial counsellors and committees. Newspapers and the journalists were also taken over by the Russians; at first Berlin had only received the Soviet military newspaper,[3] but now other papers were allowed to start again, although they were subject to strict censorship and had to be printed and published in the Soviet Sector. Concerts and recitals, the theatre and the cinema had also started again in a primitive fashion by June 1945, although again under strict control.[4] No effort was spared to ensure that Berlin was operating under tight Russian surveillance by the time the Western forces arrived. However, the Russians' gift for improvisation coupled with their total dedication to Communism did mean that the city had emerged from the chaos of war with a centralized and, considering the short time available, remarkably efficient governmental system.

[1] The *Polizei präsidium*; later to be followed by the *Volkspolizei*.
[2] Free German Trade Union Federation (FDGB).
[3] *Tägliche Rundschau*.
[4] The Cultural League for the Democratic Revival of Germany was formed on 4 July.

V

AN IRON CURTAIN DESCENDS
ON EUROPE

WHEN THE various Western Allied commanders set to work
in their zones of occupation, their first priority was naturally
enough to try to bring order from the reigning chaos, their
second to undertake the necessary long-term measures for the
'democratization' of the country. Indeed, the problems now
facing these one-time soldiers who overnight had had to
become administrators were immense. They included not only
the rebuilding of the German administration to carry out the
Allies' orders, but also the restoration of communications, the
re-opening of the factories, and the feeding of the civilian population. The social problems were just as complex, for besides
being concerned with the harmonious repatriation and
demobilisation of their own armies, they also had to return to
their own countries the thousands of displaced persons who had
found themselves at the end of the war in Berlin. In the American Zone alone there were two million people who had been
brought in by the Germans, either as prisoners of war or forced
labour. The Allied Commanders also had to find homes for the
millions of refugees who had recently fled from the east.

The British Zone was the largest in terms of population, with
22·3 million, compared to 17·1 million in the American Zone
in the south. There were of course considerable differences
between the three Western zones and the way in which they
were handled. Comments from various German writers suggest
that the British were considered the most technically competent
of all. They tended to treat their zone very much as if it were a
Crown Colony, displaying the same air of order and calm, and
often contempt for the 'natives'. Although 'non-fraternisation'
had been revoked by December 1945, the British nevertheless
tended to remain rather aloof and distant from the German

people and often chose to live apart in special areas. The degree of competence amongst the 22,000 British administrators declined sharply after 1946, when the best of them returned home to take up more permanent careers. Their replacements were of inferior quality since many of them were people who had found it difficult to settle in post-war Britain and had therefore merely drifted out to Germany.

The Americans, who only had 5,000 administrators in 1946, also lacked really first-class men in sufficient numbers. The contrast between the affluence of the 'American way of life', as pursued by the US administrators, and the life-style of the average German, who was usually starving, was glaringly obvious, and at times a distinct hindrance to civil-military relations. The discrepancy resulted in a proliferation of black market practices and a marked increase in the incidence of venereal disease in the American Zone.

Among the Western powers the Americans found the most difficulty in carrying out the tasks of de-Nazification as laid down in the inter-Allied directives. Many senior officers sympathised with the controversial yet brilliant *prima donna* of Allied generals, Patton, who was dismissed from his position as Military Commander in Bavaria because of his outspoken and tactless opposition to this programme.[1]

The French were the most stringent and uncompromising of the Western occupation powers. Centuries of tempestuous Franco-German relations now found their traditional safety valve, with one side becoming the occupier of the other. To the six million Germans in the French Zone, the C-in-C in Baden-Baden seemed to behave like some proconsul, and his provincial commissioners were as lax in obeying his directives as he was in obeying those which came from Paris or the Allied Control Commission. The French Zone contained the best and the

[1] Patton had been one of the most vehement opponents of Nazism and all it stood for during the war. For him, the campaigns he fought were a personal crusade and, with his deep awareness of history, he saw the whole conflict as a religious war. Yet at the cessation of hostilities his attitude changed completely and he became one of the chief protagonists for the rapid 'normalization of relations' with the conquered peoples. In part this was a natural result of his great capacity for compassion, but it was also influenced by his awareness of a rapidly-emerging Soviet threat to the Western powers.

worst of Western Allied administration, for while some of the wisest government was to be found there simply because the French had a profound grasp of the true nature of German psychology, this went hand in hand with the most blatant excess and corruption amongst any of the forces of occupation from the West.

There can be no question that the achievement of the Western military governments was considerable—although they failed adequately to carry out the task of de-Nazification, which meant that the trials at Nuremberg (after the major criminals had been dealt with) became something of a sham—and if they tended to concentrate more on the short-term measures rather than on long-term democratization, in the circumstances it was understandable.

Re-education of the German people was an essential function of the Allied occupation. For some years to come, German youth, which had been raised in a claustrophobic world of slogan and propaganda, be it of National Socialism or the German imperialism of an earlier age, was to be confronted with the more subtle approach of three remarkably differing cultures and interpretations of democracy. For example, the Americans poured money in to found *Amerikahaüser* ('American houses'), which catered for young people and their needs; but by universal acknowledgement the most fruitful method of approach to the younger generation of Germans was that practised in the French Zone. Yet Allied progress towards a restoration of German life was bound to be only marginal in its impact so long as the overriding need of the people went unfulfilled—food. At the end of 1946 there were in Hamburg alone a hundred thousand people suffering from oedemas caused by malnutrition, and in Cologne only twelve per cent of the children were anywhere near the normal weight for their age.

According to the medical teams from the United Nations Relief and Rehabilitation Administration which were operating by 1946 in Germany, the daily requirement of calories for health and normal work was 2,650; the official ration however was 1,500 calories per day and more often than not the actual calorific intake was below 1,000 per day.

In Berlin these problems were at their most acute. Throughout the long winter of 1945–6 survival depended on the dreaded

Russian ration card system. For Berliners hunger became the decisive factor in life, a constant companion day and night. Although less dramatic than burning streets and falling masonry in the long run it took more out of people, since bombs could not fall for ever, but hunger seemed everlasting. In a city where the population was still predominantly composed of women and children, the women became the breadwinners for their families. However, there was no employment available in any recognizable sense of the word, except for that connected with the physical needs of a large male population of occupying forces. For these women a 'liaison' with an occupation soldier meant food for their children, an occasional bar of chocolate by way of a treat and, most important, cigarettes, the essential currency for barter on the black market. Even for the single and unattached girl this degrading form of existence represented the only ticket for survival. And so fear of starvation overshadowed everything, and was directly responsible for the phenomenon peculiar to this time—the *Fraülein*. However, there was nothing which could be censured as licentious about their behaviour; sensuality could hardly flourish on fifteen hundred calories a day in cold damp surroundings in the depths of a Berlin winter, and conventional morality had lost all significance to a womanhood which had already suffered the atrocities of a Russian sacking which went unchecked for seven days.

Other distinctive phenomena of the period 1945–6 in Germany were the exchange stores and the black market, both of which flourished in Berlin. Empty shops, many nothing more than rubble-strewn shells, were transformed into centres of exchange. Everything imaginable was bartered. The exchange store operator took between five and ten per cent of the value of the goods by way of commission and offered in return some rudimentary shelving and a few desks. These shops, legalised by the Allies, were constantly packed with people, yet represented just one very small part of the 'unofficial market'. By far the biggest area of operations was the black market proper, which became possibly the most important institution in the life of a Berliner. The occupation forces of both East and West tried constantly to stamp out its activities, but never succeeded. The black market was immune from such pressures simply because its operations were all-embracing; police, prosecuting attorneys and even the judges were dependent on it. On the rare occasions when an operator was tried and convicted,[1] his operations did not stop, since the prison staff relied as much as everyone else on illicit trade. In fact, in that first post-war winter, Berlin would almost certainly have starved had it not been for the black market.

Its main centre of operations was in and around the Brandenburg Gate and the burnt-out Reichstag,[2] but some kind of black market flourished wherever people met. Like any other underground movement, its true leaders were never to be seen, but their power must have been far greater than that of any four-star general in that war-ravaged city. In some commodities the average Berliner was priced out of the market, this being particularly true in the case of domestic fuel; while the citizens froze that winter, coal was available in fair quantities on the market, but at market prices, often as much as fifty times the normal price. The real currency of the market was cigarettes. The level of goods and prices fluctuated according to the simple laws of supply of and demand for cigarettes. Prices were uniform throughout the market and yet the occupation forces could never fathom out how the rate was decided on or indeed how it was transmitted to the centres of operation.

As the city began to live again, so work became available. For the most part this meant clearing away the debris of war. Men and women cleared the streets and rebuilt the city with their bare hands. Corpses were dug out and buried, the rubble was turned into building materials, and slowly but surely the new city arose out of the ashes and returned to a degree of normality. Schools reopened and municipal services began to operate on a more secure basis. Some people, usually the skilled engineers of the former Wehrmacht, were able to demand higher wages than the menial labourers. Extra money could be

[1] This would usually only occur when he had been caught handling stolen goods.

[2] Members of the occupation forces, especially the Americans in the early days, grew rich through the black market, which was interested in watches for Russian soldiers. A GI watch which cost four dollars in the USA could be sold (before the Russians got wise) for as much as ten thousand marks; the GI soldier would then receive in exchange from US Currency Control a thousand dollars.

made through the extremely hazardous occupation of rendering harmless the hundreds of unexploded bombs and shells which adorned the ruins of the city.

The swift and thorough Russian reorganization of the Eastern Zone and of Berlin itself provided a backdrop for the front-stage activities of the four powers in their task of re-establishing the administration of Germany and its erstwhile capital city. At first sight the institutional arrangements then drawn up look reasonable enough. Each zone was controlled by a commander-in-chief, and the four commanders would meet in the Allied Control Council; while Berlin was adminis-tered by a four-power *Kommandatura* which was theoretically subordinate to the Control Council. When the Control Council was unable to reach unanimous agreement, questions were referred to the respective national governments, which meant in effect the Council of Foreign Ministers. However, although the Foreign Ministers met three times in 1946 and twice in 1947, they made no more progress than did the Control Council.

The reason for this was that the Control Council was con-fronted by three problems to which the Russians proposed solutions completely unacceptable to the West. These were to establish an effective administration of Germany, to arrange payment of reparation, and finally to reduce German industry to a peace-time level acceptable to the Allies. In this situation lay the seeds of discord which, within a year, would blossom forth into the first major crisis of the post-war world. Indeed, these tasks confronting the administrators contained an inbuilt intractability which would have taxed the ingenuity and diplomacy of any government, even had their relations with one another been at their most cordial; the growing estrange-ment of East from West made the problem insoluble. The economy could hardly be run on a normal footing until the question of reparations had been mutually settled, yet the question of reparations could not be determined until the pro-ductive capacity of the whole nation was established.

Russian intransigence reached a peak over this, the most delicate of international questions. For while they continued to exact reparations from the Western zones, they sealed their own zone from the West. In September 1945 an inter-Allied Level of Industries Committee was established, to consider the matter

of industrial production. Negotiations by this Committee bore
little relation to reality, since German industry was at a standstill anyway; it would presumably have to be started up again
and then cut back. The Committee was therefore forced to base
its calculations upon an imponderable, the future industrial
potential. This task of accurately forecasting economic trends
was not helped by the fact that discussions about the figures
to be reached usually parted company with statistical economics and degenerated into political wrangling.

The crux of the matter was the figure for steel production;
once that had been established, agreement would be possible
in other areas of industry. In January 1946 the Committee
fixed the future steel production of Germany at 7·5 million tons
a year.[1] Under other agreements passed by the Committee in
March 1946 fourteen industries were prohibited and a further
twelve were severely limited. Any plant that was surplus to
requirements was to be dismantled and used to meet the
demand for reparation.

Problems arose over the implementation of these decisions.
The Russian Zone was sealed off to the West, and the Russians
were known to be taking more for their own areas than the
agreement allowed for. Moreover, they not only took capital
equipment as reparations, but also consumer goods produced
in their own zone, all the while drawing on reparations from
the West. Thus the Russians were contravening two basic
principles concerning reparations agreed at the Yalta Conference, namely, that finished products should not be liable to
confiscation, and secondly, that the amount of reparation
should be as originally agreed.[2]

The Western commanders, in particular the Americans,
lodged vehement protests. The Russians had, by sealing off
their own zone, cut the West off from the source of essential raw
materials in the Eastern Zone. This meant of course that the
West had to produce raw materials and food from their own
resources, thereby subsidizing their zones. What the Russians
had effectively done was something which they were later to

---

[1] As compared with a pre-war figure (1938) of 19·8 millions.

[2] The Russians based the figures on the $10,000 million dollars agreed at
Yalta. The West claimed that this figure had never actually been *fixed* but
was to be used purely as a working basis.

accuse the West of, that is, of dividing Germany into two parts and thereby failing to treat it as a single economic entity.[1] In the face of such blatant contravention of existing agreements the American C-in-C, General Clay, ordered the suspension of all deliveries of reparations to the East from 3 May 1946. This step was of vital significance since it implied a tacit recognition by the Americans[2] that the future of the western parts of Germany lay in Western, as opposed to joint Allied, hands.

This was soon followed by further action on the part of the West; again it was an obvious course for them to adopt, but from which the Russians made political capital. On 11 July US Secretary of State Byrnes offered to merge the US Zone with any other zone for the purposes of economic administration. Britain accepted with alacrity, mainly because the Americans offered to share equally the costs of such administration; as the British had the biggest zone, the suggestion obviously had considerable appeal. As a result of this merger administrative agencies were established which went far beyond the Potsdam Agreement. Once again the Russians protested, but the contest between the great powers was now on for the 'hearts and minds' of the German people; faced with the obstructionist attitudes of the Soviets, the Anglo-Americans felt quite rightly that Germany could not continue to exist indefinitely in the political vacuum which so obviously suited the apparent Russian design. Nevertheless, the diplomatic charade was maintained, with the Americans countering Russian allegations concerning the new bi-zone by claiming that its administrative agencies were intended as prototypes for those of a future united Germany.

American initiatives in this area were not prompted by events in Berlin and Germany alone; there were factors in the outside world which conditioned their changing attitudes. In the two years that followed the end of the war the United States had spent the vast sum of $15,000 million in restoring the economies of liberated countries. But by the end of 1946 it became clear that not only were these sums not enough but that there must be a properly constituted organisation through which the funds could be administered. Indeed, the amount of

[1] Which had been the intention behind all previous agreements.
[2] The British quickly followed the American lead.

aid was by now reaching a level where it was fast becoming a major element in US foreign policy. Those concerned with deliberating this vital question could not afford the luxury of a careful scrutiny, because time was working against them. Many of America's former wartime partners were in desperate financial straits and their needs were becoming ever more urgent.

This was especially true of Great Britain. Although there had never been any formal agreement between the two powers, the Americans had expected Britain to sponsor the recovery of Europe, especially where the Communist threat was at its most menacing, as in Greece and Turkey. In 1946 the deficit in the British balance of payments had reached an all-time high of £380 million and an American loan originally negotiated to cover the period 1945–50 had been used up by the spring of 1947. The country was in a serious plight; severe shortages in coal not only affected the domestic market (where it was heavily rationed) but were also having an adverse effect on industry, thereby obstructing moves towards national recovery. Rationing of all consumer products was as severe as in the darkest days of the war, and unemployment was increasing. Not only could Britain no longer support Greece and Turkey, but she was in immediate need of aid herself. A Labour administration was courageously trying to create a new Welfare State, but the atmosphere of the darkest days of the Depression was inexorably returning and national morale was weakening.

France seemed in an even worse position. De Gaulle had resigned from office in January 1946 and had retired in disgust to his country retreat to await his destiny. Successive governments of the highly unstable Third Republic came and fell with increasing rapidity. A vicious spiral in prices and wages led to a wave of strikes and social unrest. In Italy, the Communist and left-wing coalition seemed to have abdicated all political responsibility and now sought only to foment discord amongst the population.

Into the turmoil of Europe stepped the crusading United States with proposals for a massive aid programme. A combination of new initiatives and new personalities would lead to a revolution in American foreign policy, in the form of a formally-established peacetime relationship with Europe. This revolution began in 1947 when, after two years of hesitation, the United States began to formulate those policies, gathered under the general heading of 'containment', which were to lay the foundations for the new post-war diplomacy.

How had this radical change come about? It was primarily due to the personalities involved; and here it is necessary to examine the events of the spring of 1946. Churchill, then touring the world in a mood of resentment at the ingratitude of the British electorate, gave a lecture on 'The Present International Situation' at Westminster College in Fulton, Missouri.[1] Truman made a special journey to be present. In his speech, which has become a byword in the discussion of international relations, Churchill talked of 'an iron curtain that has descended across the continent of Europe'. He went on to say: 'From what I have seen of our Russian friends and allies during the war, I am convinced that there is nothing they admire so much as strength and nothing for which they have less respect than military weakness.' The whole tenor of this address, to 43,000 Americans,[2] was that time was short and that the English-speaking peoples must urgently unite in order to remove 'every temptation to adventure'.

Many commentators have since claimed that Churchill, by making such an inflammatory speech at a time when international relations were at their most delicate, helped to precipitate the Cold War. Considering the hysteria with which his pronouncements were received this is an understandable opinion to adopt. However, all they had really done was to record for history, in the language of a romantic visionary, the true extent of the deterioration in relations between the wartime allies.

In the resulting diplomatic furore, both the British and American governments hastened to dissociate themselves from Churchill's views. But the very fact that Truman had gone to hear Churchill, plus rumours to the effect that the two men had met some three weeks previously to discuss the speech, led the press to regard the speech as promulgation of a new doctrine of Western diplomacy. Certainly the Kremlin, recalling with convenient clarity Churchill's campaign for intervention with Germany in Russia in 1918–19, made considerable political capital

[1] The Alma Mater of President Truman.
[2] More than four times the population of the town of Fulton.

out of the incident.[1] However, Churchill was in all probability speaking to a converted and already contentious Truman, since a month before the President had written to Secretary Byrnes that he was 'tired of babying the Soviets'.

Another personality who came into prominence at that time was General Marshall. He had been Chief of Staff of the US armed forces before and throughout the war, and had been responsible for choosing the military leaders of the victorious American armies; brilliant generals such as MacArthur, Eisenhower, Bradley and Patton owed their pre-eminence, and the Allies a debt of gratitude, to this great soldier. He had retired from the Army and had succeeded Byrnes as Truman's Secretary of State. Marshall was a servant of the state in the true sense of the word; he had worked unselfishly for victory and had become a trusted adviser of Roosevelt[2] and now, in a new situation, he was to serve Truman in the same way.

In 1947, along with another great general, Bedell Smith (who was now Ambassador to Moscow), he had represented the United States at the Foreign Ministers Conference. In Moscow, Marshall became convinced not only of the reality of Soviet ambitions for a Communist-dominated Germany but also of the serious threat that Russia posed to the United States. His convictions were substantiated (in his opinion) by the wave of industrial agitation and left-wing protest which had spread throughout Western Europe, which he saw as Communist-inspired. Stopping in Berlin on his way home on 25 April 1947, Marshall instructed General Clay to speed up the establishment of the bi-zone and the restoration of industrial capacity. At the same time Bedell Smith wrote in his despatch to the White House: 'The alternatives of a divided Germany, or a Germany under the effective economic and political domination of the Soviet Union, have become unmistakably clear.'

So by early 1947 the Russian objective had become painfully obvious to Western eyes. It was, in their view, to secure a new and centralized German government within the Communist

[1] 'I do not know whether he and his friends will succeed in organizing a new campaign against Eastern Europe—but it may confidentially be said that they will be thrashed just as they were twenty-six years ago'—Stalin.

[2] Although never sharing the same fascination for 'the State' which Roosevelt always felt.

satellite system. Since both East and West still envisaged Berlin as the capital of any new Germany, control of that capital, from the Eastern point of view, and at least the maintenance of the *status quo* from the Western point of view, became an essential objective of the respective foreign policies. Russian attitudes were so blatant that there could be no disguising their intentions. For the aim of the Kremlin to be fulfilled it was absolutely essential that Germany should be a single unit. The Berlin Blockade was therefore a logical progression in Russian policy, since by then the Americans had drastically reversed their original decision to maintain a presence in Germany for two years only. Indeed, by 1947 this Western presence showed distinct signs of becoming permanent. The Blockade can therefore be seen as an attempt by the Russians to force the issue, to test the West's integrity towards the German people. Their failure to break the Allied hold on Berlin was followed by a partial recognition of the new order and the stable division of Germany into two blocs.

VI

THE MARSHALL PLAN

BY APRIL 1947, within two years of the end of the war, a new battle had developed over Berlin. This time it was not fought with tanks and guns for the conquest of a capital city, as in 1945, but with declarations of intent and promises, with threats and counter-threats, for the prize of the allegiance of a people and the integrity of a principle. This new, political conflict developed at various levels. On the one hand the forces of occupation engaged in diplomatic wrangling in the *Kommandatura*. The newly-formed political parties fought amongst themselves to capture popular support. The victorious nations of the West were slowly forced to divert their attention away from the complex problems of domestic politics, to become drawn into a wider political arena. With Berlin as the focal point, tension heightened into a crisis situation.

By 1947 the tremendous advantages which the Russians had secured for themselves in the first few months of the occupation of Berlin had been eroded by a series of major errors of political judgement. It had been an adroit move on their part to allow the simultaneous creation of four political parties. Because political activity under Hitler had been confined to National Socialism to the exclusion of all else, the people of post-war Germany were assumed to be naïve in the matter of party politics. As the two middle-class parties with their 'bourgeois' emphasis had not existed in the past, the Russians fully expected that the two workers' parties of the Left[1] would receive the majority of the working-class vote in Berlin.

By the spring of 1946, the Russians began to have doubts about the wisdom of these earlier moves and so decided to safeguard the position of their protégé Communist party by

[1] Communists and Social Democrats.

trying to force the Social Democrats to merge with it. At first the leaders of the Left refused to agree to such a forced marriage, so the Russians retaliated with intimidation. Physical pressure, in the form of long hours of interrogation, weakened the resolve of some of the older and more frail men, who changed their minds and agreed to lend their support to the Russian plans. However, the more stout-hearted, backed by the middle level of party leaders and the active workers, decided that the only way to resolve the question was by holding a referendum among the rank and file membership, on the alternatives of independence of the party or union with the Communists. On 31 May 1946 the first genuine democratic vote in Berlin for fourteen years took place when the Social Democrats went to the polls. The Russians viewed the whole affair with some alarm but could do little more to impede the referendum than to close the polling booths in their own section of the city. In the three western sectors, more than seventy per cent of the registered members of the Social Democratic Party went to the polls and, of these, eighty-two per cent were against any form of union with the Communists.

This referendum was of great significance in the atmosphere of gathering crisis, for although it only concerned 25,000 people, but a fraction of the total electorate, it was the first popular rejection of the Russians by the citizens of Berlin. Whilst the results were received with great jubilation by the majority of the people, the East German Communists under Ulbricht responded by ignoring them and forming their own party, a merger of the Communists and those Social Democrats under Russian control. The new party was called the Amalgamated Workers Party (SED).

This first political mistake was compounded by another in the autumn of that same year. The four-power occupation forces in the *Kommandatura* had agreed on the need for a full-scale election in Berlin to choose the city's first Municipal Parliament, which was to have 130 deputies. In the month preceding polling day the election campaign came to have far more significance than that for a mere local government election. For the citizens of Berlin the election meant taking sides between East or West. Consequently, both East and West became increasingly involved in subtle (and often not so subtle) intrigues to influence the electorate. And though the election was of very real importance for the Berliner, for the rest of the world who read about it in an extensive press coverage it seemed a symbol of the new international power struggle.

Russian propaganda took various forms during the campaign. Inducements were distributed on a large scale—shoes for children and whisky for men. There were frequent electricity failures, a reminder to the citizens that the generators lay in the Russian sector. The Russian press even hinted that there would be a more comprehensive publication of the names of POWs from Berlin in Russian hands if the people voted correctly.

The Americans and the British, faced with these Russian manoeuvres, gradually became more and more drawn into playing an opposing game, albeit rather reluctantly. In the month before the election the Americans transported into Berlin, for distribution to the people, a million boxes of matches, 155,000 pairs of shoes, 10,000 bicycle tyres, 3,000 car tyres, 17,000 tons of cement, 12,000 square metres of glass, 200 tons of paper and 5,000 tons of structural steel.

The SED carried out a vast advertising campaign in which the whole of Berlin was festooned with mammoth placards and posters. This left very little space for the other parties, but what little there was, was put to crushing use, often completely nullifying all the extravagance of the SED.[1]

The results of this election, which in so many ways was reminiscent of the Hogarth cartoon of an election in a 'rotten borough', came as no surprise to the West. The American occupation forces had indeed forecast the results to within three per cent of the actual figures:

Social Democrats	47%
CDU	21%
Liberal Democrats	9%
Communist SED	19%

This represented a catastrophic defeat for the Russians. Accordingly, they proceeded to ignore the figures and, by some statistical juggling, they soon convinced themselves that they had in fact won, at the same time carrying out a brutal reprisal

[1] A CDU poster which was particularly effective asked, 'Were you raped by a Russian? Vote for the SED.'

for the 'ingratitude' shown by the citizens of Berlin. Two years earlier those skilled workers[1] who had survived the war in Berlin had been forced to sign a declaration that they would, under certain conditions, agree to work in the Soviet Union. As a direct result of the election defeat, Operation Ossavakim was implemented. In the dead of night, just two days after the election, army trucks arrived in various streets of Berlin and more than 25,000 skilled craftsmen and their families were forcibly transported into the eastern zone and beyond. The Western occupation forces protested through the proper channels, the *Kommandatura* and the Control Commission, all of which protests were promptly vetoed by the Russians. The carnival atmosphere of the people of Berlin, rejoicing in the bright future opened up by the election victory, disappeared with the exodus of this forced labour. It was replaced by a feeling of insecurity, an awareness of the feebleness of the West's protests and a new fear of the physical menace of the Soviet Union. That second winter of the post-war period was harsher than ever, and conditions in Berlin were desperate. By January 1947 more than 15,000 people were in danger of freezing to death and ten per cent of all hospital beds were occupied by pneumonia cases. The widespread despondency led to an alarming increase in the suicide rate.

Yet, as Berlin thawed out in the spring of 1947, momentous developments were afoot in international politics; the Truman Doctrine became a reality. This fell into two parts. The first was the declaration by President Truman to Congress on 12 March 1947, in response to the British decision that she could no longer underwrite the integrity of Greece and Turkey. The significance of the President's address was contained in this assertion: 'I believe that it must be the policy of the United States to support free peoples who are resisting attempted subjugation by armed minorities or by outside pressures.'

The implications of this promulgation of a policy of 'containment' were enormous; the United States was now constitutionally equipped to take up its new diplomatic function as chief prop to the tottering *status quo* throughout the world. Once this had been accomplished, a drastic redefinition of the global

[1] Including engineers, technicians, precision tool makers, architects and surveyors.

balance of power and of international spheres of interest could proceed quickly. The new patterns of realignment and 'containment' were to be most clearly seen in divided Germany and partitioned Berlin.

The initial reaction to the Truman Doctrine in the West was cautious and often ambivalent. The Conservative opposition in Britain, already pre-conditioned by Churchill's 'iron curtain' speech, had visions of a new era of Anglo-American co-operation. The Labour administration, whilst not whole-heartedly in favour, tended to follow the lead of their foreign minister, Bevin, who recognized that the American alliance must be one of the essential cornerstones of post-war British foreign policy.

Opposition to the doctrine came from what might be called the 'true' Left who, in Britain, France and the United States, saw it as nothing more than a peacetime revitalization of military Lend-Lease, which would result in a bipolar division of the world.

To a certain extent these critics of the Truman Doctrine[1] were proved right. The policies that proceeded from it did harden and maintain a division of Europe which had at first been merely an accidental consequence of the movement of armies in the Second World War. It imposed a heavy and increasing burden, both economic and military, on the United States. It turned the partition of Germany from an expedient of occupation into a political reality of the future. It ushered in a period of every level of hostility, short of all-out war, between the USSR and the West. Yet for all this, the Cold War did create its own kind of stability, since it avoided both general war and defeat without war.

The other part of the Truman Doctrine was the concrete promise of material aid known as the Marshall Plan. Although Churchill observed that the Marshall Plan was the most unsordid act in history, it would be wrong to regard this massive aid programme by the United States as being simply an example of open-hearted generosity from a rich nation towards its brethren in distress. Indeed, disinterested generosity could hardly have received the blessing of the US Senate, composed as it predominantly was of hard-headed businessmen turned

[1] Truman had seen the future international scene as based on a triangular situation of USA, USSR and the third force of a United Europe.

politicians. The war had weakened the isolationist lobby in the Senate and there were many, from both political parties, who recognized that in the new super-power world the United States could not hope to survive without allies. The growing awareness of the Soviet threat had created a large body of opinion which saw excellent sense in diverting part of the national wealth to support the economies of the nations in 'no-man's-land', thereby creating a first line of defence in Western Europe.

The American State Department recognized that although this no-man's-land in Europe needed to be bolstered up economically, it could easily become a bottomless pit into which the vast resources of the United States would disappear without trace. As Truman put it in his memoirs: 'If the nations of Europe could be induced to develop their own solution of Europe's economic problems, reviewed as a whole and tackled co-operatively rather than as separate national problems, United States aid would be more effective and the strength of a recovered Europe would be better sustained.'[1] As there were strings attached to this US offer, it was necessary that the Western Europeans should co-operate in some institution which could then present a collective 'shopping-list' to the United States. The same institution would then be used to distribute this aid to the member states. The Secretary of State himself made this precondition absolutely clear in his speech at Harvard on 5 June 1947. European reaction was immediately favourable and the initiative was seized by Britain and France, the result being the formation of the Organization for European Economic Co-operation (OEEC); thus the first 'Community of Europe' was born.

Another important assertion in Marshall's Harvard speech was that the Plan excluded no one from the offer of aid: 'Our policy is directed not against any country or doctrine but against hunger, poverty, desperation, and chaos.'[2] The tone of Marshall's offer hence softened considerably the vehemence of Truman's initial statements; indictment and crusade had given way to a call for reconciliation and co-operation for the common good. Not that Marshall believed the Russians would agree to

[1] Truman II, p. 113.
[2] Congressional Record, 30 June 1947.

enter the new European organization with any real integrity; his own brief experiences at the Moscow Conference had shown the unlikelihood of this. Events inside Eastern Europe seemed further to confirm this, when politicians in Rumania and Bulgaria who were not disciples of the Moscow School[1] were liquidated. In fact, the Russian reaction to Marshall Aid was easily predicted, since Stalin feared that subscription to the Plan would only result in a consolidation of American influence in Europe. On 16 June 1947 *Pravda* branded it as a new manifestation of Truman's tactic of political pressure backed up with dollars, leading to interference in the internal affairs of other countries.

The Russians were determined that their opposition to the Plan be demonstrated in a manner which would create maximum impact. Therefore, obviously playing a diplomatic game, with the aim of inducing in the Western powers a false sense of security, the Soviet Foreign Minister, Molotov, attended the meeting called by the British and French in Paris on 26 June. Within three days the Russian intention to disrupt became plain; they suggested various conditions for European acceptance of the aid which, though wrapped up in high-sounding principles, would inevitably be rejected by the Americans and thereby give the Soviet Union a major propaganda victory. What the Russians really wanted was bilateral aid without conditions or controls. The French tried desperately to reach some form of compromise. In this they received help from Bevin, who shrewdly appreciated that any departure from the clearly-defined American conditions, which included Soviet participation, would result in rejection by the US Senate and a termination of the whole offer.

Finally, on 2 July the Soviet delegation broke off negotiations and forbade all the East European countries to accept the aid. As a direct consequence of this, were the West Europeans to go ahead with the programme they would be creating an overt division of Europe into two blocs, with the eastern and western zones of Germany on opposite sides of this partition.

But what of the western sectors of Berlin? In the summer of 1947 their fate was still to be determined. Since it now seemed obvious Marshall Aid would result in Germany being divided

[1] Most of them connected with the non-Marxist Agrarian Party.

into two and the Iron Curtain descending on the Elbe, Berlin would then become an oasis of Western influence deep inside alien territory. The acceptance of the Marshall Plan by the West was a thoroughly understandable decision on their part, but it did inevitably mean that sooner or later the central battle of the Cold War would be fought over Germany.

That conflict was to come sooner rather than later and it was to be a battle for Berlin. Throughout the spring and early summer of 1947 the city had increasingly suffered from the restrictions that the Russians placed on the freedom of its citizens. Indeed, their first move was to prevent the Social Democrats' choice as Chief Bürgermeister, Ernst Reuter, from taking office. In the turbulent years following the end of the Great War and later in the Weimar Republic, Reuter had been first a Communist and then, disillusioned by the demands of Moscow, a Socialist. He had risen to a position of some eminence as a trade union leader, eventually becoming Mayor of Magdeburg. On coming to power Hitler had had Reuter removed to a concentration camp very early on, and it was only through the good offices of the influential British Quakers that the Nazis reluctantly allowed him to go into a self-imposed exile. Reuter settled in Turkey where, although he was at great pains to retain his passport and thereby his German citizenship, he once again rose to a powerful administrative position. First he became Professor of Social Economics at Ankara University and then throughout the war held an important position in the Turkish Civil Service as an adviser. At the end of the war Reuter realized his lifelong dream, to return to a Germany which he hoped would be free. Diplomatic red tape held up his return for some eighteen months, so he did not arrive in Berlin until the municipal elections were actually being held. The Russians would not allow him to become the new mayor and vetoed his nomination in the *Kommandatura* on the grounds of what they claimed was his 'Turkish citizenship'. The West, while sympathizing with Reuter's position, were loath to press the case too much, since they were unsure whether it was within their jurisdiction to interfere. So for the meanwhile Reuter, though now resident in the city, took a back seat and allowed a woman, Louise Schroeder, to act as his representative.

Other acts of Russian provocation sought simply to increase tension. Berliners carrying western sector newspapers in the eastern zone were arrested. Normal railway passenger services from the eastern zone were carefully scrutinised before being allowed to enter Berlin. Cars from the west were forbidden to enter the eastern zone unless they carried special permits which, needless to say, were extremely difficult to obtain.

As Berlin entered its third winter of the Cold War domestic conditions had improved a little, but there was to be no let-up in Russian obstructiveness and no easing of tension.

On 24 January 1948 Russian security guards stopped a British train at the border and detached two passenger coaches which carried Germans. No sooner had the protests from the West been registered than, a fortnight later, an American military train was stopped in exactly the same manner and all German passengers were forced to submit to a humiliating search. Further complaints from the West were simply ignored.

There was now every sign that the Russians intended to blockade the city. The Western commanders had received ample and accurate warning of this from the people of Berlin, but for some inexplicable reason they were ignored. In February and March, the Russians increased their control over movement between their own sector of the city and the western areas by physically tearing up a number of thoroughfares, thus channelling all border-crossing through a smaller number of routes.

On 20 March 1948 the Soviet delegation walked out of the Control Commission, because the Western representatives would not furnish them with the minutes of the London Conference[1] called to discuss the question of reform of the German currency, the issue which was to spark off this first conflict of the Cold War.

On 1 April Marshal Sokolovsky wrote to his British and American counterparts,[2] demanding that Russian military police should control all traffic, road, rail and inland waterway, from the western sectors into Berlin; this the West refused to accept. Finally, on 5 April a Soviet interceptor collided with an

1 The Soviets had been invited to attend, but had refused.
2 General Robertson for Britain, General Clay for the United States.

R.A.F. transport aircraft coming in to land at Gatow. The crash was witnessed by many people, who were unanimous in their assertion that the accident was caused by the Soviet pilot 'buzzing' the British aircraft and misjudging his final pass. Indeed, Marshal Sokolovsky telephoned General Robertson to apologise for the incident. Yet within twenty-four hours the Soviet leader had completely changed his attitude, claiming that a Russian 'impartial enquiry' had found the British pilot to blame.

On 18 June the American, British and French occupation forces, recognizing that it was impossible to reach agreement with the Russians on the best way to stop the general inflation, promulgated a law in their zones to establish a new currency. On that evening all passenger trains between the Russian and western zones were stopped and so was traffic on the Berlin–Helmstedt Road. The Russians considered this currency reform law absolutely critical since, if it came into operation, it could only threaten still further their attainment of the objectives they had pursued since the end of the war. Strong as they were in their own zone, they were still no nearer to dominating the whole of Germany, or to participation in the control of the Ruhr. Berlin, which might have been expected to become part of the eastern zone after the withdrawal of American troops, was developing as an outpost of capitalist democracy within a Communist state.

On the night when most road and rail traffic was stopped the new Allied currency had not been actually introduced into the city, merely the necessary decrees published. The Russians insisted that the Berlin currency should be the same as that in the eastern sector and zone. This the Western powers accepted, but with the proviso that it should be subject to four-power control. The Russians rejected this and on 23 June carried out their own currency reform in their zone and indeed made it applicable to the whole of Germany. The Western powers then introduced their own currency in their sectors where such was the confidence shown in it by Berliners that on a free and confused money market it rapidly gained a position of supremacy over the Russian coinage. On the same day rail traffic of every kind between Berlin and the West was stopped. At six o'clock on the morning of 24 June, under the pretext of having to repair bridges over the Elbe, the Russians stopped all traffic on the autobahn.

General Clay, ever the man of action, suggested sending an armed convoy through. But in Washington, where the utmost confusion reigned, the word was to abstain from any provocation. The Blockade of Berlin was thus complete—except by air.

Part Two

VII

THE DIVIDED CITY

THE BERLIN BLOCKADE was neither a clear nor a continuous struggle; many and distinct were the events which influenced the overall situation in Berlin at that time, and the course of the conflict can be chronologically divided into three periods. The first covers the months from April to June 1948, when the Russians gradually increased their hold over the city. This Communist pressure was applied by two agencies in two directions; on the Western occupation powers by the Russians and on the Berlin population by the German Communist party. In many respects this period was comparatively successful for the Soviet presence. Its subtle methods of raising and lowering tension made the Western occupation forces extremely jittery, with an equally serious effect on Western political leaders, who seemed confused. As these leaders apparently had no clearly-defined policy and no contingency plans for Berlin, the Russian initiatives sent them into alternating moods of optimism and pessimism throughout the early summer months.

The citizens of Berlin themselves were influenced to a considerable degree not only by these overt pressures from the Soviet government but also by the pronouncements of the SED. The latter in effect issued an ultimatum, making it quite clear that the price to be paid for the continued unity of the city was refusal to adopt the Western currency proposals. Many Berliners were indeed tempted to accept the intended reforms, yet few had any illusions about the repercussions of such a step upon the future of their city.

From June to September of that year, throughout a long hot summer, the blockade of Berlin became complete except for the air corridors. The Allies implemented their currency reforms, and the Berliners in the western sectors quickly became united in their stand against the threat from the east. During these months, as the operation of the Airlift became more efficient, so it took on additional significance; not only was it a highly successful solution to the problem of feeding the people but also this very effectiveness gave it immense political value. The Western Allies hence used it as a bargaining point in their continued attempts to reach a negotiated settlement with the Soviets.

From September 1948 on the Allies finally realized that they could indefinitely provide by air the means to sustain the people of West Berlin, and so preserve the integrity of their presence. Thus the operation now assumed a military function as, united with the people of that beleaguered city, the Allies became determined to stare the Russians out. The Airlift could now only fail through a breakdown in the system or a loss of resolve on the part of one of the participants. Since the Russians obviously had no intention of escalating into war, everything depended on the efficiency, the *military* efficiency, of the Allied effort. However, there was certainly considerable international tension too during this period, which prompted the US Air Force to deploy B-29s armed with atomic bombs to airfields in England. Finally, the success of the operation at this time meant that Berlin, Germany and Europe had become irrevocably partitioned into two blocs.

One reason for the complexity of the events surrounding the Blockade, with its interplay of civil-military relations, was that Russian policy itself underwent a significant change of direction during 1948. The Russians began in January 1948 by interfering with certain aspects of Western communications and authority. At that time their objective was clear, to undermine the credibility of the Western position in Germany by the straightforward expedient of forcing them out of Berlin. Very few of the leaders in the West saw the Soviet intention and its implications with the same clarity as General Clay: 'When Berlin falls Western Germany will be next . . . if we withdraw, our position in Europe is threatened . . . and Communism will run rampant.' Clay and his Allied colleagues in Berlin saw the Russian blockade as an alternative to actual war as a means of dominating Germany.

By September 1948 it had become increasingly obvious to the

Soviet Union that not only was the Blockade not going to work, but that the Allies had every intention of remaining in the city. So, without abandoning their long-term aims, the Russians decided to create a separate East German state with East Berlin as the capital city. Hence the Blockade evolved into a smoke-screen behind which this stratagem could be carried out.

The Russian decision to alter their objective was by no means entirely a result of the success of the Allied airlift; indeed, a decidedly more immediate reason was the fact that, by September 1948, the Soviets and the SED had completely failed to intimidate the *Magistrat* and Assembly into accepting the Communist line. The campaign to force the people to choose between a Western currency and a united city, on the assumption that they would choose the latter, had not succeeded.

This harrowing tale of intimidation began at the time when the Allies were making their first tentative steps towards organizing an airlift of supplies into the city. The direct attack on the Municipal Government and its infrastructure followed a period of relative political tranquillity. Except for a few diehards in the SPD, the rank and file as well as the leadership of the political parties in Berlin recognized that it was in everyone's interests to preserve the unity of the city. After the initial alarms of January and February 1948, there had been a relaxation of tension along the frontiers, while inside the city the Western-orientated parties sought to find an effective compromise solution to their differences with the SED. This calm before the gathering storm saw considerable harmonious agreement within the Assembly over further measures for the economic reform of Berlin. The SED were behaving themselves and the citizens held out high hopes for a secure, stable and, above all, free and peaceful future.

Yet, as the question of currency reform became more pressing in the Western Zones of Germany, so it began to exert an influence over life in Berlin. The Allies had held a conference on bi-zone currency reform in Bad Hamburg, near Frankfurt, in the American Zone in May 1948. Their first intention was not to include the western sector of Berlin in the proposed reform but to treat it as an entirely separate issue. This attitude was conditioned in part by a marked reluctance amongst politicians outside Berlin to provoke a crisis in the city itself, simply because they at that time believed they would lose. Similarly, most of the realistically-minded Western-orientated parties in Berlin, the Christian Democrats in particular, also counselled caution. They were prompted to a considerable extent by fear of Russian reprisals and a realization of the ineffectiveness of Western protection, as proved by the events which had followed the municipal elections.

As Clay alone of the Allied leaders understood the strategic implications of the Russian threat to Berlin, so Reuter appreciated the political consequences to the city if there were any compromise over currency reform. He believed that the salvation of Berlin lay with a Western-orientated government indissolubly linked through a common currency with the western zones of Germany. His influence was such that a number of representatives were sent from the *Magistrat* to the Bad Hamburg conference. Here they received support from an unexpected quarter. The provincial Chief Ministers in the Council of State[1] advocated an all-German solution to the currency question and that the western sector of Berlin should be included in any western zone reforms. This support carried far more weight than any that could have been rallied from within Berlin at the time.

On 18 June Frau Schroeder, the acting mayor,[2] was summoned to Sokolovsky's headquarters and told that the East Zone currency which the Russians were about to introduce was to be used throughout the whole of Berlin. The Western commanders supported Frau Schroeder in her refusal to accept this Soviet directive and declared that the Western currency would be introduced instead. Everything now depended on the *Magistrat* and the Assembly; would they support this new alignment of the SPD with the Western occupation powers, or would they compromise their principles for the sake of the continued unity of the city? If the *Magistrat* refused to accept the Western currency the Russians would have gained a considerable political victory. In the event, the *Magistrat* compromised and suggested that the two currencies should be circulated on an equal basis throughout the city. The Russians

---

[1] Set up by the Anglo-Americans as one of the first administrative organs of the Bi-Zone.

[2] The Russians were still refusing to sanction the election of Reuter.

however did not see this as a compromise, since the mere fact that it implied a *de facto* recognition of the Western currency was regarded as a flagrant defiance of their authority.

The honeymoon was over. On 23 June the City Assembly met at the old Rathaus[1] to ratify the compromise solution of the *Magistrat*. When the delegates arrived they were confronted by a demonstration stage-managed by the Communists. East Berlin police stood by as the Assembly and its proceedings were disrupted by the agitators. All this was stage-managed in the sense that it was not the Soviet intention to have the meeting broken up but merely to intimidate the members by a visible sign of Russian power. When the meeting was over and the decisions ratified, the delegates were once again confronted by a hostile mob outside the building. Many were physically set upon and beaten up, this time with the active help of the Communist police. That night all Western power supplies coming from the eastern sector were cut off and large areas of the city blacked out.

The people of Berlin replied to these violations of their liberty by immediate defiance of Soviet authority. A number of counter-demonstrations were organized and the whole issue ceased to be merely one of currency reform but escalated into a struggle for the very survival of democracy in Berlin. This popular response had an important influence on the political and military leadership of the West. As the Airlift operation swung into a professional rhythm, these leaders realized that they possessed two important factors in their favour. Firstly, they had the support of the people of Berlin, and secondly, it became manifestly obvious that the Russians had no intention of provoking actual war. During July 1948 the Airlift gathered momentum and beneath the constant streams of transport aircraft the morale of the city rose.

But the Russians had not yet finished. During August they increased their pressure on the *Magistrat* and Assembly. For neither body was there to be the luxury of a summer recess, but instead a violent campaign against selected ministers. Midnight interrogations, the constant presence of Russian liaison officers and a bitter and abusive press campaign characterized that troubled summer. In mid-August, as a result of these

[1] Situated in the Soviet sector.

constant pressures, Frau Schroeder's health broke down. It was astounding that this frail woman had continued in office for so long, under almost impossible conditions. A fervent Socialist since the days of the Weimar Republic, she was completely dedicated to the welfare of her people. Quiet and unassuming, she used none of the trappings of pomp and ceremony[1] that went with her high office, and was tremendously popular with the ordinary people of Berlin, who referred to her as 'Aunt Louise'.[2] It seems ironical that a middle-aged spinster should have become the symbol of defiance in this divided city.

When Frau Schroeder left for the comparative serenity of the western zones, her deputy, Friedsenburg, became acting mayor. The Russians put pressure on him, since he was the leader of the CDU and if he fell, he would be replaced by the next deputy in line of seniority, who was a member of the SED.

Friedsenburg not only weathered the storm but retaliated in kind. Backed by the vast majority of the Assembly, he dismissed all Communists from ministerial posts and suspended the Chief of Police, the Communist Markgraf, when he attempted to move his headquarters into the Soviet sector.

After the suspension of Markgraf, the Western Allies recognized his successor, Stumm. This caused a split in the police force, with a sizeable proportion following Markgraf into the Soviet camp. A number of Ministries, including those of Finance and Food, moved their offices into the Western sector. In addition, the Assembly sent an appeal to the General Assembly of the United Nations, so that the whole world might learn of the plight of democracy in Berlin.

On 25 August the SED newspapers prepared the way for further intimidation by calling for 'direct action' and a 'popularly-elected' *Magistrat* and Assembly. The democratic parties saw this as the preliminary to a *putsch* by the East and a revolution in the city and government. The events of the following

[1] Even to the extent of still living in a single furnished room and travelling to work each day on public transport, although an official car was provided.

[2] A popular saying of fifty years before once again became all the rage: 'Oh Louise! Keine Frau ist so wie diese.' (Oh Louise! There is no woman like her.)

day seemed to confirm their fears, when another meeting of the whole Assembly was broken up by mob-violence, and tension in the city reached an unprecedented level.[1]

As August 1948 drew to a tempestuous close, Reuter emerged actively on to the political scene by leading a number of large-scale demonstrations[2] sponsored by the SPD to protest against Communist actions. On 25 August the Soviets once again broke up a meeting of the *Magistrat*; it was by now clear to all of pro-Western sympathies that the *Magistrat* could no longer function in the eastern zone. But for the time being many of the delegates showed considerable courage in running the gauntlet of abuse, missiles and blows to attend the Council Chamber. 6 September was the worst day for violence, when every member of the delegates' escort of Western police officers was beaten up and a number severely injured.

The Assembly now moved into the British sector and took over the Technical University in the Steinplatz. The SED remained in occupation of the Rathaus in the eastern sector; thus the city was effectively divorced from its main centres of administration. On 7 September a number of Western police, who had taken refuge in the Western liaison officers' quarters in the Rathaus after the beating-up of the previous day, departed to their own sector under the protection of a safe-conduct from the Soviet authorities. As soon as they left the sanctuary of the building they were arrested and spirited away into oblivion. Word quickly spread of this Soviet outrage and within a short time more than 35,000 people had gathered to demonstrate in the Platz der Republik. After impassioned speeches from various political leaders, a large crowd moved on to the Brandenburg Gate. Soviet guards were manhandled and the Red Banner torn from its flagpole. The Russian guards opened fire, killing one man and injuring several more. Street fighting broke out and quickly spread, ebbing and flowing for more than an hour. The incident might easily have escalated into a military clash, had it not been for the prompt action of

[1] The Western commanders were particularly alarmed by these events because, if there had been any trouble, they could not have suppressed it by military force; there were only 6,000 Western troops as against 18,000 Russians, of whom there were of course far more in the immediate area.

[2] Some of these demonstrations involved over 50,000 people.

the British military police, who succeeded in separating the crowd from the Soviet troops.

Even after this incident some ministers still went stubbornly each day to the Rathaus on behalf of the West, but the administrative dissection of the city was complete. On 3 December the SED elected a new *Magistrat* and two days later the Western sectors conducted their second municipal election.[1] The result was a foregone conclusion, with Reuter's SPD now firmly established in a majority position in the western half of the city. This was something of a rebuff for the Christian Democrats, who lost seats to the SPD; however, this was not really surprising, since the CDU had counselled caution over currency reform, in the interests of preserving the unity of the city, and the electorate had obviously misconstrued this as a sign of weakness. Nevertheless, the CDU and the Liberals (who had thirty-five seats) still retained an active share of administrative responsibility, since Reuter insisted that the only workable form of municipal government in a crisis situation was an all-party coalition.

Meanwhile, the airlift itself, during the summer and winter of 1948, had gained momentum as the Allied relief organization got into its stride. Put simply, their problem was to feed two and a half million citizens as well as the occupation forces. At the minimum the Allied planners believed that this would require the US Air Force to fly in 4,500 tons of cargo a day and the RAF a further 1,500 tons. But this would simply meet the demand for food; it made no allowance for winter fuel and any other economic needs of the city.

Just as in the three years since the end of the war a group of generals acting in a political capacity had wrestled with the complex problems of restoring German political and economic life, so now, with the advent of the Blockade, a group of Air Force commanders had to direct what was essentially a gigantic civil transport undertaking. Their task was to organize a non-stop air freight service filling every minute of the day and night, every day of the week, to get supplies into Berlin.

By using an airlift as the means of breaking the Blockade, the West possessed an avenue of supply which the Russians could not impede without resorting to armed force; being thus

[1] As provided for in the Constitution of 1946.

beyond Russian control, its only limiting factors were those of the capabilities of the Allies themselves, who could in effect send as many planes to Berlin as their air forces were capable of handling.

Yet General Clay had been anxious, before the airlift became an established fact, to attempt an alternative solution which he thought was open to the Allies. Accordingly, in early July, he wrote to Washington suggesting that the Allies inform Moscow of their intention to send an armed convoy through from Helmstedt, carrying engineering equipment to help the Russians repair the bridges. Clay was convinced the Russians did not want war and he later wrote in his memoirs:

> I made it clear that I understood fully the risk and implications, and that this was a decision which could only be made by Government. No armed convoy could cross the border without the possibility of trouble. In my view the chances of such a convoy being met by force, with a subsequent development of hostilities, were small.
>
> I was confident it would get through to Berlin and that the Blockade would be ended.
>
> When our Government turned down my suggestion I understood its desire to avoid this risk of armed conflict until the issue had been placed before the U.N. I shall always believe that the convoy would have reached Berlin.

One must obviously feel sympathy for Clay's opinions, since he was the man on the spot. However, it was generally thought that he was taking an over-simplified view. The convoy would in all probability have got through, but the Russians would then on some pretext or other have refused permission for the use of the equipment which it carried, and the Blockade would have been re-imposed. The inevitable next step would have been a food convoy under armed guard, representing a far more direct challenge to Russian authority, and one in which the risk of provoking a military clash would have been very real.

But all this belongs to the realm of the hypothetical. The actual course of events in the five years from 1948 established Berlin as the barometer for the mood of the occupying powers and also to a certain extent, as their conscience.

VIII

THE BERLIN 'BRIDGE TO THE WEST'

DURING THE last quarter-century Western society has been revolutionized by the impact of air communications. Giant airliners, capable of carrying in luxury three hundred or more people, are now an accepted part of everyday life, just as supersonic warplanes, able to deliver death on an enormous scale, have been an essential part of any nation's defence arsenal for more than a decade. Although the Berlin Airlift occurred only twenty-five years ago, it is difficult for us now to appreciate that air travel was then still in its infancy. Before 1939 passenger and freight communications had been carried out in something of a pioneering spirit; however, war being the pacemaker of technology, the Second World War had stimulated tremendous improvements in the capabilities of aircraft and air travel. These had been mainly confined to military machines, and in 1948 the airliners and freighters in use were nothing more than developments of the bombers and military transports which had been manufactured during the war.

The transport aircraft in most common use in 1948 was the C-47, the Douglas Dakota. A rugged and durable machine, it had been the aerial general factotum of wartime before it became the workhorse of the armies of occupation. But the Dakota's twin engines could only lift a mere 6,000 pounds[1] of payload, which was simply not enough to meet the escalating demands of a city under siege. The need for bigger and faster machines was immediately recognized, and the US military authorities scoured their scattered outposts throughout the world for improved aircraft. One that was immediately available was the big brother of the Dakota, the Douglas Skymaster

[1] Where weights in tons are given, these refer to the American 'short ton' of 2,000 pounds.

(C-54), which was capable of carrying 19,000 pounds of freight, three times the capacity of the Dakota, at more than twice the speed. Skymasters were ordered to West Germany from bases as far away as continental United States and the islands of the Western Pacific and Asia.

The new standard Royal Air Force transport was the Avro York. This clumsy, box-like aircraft, with its four powerful Merlin engines, was developed from the very successful Avro Lancaster bomber. It could cruise at a greater speed than the C-54 and carry an equivalent payload.

In November 1948, the RAF's newest transport—the Handley Page Hastings—arrived on the scene. This aircraft carried a payload equivalent to that of the other four-engined transports, yet could fly even faster, thereby effecting a marked improvement in the speed and efficiency of the airlift operation. The Berlin Blockade was the baptism of fire for the Hastings, its first operational assignment. Initially, only one squadron of fifteen aircraft was available but this number was gradually augmented during the following months of the crisis.

On June 28 the airlift into Berlin began. At first it was conducted in a carefree, almost haphazard manner. One small room at Gatow, equipped with a small perspex board, had been set aside as the Operations Room. From here, as one of the pilots afterwards put it: 'Pilots full of doughnuts and tea went forth to seek any aircraft which happened to be fuelled, serviced, and ready to fly. Hot was the competition, and great the joy when one was found. Soon the summer skies were full of a monstrous gaggle of aircraft heading in the general direction of Berlin.' It was all something of a lark, and anyway it would not last long.

But as these pilots full of doughnuts and tea were heading merrily towards Berlin, air commanders in England and Germany were calling conferences to complete plans for a massive ferry service to Berlin which, far from being a lark, would become a strenuous and minutely organized routine.

Towards the end of July arrangements were made to supplement the operational strength of the airlift service with aircraft and crews from several of Britain's charter air companies. These organizations entered into contracts with the British Government through the agency of British European

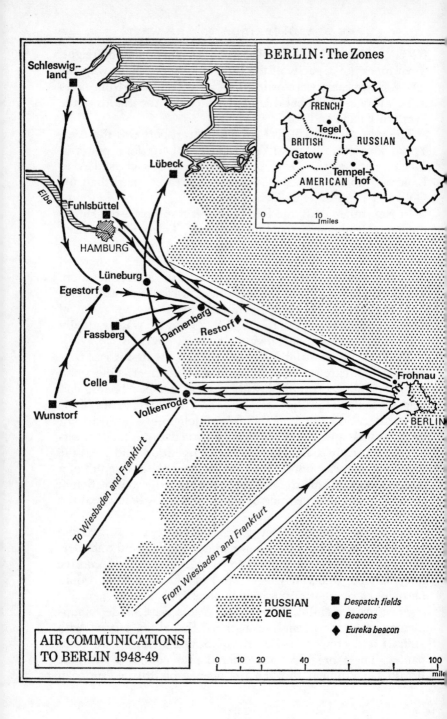

BERLIN: The Zones

FRENCH

Tegel

BRITISH   RUSSIAN

Gatow

Tempel-
hof

AMERICAN

0   10
                    miles

Schleswig-
land

Lübeck

Elbe

Fuhlsbüttel

HAMBURG

Lüneburg

Egestorf

Dannenberg

Restorf

Fassberg

Frohnau

Celle

BERLIN

Wunstorf

Volkenrode

To Wiesbaden and Frankfurt

From Wiesbaden and Frankfurt

RUSSIAN
ZONE

■ Despatch fields

● Beacons

◆ Eureka beacon

AIR COMMUNICATIONS
TO BERLIN 1948-49

0   10   20   40   100
                                                            miles

Airways and the then Ministry of Civil Aviation. For them the Berlin airlift meant fat profits and a valuable boost to their status in the world of civil aviation. At the same time these civil airmen and aircraft were often of particular value of the operation because of their specialized experience in, and equipment for, carrying large quantities of liquid fuel, petrol and oils of various kinds, that could be pumped to the aircraft, and discharged, through pipelines. The need for liquid fuel was growing acute in Berlin, and the commitment to supply this was undertaken entirely by British civil airlines flying Avro Lancastrians, a hasty conversion of the wartime bomber which could nevertheless carry a payload of 12,000 pounds of liquid. The transport of fuels was by no means the sum of the work carried out by civilian aircraft. Other machines, such as the Handley Page Halton, a civilian conversion of the Halifax, and the ubiquitous C-47, hauled increasing quantities of general freight. The first civilian flights were made on 28 July, and merchant airmen were involved in the airlift in increasing numbers from then onwards.

Finally, there were a number of specialized aircraft like the Bristol Freighter which, specially designed for awkward loads, was used mainly for 'back-loading' of freight out of Berlin. The American Fairchild Parker (C-82) performed a similar rôle. Even Coastal Command's Sunderland flying boats were deployed, flying to the Berlin lakes, until the onset of winter brought ice-floes to the Havel River. They flew from Furkenwerden, a former Luftwaffe float-plane base on the Elbe near Hamburg. The value of these flying boats was that they could carry salt. It had been calculated that Berlin needed about thirty tons of salt per day, but it was an extremely difficult commodity to handle. It tended to seep through its packages and was highly corrosive. If salt were allowed to collect below the floorboards of conventional aircraft, it destroyed the control wires and attacked the airframe. But because the flying boats normally operated from river and estuary bases, their hulls were treated to resist corrosion and they carried their control wires in the roof, where the salt could not get at them.

As the aircraft reinforcements flowed into Western Germany it became increasingly apparent that more airfields would be needed to cater for the ever-increasing traffic. At the dispatch

THE BUILD-UP OF THE AIRLIFT

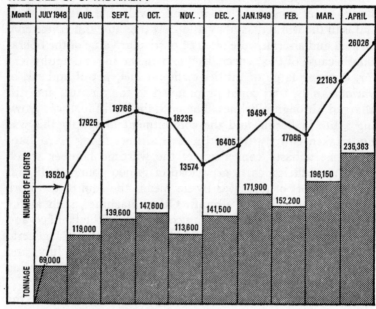

FLIGHT PATTERNS IN THE NORTH CORRIDOR

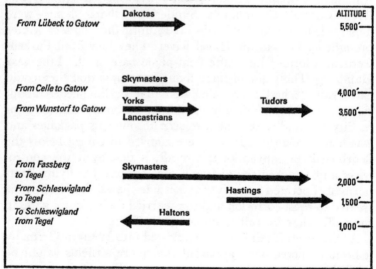

end in the western zones there were ample facilities, not only
with regard to the number of airfields immediately available
but also in the means at hand to improve them. There six
fields[1] in the British zone, plus the flying-boat base, and two in
the American zone.[2] The additional airfields having already
been chosen, British and American engineer battalions, together
with the German railway organization, constructed special rail
and road approaches and unloading facilities. At the same time
men of the Airfield Construction Wing were adding to existing
runways at high speed. The real problems occurred in the
eastern, receiving end of the operation, in the western sector of
Berlin. The whole value of this airbridge would depend on the
operational efficiency of this eastern support. In Berlin there
was no superfluity of airfields to choose from—just two, Gatow
and Tempelhof.

It was vitally important that these two airfields should be of
maximum utility; which obviously depended on their size and
facilities. Gatow had been a grass airfield during the war; the
RAF had already laid upon its surface a runway of pierced
steel planking, but this was far too weak to support any intensive use by heavy four-engined aircraft. Fortunately, the construction of a modern concrete runway had been started in
1947 and, when the Blockade was imposed, was nearing completion. This had in itself been a mammoth task, since the
supply of cement and building materials in Berlin was de-
pressingly small. The answer was found in improvisation, and
the road surface from bombed areas of the city was torn up and
used for the new runway. The Russians had in 1945 removed
everything of value from Berlin, and so boilers to melt bitumen,
crushers to pulverise the ballast, dumpers to cart the mixture
into position on the runway and steam-rollers[3] to flatten it out
had to be begged, borrowed, and occasionally stolen, from
various sources.

[1] Schleswigland, Lübeck, Fuhlsbüttel, Wunstorf, Celle, Fassberg, and
Furkenwerde for flying boats.
[2] Frankfurt and Wiesbaden.
[3] These were mostly of First World War vintage, and even the Russians
had no use for them. The problem was eventually solved by the arrival of a
brand-new steam-roller, complete with driver, which had trundled all the
way from Leipzig in the Russian zone—no one ever found out how it had
passed through all the checkpoints.

The American air terminal in the early days of the occupation was Tempelhof, the old civilian airport of Berlin situated in the centre of the city. Although this field possessed the great advantage of being central to the population, thus reducing the problems of distribution, it was nevertheless very close to the eastern zone and its location in a heavily-populated area meant there was little or no room to increase the facilities.

Despite the many improvements that were carried out at Gatow and Tempelhof, these two airfields were still insufficient to handle all the traffic that the Airlift was bound to entail. A third field was now therefore constructed at Tegel in the French sector of Berlin. Though built by the Americans and the French, Tegel soon became familiar to British airmen since a large proportion of their aircraft were diverted there from Gatow. The new airfield gave a much-needed increase to the tonnage that could be flown in.

Runway space was only one requirement of the airlift operation.[1] Possibly even more important was the need for control and navigation equipment. The bulk of the flying took place in the winter months, when weather conditions were at their worst and aircraft density at its highest. As aircraft in ever-increasing numbers arrived at the circuits over the airfields it became vital to ensure that they were landed and despatched with the greatest possible efficiency. For example, the RAF target at Gatow was to land one plane and dispatch another every three minutes day and night, that is, an aircraft movement, in or out, every ninety seconds. In bad weather this three-minute interval could be stretched to five. Such a remarkable density of traffic was achieved by the installation of the most up-to-date navigational aids. The RAF at Gatow possessed the finest possible equipment of its kind in the world, manned by highly-skilled operators. By the use of a complex of radio beacons and the radio-telephone, the ground controller could beam in a stream of aircraft towards Gatow like beads slipping at regular intervals along several strings. When the weather deteriorated, these aircraft could be taken over one by one for their final approach by a radar controller in a small caravan at the end of the runway. The operator could watch the movement of each

[1] Code-named Operation Vittles by the Americans and Operation Plainfare (originally Carter Paterson) by the British.

machine on his radar screen and give the pilot precise instructions on how and where to fly, second by second. Thus a pilot could be 'talked down' on to a runway that, until the last moment, he could not even see through the fog.

Without these aids, and the men to operate them, the airlift could only have been carried out in good weather. So tight was the schedule that there was no opportunity for a pilot to overshoot the runway and come around for a second attempt to land; if he missed on his first run in, he had to join the outgoing circuit, fly back to the western zone and come in again from that direction.

Perhaps the best way of depicting the hectic activity in and out of Gatow at the height of the Berlin airlift is to follow the progress of an imaginary observer making the journey from Wunstorf, say in an RAF York, late one afternoon, when dusk was not far away. From the busy operations room at Wunstorf, with its jangling telephones, he followed his crew to a small lorry, which ran them out to their aircraft, one of a line already laden with sacks of flour. The flying instructions which the crew had been given hinged upon one central fact, the time at which their aircraft had to be over the Frohrau radio beacon, just to the north of Gatow. From that datum, with an allowed margin of error of plus or minus thirty seconds, they had worked out the speed at which they must fly, taking into account the strength and direction of the wind. The height at which they must fly was constant. The aircraft took its place in the current wave of Yorks destined for Gatow, each plane leaving precisely three minutes after its predecessor. Once airborne, the York turned northwards towards the entrance of the northern air corridor to Berlin (the entrance opposite Hamburg) and there, at the local radio beacon, it swung into the procession down the corridor. The journey to Berlin would take about fifty-five minutes, a few minutes less than the non-stop train journey from London to Brighton.

The territory beneath the corridor was, of course, under Russian occupation; but the crew paid no more attention to this than the occasional idle glance downwards from the cockpit. They had probably made this journey something like two hundred times already; it had become a matter of routine.

Twenty miles out from the Frohrau beacon the pilot called

up the control tower at Gatow, reported his presence, and
stated the load he was carrying; this last was to facilitate unloading arrangements. At the beacon he called up again, and
was instructed to turn in a south-westerly direction and to start
to lose height. From now on he would be in close touch with
the two controllers on the ground; had the weather been foggy,
he would have been handed over in the final stages to a third
controller, the GCA radar man out in his caravan by the runway, who would have talked him down through the murk.

But this time the pilot came in visually. He turned again over
another radio beacon near the centre of Berlin, still losing
height, and now headed directly for the Gatow runway. He
called up again as he crossed over the Kaiser Wilhelm I
memorial, a big tower brightly lit with red lamps a short
distance out of Gatow. 'Over the Christmas Tree', he reported
on his radio, the standard phrase for that moment in the airlift
journey. As usual, a good deal of light-hearted patter had
worked its way into the language of this radio approach.

Once over the 'Christmas Tree', our York had practically
arrived. Below it in the gathering dusk stretched the lights of
Gatow. The aircraft ahead was just rolling to the end of the
runway, the one ahead of that was taking up position on the
unloading apron, and in the reverse direction down the landing
track was taxi-ing the next aircraft to take off for home. Meanwhile, behind the York the following aircraft was already over
the first beacon, over the second, undercarriage down, dropping gradually through the sky. Behind him came yet another,
and so on interminably through the evening.

The York touched down, rolled to the end of the runway,
taxied rapidly off to the unloading apron, and took up its
position in the line. Two lorries, laden with gangs of German
labourers, were already on their way to meet it. As the aircrew
strolled across to the dispersal huts for a coffee, the sacks of
flour tumbled out of the aircraft and into the waiting lorries.
The aircraft would be on the ground for between thirty
minutes and an hour, during which time it would be unloaded
and reloaded for the return flight.

Before that hour was up, the crew were seen to climb back
into their aircraft, laden now with electric lamps, valves and
other equipment manufactured in the factories of Berlin and

destined for the world market. The doors were slammed shut, and the York, taking its turn in the line, lumbered down the row of small blue lamps marking the taxi track.

An empty Tudor tanker had just taken off. A wave of Dakotas from Lübeck was landing. Soon there would be Sky-masters from Fassberg, then perhaps more from Celle. The York, obedient to the instructions of the controller, roared its engines at the end of the runway and took off for the fifty-five minute flight home.

Thus, Gatow on any evening during the airlift presented a spectacle unprecedented in the history of aviation.

When the airlift began it was seen as a temporary expedient to tide Berlin over an emergency and to give diplomacy a breathing-space. But since it very rapidly became an integral part of the pattern of European life, to continue for nobody knew how long, it had to be developed into a highly-organized machine, an instrument that could be relied upon at all times and in all conditions.

This machine had two component parts, the men and the tools. If either were to fall below the highest possible standard, the whole structure could conceivably collapse. The material side, the aircraft and the ground facilities, we have already discussed, but the human resources were just as vital, and by no means comprised just the pilots who did the actual flying; the work done on the ground, though less spectacular, was fully as important to success.

There were the military organizations who decided exactly what commodities were necessary to sustain the existence of West Berlin. The initial planning of commodity supplies was carried out in Berlin on a tripartite basis by the three Allied commanders, who met regularly to draw up a list of priorities. In the bipartite Control Office in Frankfurt these schedules were communicated to the various authorities concerned, in-cluding the Headquarters Staff of the British Army of the Rhine and a special British unit, the Army Air Transport Organization. The latter was responsible for collecting the necessary goods from wherever they could be obtained and for delivering them to one or other of the dispatching air bases in the western zones of Germany.

On arrival at the airfields in the British zone the freight had to be stored, graded and checked. On each dispatching field the Army deployed units specially created for this task and manned by officers and men of the then Royal Army Service Corps, together with a vast number of German civilian labourers. They were known as the Rear Airfield Supply Organization (RASO). At the British airport at Gatow a similar organization, known as the Forward Airfield Supply Organization (FASO), was established.

In addition to the men at the airfields, there also had to be, just as in wartime, an operational and administrative head-quarters to control the whole operation and to keep careful watch, twenty-four hours a day, on its every detail. Initially, this task was undertaken by the Headquarters of the British Air Forces of Occupation, but later a special Transport Group Headquarters was formed, located in an ancient palace in the small town of Bucheberg, a few miles west of Hanover.

From this palace the British Air Commander and his staff, together with British and American controllers, planned the British contribution to the airlift and kept watch over its implementation. The military staff were ably supported by scientists and technologists, who were able to calculate future airfreight requirements with remarkable exactitude. Further down the chain of command were the soldiers and airmen who worked continuously in all weathers maintaining, improving and administering the airfields. In fact, this chain stretched all the way back to England where various airfields, both British and American, were used for the maintenance of the aircraft.

These then were the men who constituted the supports of this amazing aerial bridge. There remained of course the aircrews, whose onerous task it was to fly two round trips a day from the bases in the western zones to Berlin, and back again.

The British and US Air Forces concentrated squadrons of superbly skilled airmen from all over the world into the airfields of West Germany. In addition, there were the crews from the new civil airlines, for whom the airlift meant so much in terms of contracts. Indeed, many of the latter quickly expanded their fleets of aircraft and recruited more crews to fly them. For many an ex-RAF aircrew member the end of the war had meant a return to the humdrum existence of an office job in austere post-war Britain. The airlift offered a welcome chance to break out of the rut and to return to their first love, flying. Of the RAF and USAAF aircrews, many were wartime veterans, who transferred from some administrative task with their Service to active flying with gusto, whilst others had been in training schools (or still schoolboys) when the war ended.

One of the most noticeable features of the airlift operation was the degree of inter-Allied co-operation which developed; with the experience of wartime to draw on, the extent of effective collaboration soon surpassed all previous standards. Between the respective national contingents there was nothing but healthy rivalry, with little or no pettiness, and on any given day, in the streams of aircraft converging on Berlin, could be found airmen from America, Britain, Australia, South Africa and New Zealand. For geographical reasons, many of the American aircraft were based on British fields in the west[1] and flew into the British base at Gatow. The airfields themselves were commanded and administered by the Royal Air Force, with British and US Air Controls and a joint operations staff. In spite of the obvious difficulties of co-ordinating military forces with differing sets of regulations, particularly with regard to discipline, generally speaking the relationship was harmonious. The British took to eating sweet breakfasts while the Americans quickly became addicted to afternoon tea. The two nationalities shared everything, living together, often in desperately overcrowded conditions, and taking their leisure together.

As the British and American aircraft reinforcements flowed in, airfield congestion in the western zone became an increasing problem. Teams of military engineers from both countries made drastic improvements to existing facilities, swiftly laying down new runways and special road and rail approaches to the fields; but this was not enough. By midsummer various airfields began to specialise in the type of aircraft they handled. Wunstorf was used exclusively for four-engined aircraft, whilst the Dakotas were moved on and concentrated at Fassberg. American Skymasters had saturated the airfield facilities in and around Frankfurt, so in mid-August many were sent to Fassberg and the Dakotas were once more moved on, to Lübeck on the Baltic. By the middle of September, American aircraft were based at

[1] Particularly Celle and Fassberg.

another British field, Celle; together with Fassberg, these airfields fulfilled the needs of the USAAF. Meanwhile, a further rationalisation of the infrastructure was introduced in early October, when all civilian aircraft were concentrated at Fuhlsbuttel. The last major development before the end of 1948 was the opening of the most northern of all the airfields, at Schleswigland. The RAF squadrons that went there in November were flying the heavy post-war Hastings, then being used operationally for the first time.

Long before this rationalisation of aircraft and airfields was completed, the whole character of the airlift had changed. Aircraft at first had only flown in the hours of daylight and in summer weather, but now, with the onset of winter, the need for supplies had increased and they flew twenty-four hours a day, at shorter intervals. The airfields were larger and more complex and the operation itself, at first treated as a light-hearted adventure, became a military offensive. Improvisation had been sufficient in the early days but now, in the depths of a German winter, the demand became such that the whole task had to be treated with the cool efficiency proper to an exercise of war.

IX

A CITY UNDER SIEGE

PARADOXICAL THINGS were happening in beleaguered Berlin in the autumn of 1948. They were usually provoked by the division of the city, by a situation in which there were two separate city councils and two different kinds of money, newspapers and trade unions. In this city, Russians and members of the armed forces of the Western powers no longer greeted one another, and the four-power Central Council had long since ceased to exist. Yet there still remained one area where the four powers peacefully shared the responsibilities of administration and custody. This was Spandau, the grim prison which housed the seven war criminals whose lives had been spared at the first Nuremberg trial. Each of the four military governments in Berlin had to supply a prison warder, a doctor, a prison guard, fifteen labourers, an equal number of clerks, and some seventy soldiers three times a year for the guarding of these prisoners. Each month a different nation was in charge of the prison; each month warder, doctor, soldiers and the rest rotated. The seven men, Rudolf Hess, Walter Funk, Erich Raeder, Baldur von Shirach, Alfred Speer, Konstantin von Neurath and Karl Doenitz, had been in prison since July 1947. Spandau had previously held six hundred inmates; these had been hurriedly moved on and the building prepared at some cost to welcome its new internees, who proved to be the seven most expensive prisoners in the world. They had at their disposal a personnel of about two hundred and fifty men, one hundred of whom were on duty at any one time; far more personal attendants than they ever had while at liberty.

Another contradiction of the time was the fact that, while on the one hand the Russians were doing all in their power to starve out the Western allies, on the other they were fostering the black market in order to supply the Berlin populace—or at least those amongst them who could afford the exorbitant prices asked for food, cigarettes and consumer textiles. The Russians did not show themselves as the profiteers but instead used as front men nationals from the satellite powers, particularly Bulgaria, Poland and Jugoslavia. In the eastern part of the city, special shops were opened with impressive names like 'Ballorex' and 'Texta' to sell these goods. Although Markgraf was trying to clamp down on the black market, these shops were outside his jurisdiction.

Just as the Russian version of a black market operated at full stretch, so too did the propaganda media. The Eastern newspapers were in daily need of material to support the three pillars of the Russian message, which were that supplies into Berlin were on the point of collapsing, that the airlift was completely inadequate and meant higher prices, and that the West Berlin populace lived only for the withdrawal of the Americans and the British. At first these reports made some impression on the Berliners, but as the airlift became more effective they recognized the Eastern newspaper stories as nothing more than fantasy.

Only the top Communist officials refused to learn. Ulbricht, Grotewohl, Puck and their like seemed convinced that Berlin, which they had lost on 20 October 1946, would drop into their laps with the inevitable failure of the Western airlift.

However, Reuter and the newly-elected *Magistrat* and Assembly in the western sectors were as determined in their own way as the Allies were to ensure the success of the airlift. The most urgent task for the new municipal government was the construction of an efficient and reliable administrative structure. The old system had broken down, first through the obstructionist activities of the Communist functionaries in every department, then through the vacuum caused by their subsequent dismissal.

The city government had also to deal with economic difficulties of staggering complexity. The fact of the circulation of two currencies in the city, one of which sank to a fifth of the other's value by January 1949, had forced the administration to adopt a system of subsidies which threatened to drain the city budget. No one could receive more than a proportion of his wages in

West Marks, and the whole population was anxious to exchange East for West Marks at the best available rates on the
black market; so that a rapid inflation of the former set in,
while the latter became alarmingly over-valued. As soon as the
two new currencies had appeared and goods could be bought
with one or the other, the black market established a relation
between them. The Russian Mark was the subject of countless
jokes; Berliners referred to it as 'wallpaper money' or *'foul
mark'*.

The endurance and solidarity of the population during that
winter, when the temperature often dropped to thirty degrees
of frost, was admirable. They were to a large extent fortified in
their resistance by the visible success of the airlift and the
growing knowledge that the West's counter-blockade of produce into East Germany was seriously affecting economic
activity there. These counter-measures had been imposed in
the summer and, though having little effect at first, they were
progressively tightened until no important industrial supplies
were allowed through the custom points. These restrictions
coincided with the breakthrough in the airlift. In the early
months this had barely succeeded in maintaining Berlin but
now, in the middle of winter, it regularly began to bring in
more supplies than were ever carried by rail in the immediate
postwar period.

One of the major contributing factors to the Allied success
was the care and planning that went into the operation,
especially with regard to its effect on the economy of the city.
The import cost of raw material was no longer reckoned against
the selling price of the finished article; this became but a minor
consideration. The deciding factors were freight space, demand,
and effect on employment and morale. For example, was it
'cheaper' to import ready-baked bread, which contained thirty
per cent water, or to bring in the coal and flour to produce the
bread in Berlin? Careful analysis showed it to be cheaper to
bring in the raw materials and bake in Berlin. A similar calcu-
lation analysed the alternatives of bringing in real coffee, or
the fuel to produce *ersatz* coffee; in this case the planners
decided on real coffee. Painstaking calculations of this kind
laid the foundation for the success of the airlift.

Initially the airlift had been intended for the transport of food, but it was soon found that the western sector needed fuel just as badly. So within twenty-one days of the start of the operation, coal too began to be carried, a commodity which had hitherto been regarded as impossible to airlift.

The first loads were carried by RAF Dakotas, but it soon became apparent that larger aircraft would be better employed on this bulky and, in terms of efficient use of space, most extravagant cargo, so the four-engined Yorks and later USAAF Skymasters, flying out of Fassberg into Gatow, took over the responsibility. When the RAF Hastings arrived they were also consigned to this none too pleasant task. Coal is one of those substances which seeps everywhere. Aircraft soon became totally engrimed with coal dust and tons of it were cleared out of innumerable crevices during the frequent servicing and maintenance in England. Once one of the pilots, requested over the radio telephone to state his load, burst out in reply with a couplet that became famous throughout 'the lift':

> Here comes a Yankee with a blackened soul
> Heading for Gatow with a load of coal.

Other fuels flown into Berlin included petrol and diesel oil, with some kerosene and other petroleum products. The power from liquid fuel is compressed into a far smaller space than that of coal, but the dangers of carrying it by air are obvious. In the early days the Americans flew liquid fuel to Berlin in drums, but this method was obviously uneconomic since much space in the aircraft was wasted. The task was handed over to the British when their civilian air charter companies arrived. Aircraft were specially adapted and crews trained for this highly dangerous task. Some of the machines were genuine tankers, with fuel carried in the wings, but most were ordinary aircraft, either civilian airliners with hastily-constructed tanks inside the hull replacing the passenger accommodation, or conversions of war-time bombers such as the Lancaster and the Halifax. The transport of liquid fuel increased rapidly, as utility furnaces in West Berlin were converted to partial consumption of diesel oil to save as much coal as possible; for example, coal consumption of a power station could be reduced by as much as a quarter by these means.

Methods for meeting the various needs of Berlin had to be

kept flexible throughout the operation. Generally speaking, the amounts required of each commodity and the priorities of delivery were known, but these were altered from time to time to suit the prevailing circumstances of the aircraft. The basic principle was to accumulate in Berlin about thirty days' reserve of the main commodities and then to maintain stocks at that level. But reserves of coal could dwindle simply because bad weather for a few days would prohibit flying operations from Fassberg and Cassel. In that case those airfields which had clear weather would increase their flights and build up stocks of, say, flour. Then, with a general improvement in weather, a special effort to transport coal would restore the equilibrium.

The major difficulty encountered in lifting food supplies was the sheer variety of the cargo; some items were light, some could be compressed, whilst others were bulky. The primary target was to carry in enough food to maintain the daily ration of 2,100,000 Berliners at a *per capita* level of about 1,800 calories, increased by 220 calories in November 1948.

By far the biggest single item of food flown in was flour, which occupied more than half the cargo space. Indeed, flour, cereals and dehydrated potatoes together for long made up more than eighty per cent of the total bulk airlifted. Dehydrated vegetables are not a particularly attractive diet but they are light to carry; for example, 900 tons of ordinary potatoes could be reduced to 180 tons when dehydrated. In terms of the airlift this meant a saving of more than eighty return trips a day, a significant contribution to solving the logistical problems of the planners. Economics made in other areas included packaging, which often accounted for a quarter of the weight of an article. Goods stacked in light cardboard containers or sacks showed a considerable saving in weight which more than compensated for any loss or damage in transit.

A final category of goods lifted into Berlin was that known as 'special freight'. This often involved the strangest loads and gave the operations staff many headaches. Electric generators, iron girders for power stations, steam-rollers and fire-engines; in addition to these loads, often carried in the special aircraft mentioned in the previous chapter, were others as diverse as the regimental mascot of the 1st Battalion The Royal Welch Fusiliers—a goat—and rolls of newsprint. Particularly vital amongst these specialised commodities were medical supplies. Many drugs and chemicals are completely unsuitable for air freighting and available substitutes had to be found quickly. For example, ether, though essential, could not be carried by air at that time, so instead alcohol was flown in, from which ether could be manufactured in the city.

The longer the Blockade was maintained, the greater the need became within Berlin for consumer goods. Large quantities of boots, shoes and clothing were carried, and even 2,000 hot water bottles for the sick and the aged. There was no regular supply of tobacco, but the Americans on one occasion took in a large haul of cigarettes from surplus Army stocks. The pre-Blockade tobacco ration was maintained throughout from stocks already in the city. In addition, six million cigars made from homegrown German tobacco were flown in during the early months of 1949.

The intensity of the combined Anglo-American airlift rose from June 1948 on to reach an average daily total of about 4,000 tons by the end of August. It levelled out at around this figure, and even dropped a little during the winter months, but new peaks were reached and passed in the spring of 1949.

The final operation essential to the success of the airlift was the efficient unloading of the aircraft on the airfields at Berlin and distribution to the people in need. Perfect timing was required to ensure that each aircraft was unloaded as soon as it came in, so that no traffic jam was created. The basic principle was that none of the load should remain anywhere on Gatow or Templehof for a moment longer than necessary, but should be immediately cleared away into the warehouses and yards of Berlin. However, at Gatow the labourers and crews that unloaded the aircraft could not be spared for this latter task because there simply were not enough of such trained gangs available. So, with the exception of coal and liquid fuel, the goods were carried to one of the big hangars and transferred to civilian trucks, which then drove down to the Havel Lake. Here there were more than forty large barges available,[1] with a fleet loading capacity of 15,000 tons; 560 tons of food a day

---

[1] These barges had originally belonged to the Dutch and Belgians before the Nazis had used them. They were concentrated at Havel ready to be returned to their rightful owners when the Blockade was imposed.

were carried by the barges to the various warehouses in Berlin. Similarly, the liquid fuels were stored in large reservoir tanks at the airfield at Gatow and thence pumped by pipeline to the Havel Lake for transit by barge to the distribution centres in the city.[1]

Right from the beginning of the airlift there had been a two-way carriage of freight over the air routes. The aircraft that brought in essentials for the survival of Berlin were not allowed to return empty. Indeed, the freight to be lifted out was almost as important to the besieged city as that brought in. Initially there was of course the mail, both from the Western occupying forces and the civil population. But it was just as vital to be able to export finished goods, which could earn much-needed capital for the city. In this sense at least Berlin was fortunate, since it had in the past been a centre for highly-skilled electrical and optical industries, whose products were at a premium in the post-war Western world. Although the Russians had removed much of the capital equipment as reparation in the early and uncontrolled period of their occupation and had also kidnapped much skilled labour in various 'retribution' raids. a sufficient residue of traditional knowledge remained to make these industries a viable proposition for ensuring the continued economic survival of the city. Their output had the added advantage of being easily transported by air. The volume of this freight backloaded from Gatow and Tempelhof in a typical week amounted to some 1,500 tons, a traffic which obviously had important political implications.

This 'backload' to the West did not consist entirely of goods manufactured in Berlin workshops; many of the aircraft carried passengers on their return journey. There were many people in West Berlin whom it was desirable for one reason or another to bring away. The first priority was for those who did not live in Berlin but who had been in the city for business or personal reasons when the Blockade was imposed; 4,000 people came into this category and they were airlifted out very quickly. Secondly, there were West Berliners who had been given permission to leave the city. Their reasons for doing so varied, but mostly they were emigrating to other countries or simply

[1] In Berlin at this time there fortunately happened to be some lengths of plastic piping.

moving to new homes and jobs in the western zones. Others were young people anxious to study in the universities of the West.

By the end of the first month of the Blockade, when no end could yet be envisaged to the operation, the authorities decided to evacuate many sick people, especially those who had tuberculosis and similar ailments and thus needed long periods of rest and good food, and those who required specialist treatment which could not be easily obtained in Berlin. However, in spite of all the privations, the public health of the city remained good. This was partly due to the fact that the one utility which remained almost unaffected by the Blockade was the water supply, which came from deep wells beneath a natural filter of sand and gravel. At the same time, accommodation in the hospitals, fifteen beds per thousand population, compared favourably with that of any British city at this time and was quite adequate for the day-to-day needs of the city. In the winter of 1948–9 there were no serious epidemics and the incidence of infectious diseases was low. Indeed, the death rate, in particular infant mortality, was considerably lower than in the previous year. Nevertheless, despite all the efforts of the Allies, real personal hardship was experienced by the average Berliner in those winter months. Most of the electricity supply was needed for the factories, hospitals and schools, and only a little was left over for domestic consumption. It was not that West Berliners suffered severe power cuts that winter, but rather that they lived through one long power cut occasionally relieved for a couple of hours, often at the least convenient time. To alleviate the suffering of those who had already borne so much, the Allies decided to fly out thousands of children, who had long endured the privations of war and occupation and were by now many of them desperately under-nourished. All these evacuees were flown out by RAF transports; the children travelled free, while the adults paid a small fare. By March 1949, more than 50,000 people had been airlifted out of the city.

The Russians occasionally tried to interfere with the flights by buzzing aircraft in the corridors. (There were three corridors or air highways, each twenty miles wide: Hamburg south-east to Berlin and Hanover due west were in the British sector, whilst the third and largest corridor was from Frankfurt in the American zone north-east into Berlin.) Yet incidents were few and far between. Three of the sixteen air crashes which occurred during the Blockade resulted in the aircraft coming down in Soviet-occupied territory. The Russians behaved in the most humane way on these occasions; they waived all formalities and allowed Western medical teams, and on one occasion the wife of a fatally-injured RAF aircrew officer, to hasten to the scene of the accident.

After the initial onslaught in the summer, the volume of British flying over the air bridge began to decline. There were several reasons for this. One was the weather; in bad conditions, when the number of aircraft which the fields in Berlin could receive was limited, it was obviously good sense to use only the largest and to drop the smallest from the programme. The first squadrons to stand down in bad weather were therefore always those using the twin-engined Dakotas, which still formed a large proportion of the airfleets, particularly the British. Another reason was a shortage of aircrews, again particularly felt by the British. Transport Command's resources were limited and it had by now become necessary to withdraw some of the experienced crews from the airlift and send them back to England to train fresh men.

Yet another reason was the fatigue which intensive operations inevitably imposed upon the aircrews after a time, although no man was permitted to fly more than two return journeys to Berlin per day and at regular intervals he was sent home to England for a few days' leave.

All these factors diminished the flying figures during the autumn. But in December, when the worst weather was to be expected, a curious thing happened; the volume of British traffic began to rise. The reorganization and the routine drill were taking effect. The amount of freight airlifted rose slowly but steadily, until by the end of January and throughout February it was far higher than ever before.

For the Americans, who had more men available with aircrew experience, these problems did not exist to the same extent. With typical efficiency, the United States Air Force fed aircrews into the Berlin operations on a regular rotational basis, drawing on squadrons from as far away as Alaska and Okinawa.

Leave facilities and rest areas at their main bases around
Frankfurt were expanded to meet the increase in demand;
whilst there was always 'furlough' in Paris, Brussels or London.

This chapter began by discussing some of the paradoxical
events which occurred during the Blockade. But perhaps
strangest of all was the very nature of the Blockade itself. All
the famous sieges of history, from ancient Troy to Paris in 1870
and more recently Leningrad, have conformed to a roughly
similar pattern: the besiegers drew up in strength around the
city and attempted to obtain physical possession of it by force
of arms and slow starvation. But the blockade of Berlin was a
siege directed at not only gaining physical control of the city,
but of its soul as well. For example, anyone in West Berlin was
given the opportunity by the Russians to lift the Blockade for
himself and his dependants at any time; without changing his
residence or employment, he had simply to register for his
rations in East instead of West Berlin. The Western powers
certainly put no obstacles in his way. But with few exceptions
the Berliner chose to reject the Russian invitation.

There were several other anomalies concerning this siege.
Electricity for the Russian radio station, which poured out anti-
Western propaganda day and night, was supplied by the
Western powers, simply because the generator happened to be
in West Berlin. On the other hand, electricity for Gatow was
supplied by the Russians because the airfield happened to be
on the edge of the Russian Zone; reciprocally, the British
sector was feeding electricity to one of the Soviet fighter
stations. At any time either side could have cut off these
supplies; however, despite the fact that alternative sources
existed, it was obvious that such exchanges were simply convenient for both sides. The Blockade itself was not vitally
concerned with such matters; it was a psychological struggle as
much as a physical one.

The most formidable weapons available to either side were
hope and despair. The blockaders hoped to win the city by
making it despair of any alternatives. Those who opposed
them, the Western powers, did so by bringing renewed hope to
the citizens.

X

ADENAUER AND THE EMERGENCE OF THE FEDERAL REPUBLIC

THE BERLIN BLOCKADE and the Allied airlift radically altered the psychological and political climate in occupied Western Germany. The Allied rescue operation was a decisive event which not only saved the blockaded city from starvation and surrender to an alien creed, but beyond this immediate achievement created for the first time a bond of genuine solidarity between Germany and the Western world. Until then, the Germans in general had regarded the Western governments as merely conquerors bent upon humiliating their nation and exacting reparations for past misdeeds.

Certainly this early period of German post-war history, from the unconditional surrender to the establishment of the Federal Republic, was one in which neither the Germans nor the Allies could clearly see their way ahead. The spectre of war-time propaganda was still abroad, distorting people's outlook; perhaps the worst example of this was a disastrous document which everyone quoted although few had seen, the Morgen-thau Plan. This notorious concoction of prejudice and absurd-ity indeed poisoned the atmosphere between the German people and the Western occupying powers for years and put endless difficulties in the path of co-operation.

Apart from this, there were glaring inconsistencies in the Allied attitude towards Germany. On the one hand, they went to unparalleled lengths of exertion and material sacrifice to succour Berlin, while at the same time pursuing with vigour and relentlessness their programme of industrial dismantling.[1]

The launching of the Marshall Plan and the admission of Germany to its benefits emphasized afresh the absurdity of

[1] 'What the right hand builds, the left hand tears asunder'—Adenauer in his Berne speech.

subsidizing that country's recovery while simultaneously dismantling its industries, especially when the maximum German contribution was clearly needed to help get Europe back on its feet. The Economic Co-operation Act called for the retention in Germany of any industrial plant that could best serve the recovery programme by being left there, and so in April 1949 provision was made for the retention of equipment in 159 plants previously scheduled for removal as reparations, in addition to the contents of forty plants in the French zone which had previously been removed from the reparations list.

Yet despite this seeming inconsistency in the Western attitude to the conquered territories, events there were moving in a positive direction, towards the creation of the new German state. Milestones along the way have already been discussed, such as the creation of the bi-zone administration, which in turn allowed for the establishment of diets in the eight states constituting the bi-zone, and later a second chamber of States Council. Such moves represented an attempt by the Allies to shape an 'anticipatory model' for the future constitutional structure of the whole of Germany.

In March 1948 the Russians had walked out of the Allied Control Council, a step which, followed as it was by their withdrawal from the Berlin *Kommandatura* in June, virtually sealed the partition of Germany. It also helped to bring about the consolidation of the western zones, to which the French at last agreed on 8 April 1949, and thus set in train the process that called into being the German Federal Republic later in the year.

In April 1948 the Western Allies announced that not only would they introduce the new currency reform, but also were prepared to create provisionally a separate West German state. The victorious powers had realized that the point had been reached where they needed the help and co-operation of the vanquished if the benefits of victory were not to be lost.

On 1 July 1948, just ten days after the introduction of the currency reforms (which at one stroke placed the whole of the West German economy on a new and secure footing), the three Western military governments summoned the Ministers President of the eleven West German states to Frankfurt, where on behalf of their governments they handed them three documents. Generally known as the London Documents, these had been drafted by the London six-power conference. Their purpose, as outlined in the communiqué issued on 7 June 1948, was to authorize the German people 'to establish for themselves the political organizations and institutions which will enable them to assume those governmental responsibilities which are compatible with the immense requirements of occupation and control and which ultimately will enable them to assume full governmental responsibility'.[1]

The gradual reacquisition of sovereignty by Germany had been originally intended to follow the growth of democratic sentiment and achievement. In reality, however, it began immediately the East–West schism developed; the wider this schism became, the more the victors on either side tried to consolidate their 'own' part of Germany by promoting its sovereignty.

A terrible dilemma confronted the German representatives. Should they proceed with the directives of three Western allies, and form a Parliamentary Council and create a new constitution, which would then only be recognized in the Western provinces? Such an act carried implications not only of collaboration but also of a permanence which might prohibit any future reunification. The alternative was to refuse to co-operate and simply wait and hope for a time when the four powers could resolve their differences and allow positive progress toward the recreation of a single free German state on democratic lines.

When the Parliamentary Council assembled for the first time in the Pedagogic Academy at Bonn, its newly-appointed President, Konrad Adenauer, outlined this dilemma facing the delegates when he stated in his opening address:

It has been a difficult decision for me, as it has been for every member of this house, whether, in the present condition of Germany, I should lend my co-operation to this enterprise at all. But we must be clear in our minds about the

[1] Document I—the convening of a constituent assembly to draft a Federal Constitution. Document II—to submit proposals for any alteration of State boundaries which might be thought necessary. Document III—defined the rights and responsibilities of the Occupation Powers after the constitution come into force.

alternative—what would happen if this Council were not to come into being? The present state of lawlessness and absence of rights, from which we all suffer, would continue and grow steadily more unbearable. Therefore, it is our duty to seize and exploit every opportunity to bring it to an end. What the results of our work will be for Germany depends on factors over which we have no control. Yet we must endeavour to solve the historic problem which has been set us under the protection of the Almighty, with all the seriousness and high sense of duty which the greatness of the task demands of us.[1]

The Bonn Assembly which listened to these words was an unusual gathering. The greater proportion of the delegates from the eleven states were politicians of an older generation, who had occupied prominent positions in German political life before the coming of the Nazis in 1933. Almost without exception, they could look back on fearful experiences during the twelve years of Hitler's rule. The more fortunate had gone into exile, but the majority had spent those twilight years incarcerated in prisons and concentration camps. It was thus a Parliament representative of a bygone age, an assembly composed of the survivors of the Weimar Republic. Indeed, the memory of that republic's failure obviously exerted an important influence on their approach to the task of framing a new constitution. The delegates were determined that there should be safeguards written into the fabric of the new German constitutional structure which would prevent any repetition of the mistakes of the past. Thus the ghosts of Weimar stalked the corridors of Bonn.

From the very outset, the influence that Adenauer exerted over the proceedings was immense. Technically, his position as President of the Parliamentary Council carried little real power; the bulk of the work on the drafting of the new constitution was to be undertaken by special sub-committees and the Steering Committee. Adenauer's political opponents in the Social Democratic Party had deliberately encouraged his appointment to this office so that he could exert minimal influence over events. But Adenauer was not the man to submit

---

[1] Paul Weymar, *Konrad Adenauer*, pp. 232-3.

weakly to such 'cold storage' treatment. Always a prodigious worker, he kept himself fully informed on all aspects of the committees' work, and so always knew precisely where and why difficulties had arisen. It was then that he intervened and, through informal discussion with the interested parties, sought solutions. These interventions were usually decisive, a brilliant mind and a keen political instinct combining to disentangle the complex constitutional problems which the 'experts' had woven. Adenauer had an immense store of practical experience to draw upon, as Mayor of Cologne and as leader of the Prussia State Council,[1] and thus was able to demonstrate, through precedence and example, the practical implications of any particular aspect of the new constitution. The clarity of his argument invariably won the day, solved the problem in hand and further enhanced his own reputation. Perhaps Adenauer's most important function was 'linkman' with the military forces of occupation. This office allowed him alone to confer with the Allied Military High Command, and in a few short months he became the acknowledged spokesman of the nascent Federal Republic to the Western powers. At the age of seventy-three, Adenauer was on the threshold of a new political career.

The work of the Parliamentary Council proceeded slowly and thoroughly, altogether too slowly and thoroughly for the taste of the military governors. They had allowed three months for the drafting of the constitution and so, by the end of 1948, with little progress evident, they became increasingly impatient. Problems had occurred partly because of a developing rift within the Parliamentary Council and partly because the Allies were unwittingly obstructing progress themselves.

The rift within the Council was in fact a head-on collision between Adenauer and his Christian Democratic Union, and the Social Democrats led by Schumacher. The parties clashed over the fundamental issue of the structure of the new state. The third of the London Documents had laid down that the new Constitution was to be of 'a federal type'. The problem arose because the Document was desperately vague in its specifications thereafter: the type of federation to be adopted and the relationship between the central or Federal authorities

[1] For a more comprehensive account of Adenauer in this period read the comments of Professor Meres concerning Weymar's biography.

and the state or Provincial legislatures was not defined, nor
could the Allied powers agree amongst themselves on the
degree of federation which they wished to see.

Adenauer wanted the component states within the federation
to retain maximum independence in relation to the central
authority; hence he sought to ensure that they should not be
financially dependent on it. The Socialists wished to see the
maximum of effective power, including budget controls, in the
hands of the central government. The Social Democrats were
convinced that they would win the first general election; once
in power, they intended to implement a far-reaching programme of social and economic reforms, including the transfer
of the Ruhr heavy industries to State ownership, and hence
required above all a government with strong central executive
power. At the same time, they were unwilling to regard the
Bonn constitution as anything more than a provisional measure,
which must not prejudice any future hopes for a unified Germany. After a month the two political parties were as far from
agreement as ever on this fundamental question of 'Basic Law'.
Adenauer therefore sought the advice of the military governors
as to the type of federation they envisaged in the German
constitution. He did this because he believed it to be in the
interest of the German people. Despite all the obstacles and
discouragement he encountered he was trying to work toward
a genuine partnership which he hoped would result in not only
a German, but also a European consolidation. Hence he saw
nothing dishonourable in giving the military governors a clear
picture of German difficulties. His opponents did not see his
action in quite the same light, and Adenauer's consultation
with the Allies created a political furore which became known
as 'The Frankfurt Affair' and, at one stage, threatened to
topple him from his position. With some justification, the Social
Democrats claimed that Adenauer was acting more like a party
politician in an inter-party dispute than the spokesman of the
assembly as a whole. But their other claim, that he was trying
to line up the military governors against the Socialists, had little
foundation. Adenauer was convinced that, by informing the
Allied leaders of the constitutional difficulties, a bond of confidence would be built up, that trust would be reciprocated
with trust. In the long run he was proved right. Indeed,

Adenauer survived the crisis and remained President of the Parliamentary Council; ironically, his reputation at home and abroad was even considerably enhanced.

The Allies themselves were unwittingly obstructing further progress owing to the fact that the Basic Law could not be properly formulated so long as the Allied Occupation Statute remained an unknown quantity. In other words, the Parliamentary Council had received no clear directives on which areas of administration were to fall within the jurisdiction of a new federal government and which would remain the prerogative of the Allied occupation. The intention of the latter was to allow the Parliamentary Council to frame a new constitution which they would then discuss, and presumably reject those clauses they did not consider to be in their own best interests.

By the end of 1948, the successful completion of the new constitution was being endangered from two sides. On the one hand the Social Democrats had stiffened their resistance to Adenauer, to the extent of using obstructionist tactics. At the same time, the continuing differences of opinion between the military governors had reached a critical point. The main problem was that the French position, as championed by General Koenig, was far too extreme for the Anglo-Americans; it favoured a degree of state independence which not only went far beyond that advocated by Adenauer but would also paralyse the federal government and render it incapable of any decisive political action. In these extremely difficult times Adenauer, together with some of the more responsible elements in the Social Democrat party, recognized the danger of prolonged delay and so pushed through the completion of the Basic Law without waiting for the Occupation Statute. On 16 February 1949 Adenauer presented the draft copy of the Law to the Allied Military Commanders. As he had feared, although the military had no complaint against the general 'democratic tone' of the document, they objected to the degree of power concentrated in the hands of the central authority. So the document was returned to the Parliamentary Council for 'adjustment', and it seemed as if final agreement on the nature and form of the new constitution was as far away as ever.

For his part Adenauer returned to the debate with as much vigour as before. This was a remarkable achievement, because at the same time he was also deeply involved in preparing his party for the first general elections. Besides being leader of the parliamentary party of the CDU in the North Rhine–Westphalia Parliament, he was also chairman of the zonal executive committee of the CDU in the British Zone. In this latter capacity Adenauer was generally acknowledged to be the effective head of the party throughout the three western zones of occupation. Unlike so many of his contemporaries, Adenauer had sufficient political acumen to recognize the implications of victory in this first general election; he knew that the winning party, the first to form a government in the new German state, would set the pattern for the country's development for a long time ahead.[1] Thus he spent an increasing amount of time mobilising his party for the forthcoming campaign; he ousted much dead wood and enlisted leading experts in various fields into the party structure. Possibly Adenauer's most adroit recruitment was of Ludwig Erhardt, Professor of Economics at Munich University and architect of the economic system called 'Social Market Economy'; Erhardt was senior adviser to the Bi-zonal Economic Council at Frankfurt and his system, which combined economic freedom with a measure of state control, was already proving a great success. Indeed, the adoption of Erhardt and his economic policy eventually proved to be a political master-stroke. The phenomenal economic recovery, which had begun in the aftermath of currency reform, was probably the only major political development in post-war Germany to have any profound effect on the consciousness of the great mass of the electorate, who otherwise took little or no interest in politics. Hence, the incorporation into the CDU political platform of an economic system which the people believed would pave the way to prosperity was a major trump-card in the coming elections.

Meanwhile, work on the Bonn Constitution was proceeding. Difficulties were still being made by the French, who considered it fundamental to their continued national security to have a weakened form of central government in Germany

[1] 'We must win power, we must remain in power for at least eight years. If we can achieve that, we shall have placed Germany firmly on a road along which she can safely proceed'—Adenauer to Dr. Alain Zimmer. Paul Weymar, *op. cit.*, pp. 247–8.

which would thus be unable to pursue a positive foreign policy and hence possibly pose a threat to France. General de Gaulle, then no longer in power, expressed the fears and doubts of many Frenchmen when he stated, in a speech to some of his old wartime associates: 'Only one question will dominate Germany and Europe, which of the two Reichs will bring about re-unification.'

Adenauer too was becoming uncharacteristically impatient with the lack of progress and, in a speech delivered in Berne on 25 March 1949, he set out a succinct critique of Western prognostications concerning the creation of the new state. The meeting took place in the auditorium of Berne University, before a select audience of the Inter-Parliamentary Union, and when 'the pale, lean German with his hard Tartar face' (as a Swiss Socialist newspaper described the seventy-four-year-old Adenauer) mounted the rostrum, no one in that audience could have predicted the explosive effect his words would have. In this, the first utterance on foreign policy of a post-war Germany, Adenauer began by outlining the state of disorder and chaos that existed in his own country in particular and the entire 'European Community of Fate' in general. With unadorned frankness, he further suggested that the social and economic plight of Germany was partly the responsibility of the Allied Military Government, for whose combined policy of dismantling a country which had the largest industrial potential in Europe he had nothing but scorn. Such an assertion was at that time very strong meat indeed, and was bound to give a profound shock, especially to a neutral audience, but Adenauer had proof to back his arguments and this he furnished in abundance.

At the same time the speech was a positive declaration of faith. He pledged the new West Germany, with all its industrial potential, to work for a new community of nations in Western Europe. This showed that the leader of the new Christian Party in Germany was determined to rise above traditional nationalist thinking and commit his nation to the supranational goal of a New Europe.

Unfortunately, Adenauer's brave words caused a political sensation throughout the Western world. Quoted out of context, he was labelled the arch-nationalist of the new Germany.

Socialist newspapers in Britain and France crucified his statements to pander to the narrow fears of their readers. Questions
were asked in Western parliaments and at one stage it looked
as if Adenauer's career would end there and then. Yet he
remained. Stoically silent, he refused to be drawn into further
argument and simply allowed the storm of irrational protest to
blow itself out.

In Germany, with the continued opposition of the military
governors to the proposed constitution showing no signs of
weakening, the Social Democrats changed their tactics. Schumacher and his party now demanded that the constitution be
completed without further reference to the military trium-
virate. It was their intention to present the Allied authorities
with a new German Basic Law which would have the support
of the majority of the Parliamentary Council. If the Allies then
rejected it the onus of responsibility would lie with them and
the Social Democrats would emerge as the champions of
national resistance. This stratagem placed Adenauer and the
CDU in a terrible dilemma; they had always believed that
co-operation with the Allies could only result in a secure
German state, yet now such co-operation would be seen as
undignified and spineless collaboration with the occupying
powers.

This Socialist pressure was hardening into a powerful opposition lobby to Adenauer, which rapidly gained popular support
throughout the Western Zones. The two parties were forced
into even further enmity over another issue. In December 1948
the Ruhr Statute, establishing the International Authority for
the Ruhr, was passed by the Allied military government. This
new body had the power to fix the levels of production, as well
as the prices, for coal, iron and steel, and hence could influence
the entire German economy. Among the mass of bankrupt
estates which the fall of Hitler's Germany had left in the hands
of the creditor nations, the Ruhr was by far the most valuable.
Coal and steel were basic commodities, the ones most desperately needed both inside and outside Germany, and despite
large-scale devastation the Ruhr was still one of their most
important areas of production. By early 1949 its industrial output, while still modest, was begining to play an important part
in the German economy. Adenauer believed that only the

maximization of the Ruhr's potential could ensure success for the Marshall Plan and the reconstruction of Europe; at the same time he was aware as anyone of the dangers inherent in a powerful concentration of economic strength within a comparatively small area and in comparatively few hands. Its evil effects had been experienced before. The Christian Democrats believed that future industrial prosperity lay in the system of private enterprise advocated by Erhardt's Social Market Economy. The Social Democrats demanded that when the time came the entire complex of Ruhr industries should be nationalised.

Despite the success of the airlift and the consequent feeling of optimism in Berlin, the overall mood of Germany in early 1949 was gloomy. The deepening rift between the Christian Democrats and the Socialists was aggravated by the combined failure to reach agreement with the military governors on the future of Germany. In March and April, as it became increasingly clear that the blockade of Berlin might well be lifted, there seemed no way out of this impasse which could lead to a new Germany.

Progress, when it eventually came, came quickly and was influenced by events outside the claustrophobic arena of intra-German political strife. On 2 April 1949 the Atlantic Pact was signed in Washington and the North Atlantic Treaty Organization came into being.

Already before this NATO treaty there had been a renewal of some old alliances. In March 1947 Britain and France signed the Dunkirk Treaty of Alliance and Mutual Assistance. A year later this had been extended to include Belgium, Luxembourg and the Netherlands as well, by the Brussels Treaty of Economic, Social and Cultural Collaboration and Collective Self-Defence signed on 17 March 1948; this group of five nations later became known as the Western Union.

Three months later, on 11 June 1948, the United States Senate passed by a large majority a resolution sponsored by the late Senator Vandenberg affirming US determination to exercise the right to individual or collective self-defence, as allowed by Article 51 of the United Nations Charter, and recommending the 'association of the United States . . . with such other regional and collective arrangements as are based on continuous

and effective self-help and mutual aid'. The way was thus
prepared for the transformation of the original Brussels Treaty
into the wider Atlantic Alliance, which Ernest Bevin, then
Foreign Secretary of Britain, had hoped and planned for.

The original signatories to the North Atlantic Treaty were
Belgium, Canada, Denmark, France, Iceland, Italy, Luxembourg, the Netherlands, Norway, Portugal, the United Kingdom and the United States'[1] The Treaty itself is a model of
clarity and brevity, its purpose well expressed in the Preamble:

> The parties to this Treaty reaffirm their faith in the pur-
> pose and principles of the Charter of the United Nations and
> their desire to live in peace with all peoples and all govern-
> ments.
>
> They are determined to safeguard the freedom, common
> heritage and civilization of their peoples founded on the
> principles of democracy, individual liberty and the rule of
> law.
>
> They seek to promote stability and well-being in the North
> Atlantic area.
>
> They are resolved to unite their efforts for collective
> defence and the preservation of peace and security.

Although Germany was not specifically mentioned in the
Atlantic pact, the new alliance benefited her in a number of
ways. To begin with, the absence of any direct reference was
taken by Adenauer and his party to mean that their nation
was no longer considered a potential aggressor by the West;[2]
this was very much a step forward. Similarly, it now seemed
clear that there was no further intention of treating the western
zones of the former Reich, for which the three senior partners
of NATO—the United Kingdom, France and the United
States—bore responsibility, as a political no-man's-land.

However, by far the most significant influence that the new
treaty would have on the future of Germany arose from the
goodwill it engendered between the three major Western
powers and the convenience of having the three foreign minis-

---

[1] Greece and Turkey acceded to it in 1952 and the Federal Republic of
Germany in 1955.

[2] Particularly compared with the Treaty of Dunkirk, which had referred
explicitly to 'a threat from beyond the Rhine'.

ters, Dean Acheson, Ernest Bevin and Robert Schuman, together in Washington for a week. This opportunity they themselves recognized and in a cordial atmosphere they cleared up their mutual differences and reached agreement over a constructive policy for Germany. A new Occupation Statute, short, precise and above all simple, was quickly produced. This document clearly delineated the areas of responsibility and sovereignty to be divided between the military administration and the new federal authorities.[1] The Statute was quickly passed on to the three military governors, who on 10 April in turn presented it to Adenauer as President of the Parliamentary Council.

On the vexed issue of the degree of central control to be exerted by the new federal government, the Allies came down firmly on the side of Adenauer and the Christian Democrats. The Allies further promised that, within eighteen months of the new constitution coming into effect, the Occupation Statute would be further revised and many of the remaining restrictions on German sovereignty would be abolished. By offering this prospect of an assured continuity of development and the possibility of further negotiations, the Allies had given the Parliamentary Council an attractive incentive towards the rapid settlement of outstanding differences.

Although the value of this incentive was recognized by the Christian Democrats, the Socialists took an entirely different attitude. With the general election looming ever nearer on the political horizon, they adopted a posture of rigid opposition, rejected out of hand the entire draft constitution so far agreed on, and announced that within a few days they would submit a completely new constitution to the Parliamentary Council. Such irresponsible action in pursuit of a cheap political prize, the position of 'champions of the people', lost them any support or sympathy they had ever had from the military governors, who in turn seemed to look upon Adenauer with increasing favour. In open disregard of military authority, the Social Democrats submitted their own draft Constitution on 21 April. The reaction of the military governors was very much conditioned by a letter they had received from their foreign

[1] The so-called 'reserve fields' of allied control included disarmament and demilitarization, foreign affairs and currency control, the Ruhr Authority and other international organs of control.

ministers at the time of the new Statute of Occupation. This letter had been intended for Adenauer in his position as President of the Parliamentary Council, and allowed the governors to make considerable concessions over the degree of federal authority and the controversial issue of equalization of finances; they had withheld this letter for reasons of their own. The implication was clear enough; the Allied foreign ministers were obviously prepared to make concessions in return for the establishment of a democratic constitution in an atmosphere of political stability. Such stability, they believed, could only be obtained if the whole-hearted support of the Left in Germany were guaranteed for the new state. Therefore, acting with the authority of the letter, the military governors acceded to the Socialist ultimatum, particularly since its demands corresponded closely to the concessions suggested in that communication.

Therefore, the new-born state was at one and the same time close to receiving its new constitution and also witnessing the imminent political demise of the hitherto all-powerful Adenauer. On the surface, it seemed as if he had been completely outmanoeuvred and the scene set for a Socialist constitution and a sweeping Socialist victory in the forthcoming elections. Even some of Adenauer's closest political allies believed that the game was up for the Christian Democrats. However, many of the party officials considered that the military governors had treated Adenauer in a shabby fashion in return for all his loyalty and co-operation; Adenauer himself reasoned that their motives were understandable enough. His adroit political mind perceived the basic fact of political life in Germany at that time, that in Allied eyes the Socialists offered a better guarantee of stable democratic development in the new state. He was further aware of the fact that, whereas the Socialists had had their origins in the Weimar Republic and had long sustained implacable opposition to the rise of Hitler, subsequently paying the price of political martyrdom, the Christian Democrat party in its present shape represented an entirely new concept in German politics.

Adenauer still sought compromise as the solution to Germany's constitutional problems. A lesser man would have been tempted to involve his party in opposition to the Socialists and thus to play the same political game. However, the Christian Democrats preferred to attempt a satisfactory co-ordination between Socialist demands and that which had already been achieved. Speed was essential at this time, since on 27 April the Russians had announced their intention to lift the blockade on Berlin provided the Western powers agreed to hold a four-power conference to discuss the reunification of Germany. The Soviet intention was to prolong the negotiations in order to obstruct the unilateral creation of a West German federal constitution.

The Allies, whilst welcoming the lifting of restrictions on Berlin, realized that this by no means represented a *volte face* in Soviet policy towards Germany and Western Europe. However, the conference would cost them nothing and so they agreed to meet in Paris on 23 May. Since they were not prepared to have the creation of the West German State made into a bargaining point, it became absolutely essential that the new constitution must be ratified by all concerned by that date.

Adenauer brought all his political skill to bear on implementing this. Despite increasing opposition from the West German Communists, who sought (presumably under orders from Moscow) to delay proceedings, at midnight on 8 May 1949, the fourth anniversary of the end of the war, the Basic Law was adopted in the Parliamentary Council by an overwhelming majority. Events proceeded quickly and smoothly thereafter. On 12 May, at the head of a delegation from the Parliamentary Council, Adenauer received from the military governors at Frankfurt a formal letter confirming official approval of the new constitution by the occupation forces.

The final problem to be solved was the selection of a provisional capital city for the new republic, since for obvious reasons Berlin could not continue to serve this function. Two West German cities were competing for the privilege, Bonn and Frankfurt. The issue could not be resolved by the normal channels and so the Parliamentary Council was asked to choose between the two with a simple vote. Just how much influence Adenauer was able to exert in this matter cannot really be assessed. Anyway, Bonn was chosen, by a narrow majority; it was almost a sister city to his native Cologne and hardly a stone's throw from his own home across the river.

Throughout his political life he had lived and worked in the Rhineland, and his outlook on many issues was that of a provincial politician.

Other interpretations have been attached to the choice of Bonn. The emphasis placed on the term 'provisional' has been remarked, and indeed Bonn could never be regarded as a permanent capital city, being very much an inferior substitute for Berlin. The fact that the level of material damage it suffered had been considerably less than in other West German towns may well have been an important factor in its selection, but nevertheless the facilities made available for the administration and diplomatic representation were of a temporary nature in 1949 and still are. Frankfurt is a much bigger city and could well be envisaged as a feasible permanent alternative to Berlin. In this way, as long as Berlin remains a divided and occupied city and Bonn remains the 'provisional' capital, the issue of German reunification will be kept alive in European politics.

The choice of Bonn, however, meant that Adenauer's political career was in the ascendancy. The general elections were held on Sunday, 14 August 1949 and the result was indecisive, since no party emerged with an overall majority. Of the 402 members of this, the first Federal Parliament, 139 belonged to the combined CDU/CSU and 131 to the Socialist Party; the Free Democrats (FDP) had fifty-two seats, whilst the remainder went to the German Party and the Bavarian Party, with seventeen each, and the Communists, with an insignificant fifteen seats. Obviously some kind of coalition had to be created to enable a government to be formed for the new republic. In accordance with established parliamentary tradition, it fell to the CDU/CSU as the strongest party in parliament to arrange that coalition.

Two solutions offered themselves: a coalition between the two major parties, CDU and SPD, which would in effect produce a kind of national government, since there would then be no significant opposition group, or co-operation between CDU and the smaller non-Socialist parties, which would then place the SPD in opposition.

There was much to be said for a coalition between the major parties. The Allied governors favoured this solution, as did many German politicians and civil servants who saw the value of starting the new republic off with a major joint effort. The Social Democrats themselves made it clear that, whereas they were in sympathy with such a coalition, they required the Ministry of Economics as a pre-condition for their co-operation. Adenauer however favoured a coalition with the smaller parties, not simply because of this Socialist demand for control over the economy, but also because he believed that the political principles of CDU and SPD were diametrically opposed on many other issues as well. Hence an alliance was formed between the CDU/CSU and the Free Democrats.[1]

The coalition government, now with an overall majority, took office in September 1949 and Adenauer was selected by his party as the first Federal Chancellor. It is interesting to speculate on how Adenauer had managed to rise in a brief three years from the obscurity of a municipal mayoralty to the political leadership of a country of fifty million people. One reason was obviously the lack of competition. The ex-Nazis were temporarily in disgrace and their most active opponents were dead. The Social Democrats were condemned to the opposition benches in the new Bundestag, partly because they entrusted their leadership to the ailing, politically naïve Kurt Schumacher, partly because they were identified with the British Socialists, who were now embarked on a thoroughly unsuccessful essay in government in London, and partly because the most prominent Social Democrats to survive the Nazi era had been exiles in London, Stockholm and Switzerland, carrying the plain, if unfair stigma of a 're-export'. Adenauer had emerged as the natural choice for leadership because he had risen above the physical discomfort of the occupation and its political squabbles. He had preserved his dignity when most of his contemporaries were losing theirs.

[1] Professor Heuss, a leading Free Democrat, became Federal President; he was the personal choice of Adenauer.

XI

THE END OF THE SIEGE

BY THE winter of 1949 it seemed as if the Blockade might continue indefinitely, for perhaps even a year or more. Direct negotiations had failed to find a solution, the Security Council had proved impotent, and the dispute had now become an endurance test. The Russians could keep the western sector in isolation for as long as they wished, the Allies could support its population for as long as they could maintain the airlift, whilst the people themselves could stand firm against the Communists for as long as they were fed and employed. The irresistible force had met the immovable object.

However, although throughout this bitter winter the airlift averted the immediate dangers of starvation and disease, it could do little to alleviate the effects of economic isolation. West Berlin's industries, starved of fuel and power, were cut off from the markets and sources of raw materials in the Soviet zone as well as those in the west. Despite the fact that many of the city's products were of small bulk and could be carried conveniently by air, the airlift obviously could not meet the demands of industry as well as those of the population at large, and so a new shadow fell over Berlin. As industrial activity declined, unemployment began to rise, in February reaching a peak of 140,000 jobless.

Although West Berlin was thus paying the price for its independence, as thousands of small firms were gradually forced to close down, the Soviet zone also appeared to be suffering from the effects of the Blockade. Reports reaching the West indicated that the zone was having acute difficulty in satisfying the demands of reparations from its own production while deprived of the coal, steel and industrial equipment previously imported from the Ruhr. Indeed, the counter-blockade was so effective that it is arguable that the eastern zone was hit more severely by the Western embargo than West Berlin ever was by the Russian blockade.

However, despite all the tribulations of the Blockade, in the early months of 1949 West Berlin was rapidly taking shape as an independent and self-contained city. Though still entirely dependent on outside help in material terms, it had at least begun to construct its own administrative, economic and social systems. One product of this new independence deserves particular mention: the Free University of West Berlin, which was begun entirely on the initiative of the Germans themselves before the city was divided, and whose eventual success was to become perhaps the most striking witness to the new spirit of West Berlin.

The original University of Berlin was on the Unter den Linden and hence in the Russian sector. The students and professors there resented the influence of the Russians perhaps even more than they had that of the Nazis, but theirs was a perilous struggle, since opposition could mean risking their liberty, if not their lives. A 'Free University' was therefore recognized as indispensable; in a city whose fight against oppression had brought it to the attention of the whole world, such a university could be a militant institution with which to do battle against the Soviet attempt to dominate the minds of Berlin's academics and students. The years 1933–45 had provided ample demonstrations of what could happen when German universities were not free, a sad decline which had begun with Bonn University, amid peals of ironic laughter from the free world, withdrawing Thomas Mann's degree of Doctor of Philosophy, and ending with experiments on human guinea-pigs in concentration camps carried out by university-trained doctors. The Russians now attempted to control the German universities located within their area of occupation by such methods as the planting of informers amongst faculty staff and student bodies; a high point of tragi-comedy was reached when Moscow professors were sent to instruct their counterparts in the Berlin University on the correct approach to Goethe!

These oppressive conditions persisted for some time because, although many of the professors wanted academic freedom, they were loath to endanger the existing university. However, during 1947 political pressure built up as student organizations affiliated to the SPD and CDA explored ways of expanding the Technical University in the British sector into a Free University. Meanwhile, students in the Unter den Linden rebelled against what they regarded as the 'Marxization' of their courses.

The German student movement was a powerful organization which had always played a leading part in the administration of universities. Although the Russians carried out frequent purges of the Berlin student body, they had up to then failed to stifle its official mouthpiece, a journal called *Colloquium*, published with American financial support. However, in April 1948 its most active contributors were expelled and from that time on the lobby to create a free university became a popular demand. The *Magistrat* swung round in favour of a radical alternative to the old Berlin University and in April voted (with the exception of the SED) to remove the university from zonal control and to itself assume responsibility for it. In January 1949 the Student Council of the university staked everything on one action and resigned *en masse*. From that time onward Berlin University was supported by the Western Allies, who sponsored the creation of a new and free alternative in the western sector, under the jurisdiction of the city itself.

Although the Blockade hastened the creation of the Free University, it had less influence on the activities of the black market. Berlin in fact demonstrated that a large city simply could not be totally blockaded, since throughout this period it was possible to buy almost anything 'on the market'. The usual route for contraband goods was from the western zones into the eastern sector of Berlin, and from thence to the western suburbs; risks were high, since many such ventures ended in a shooting match, but so were the profits to be made. Many other goods came to the western sectors of Berlin directly from the eastern zone itself; all through the summer and autumn of 1948 hundreds of peasants travelled from the rural areas of the East to do business in Berlin, since the value of the West Mark was such that it was a coveted possession well into East Germany.

Blockade-running took many forms. During the first months of the airlift, lorries from Bremen and Hamburg were allowed to enter the city as long as they were loaded with goods destined for the Russians. Hence, many an enterprising lorry-driver carried two complete bills of lading, each showing different cargoes. For the Russians' benefit the consignment might consist of building lime, while for the black market there would be vats of herrings or bags of sugar and flour, all of which could be carried under the lime.

Smuggling was by no means a monopoly of the Germans. There were certain Soviet officers who were friendly enough or senior enough, perhaps with command of a zone boundary, to be able to pass through without search in a staff car bound for Berlin. For a reasonable fee no questions were asked and no search was made. Members of the various military missions, such as the Czechs, Poles and Hungarians, also brought into the city large quantities of American products under the guise of transit goods. These they sold for dollars and the dollars they exchanged for West Marks, all under the protection of diplomatic immunity. Also, the aircrews involved in the airlift were not averse to carrying cartons of cigarettes and chocolate, and the occasional packet of tea or coffee, as a profitable means of supplementing their basic pay and as a diversion from the tedium of flying. But smuggling became less and less profitable the longer the Blockade continued. For as the city became poorer and poorer, many people were priced out of the market. Soon the black market specialised only in luxury consumer products for the chosen few.

As the winter neared its end, there were signs that the Russians were becoming tired of the siege. Their leadership underwent a subtle change, as those originally associated with the Blockade were replaced by men who had no such close identification. On 4 March 1949 Andrey Vishinsky became Soviet Foreign Minister; unlike his predecessor Molotov, he had never taken a particularly determined stand on the Berlin question. Likewise, on 29 March, Marshal Sokolovsky, so closely involved with the initial implementation of the Block-ade, was recalled by Moscow and replaced by General Chuikov, something of an unknown quantity as far as the West were concerned.

On 27 January 1949 an American correspondent, Kingsbury Smith of the International News Service, interviewed Stalin in

Moscow on the subject of Soviet-American relations, and at one point asked him whether the Soviet government would be willing to raise the Blockade if the Western powers would postpone their plans for creating a government in West Germany pending a meeting of the Council of Foreign Ministers, a meeting which could explore further the problems of Germany as a whole. The significance of the question lay in the fact of the Soviet claim that the Blockade was only necessary because of 'technical difficulties' in communications and the need to safeguard the Eastern Zone economy following the Western currency measures.

Stalin's reply was: 'Provided the USA, Britain and France observe the conditions set forth in that question, the Soviet Government sees no obstacles to lifting transport restrictions, on the understanding, however, that transport and trade restrictions introduced by the three powers should be lifted at the same time.'

This was the first time that deferment of the proposed West German government was publicly announced as a Soviet condition for ending the Blockade, although the matter had been put forward, and then dropped, at the Moscow meetings. Nor had such emphasis previously been placed on raising the counter-blockade, which had also been treated at Moscow as a secondary issue. Stalin was no doubt influenced in sending out this feeler by the rapid economic recovery of the western zones, under the double impetus of currency reform and Marshall Aid; this rising West German productivity seemed only to emphasise the industrial stagnation of the Soviet zone.

On 20 March 1949 the Western military government escalated the counter-blockade of the Soviet Zone by finally agreeing to the suggestion made some months before by the West Berlin municipal authorities of making West Marks the only legal tender in West Berlin. This action did not actually prohibit the circulation of East Marks in West Berlin, but meant they were no longer acceptable as payment for food, rent, taxes, fuel and so on; nor would they be accepted at parity with the West Marks. On the black market at this time, four to five East Marks were required to purchase one West Mark. For months now the West Marks had been flowing into the eastern sector and a substantial proportion of them had undoubtedly found their way into Soviet or Communist hands, to purchase goods smuggled from West Germany or to finance Communist party activities there.

This circulation of two currencies further aggravated the hardship which many Berliners already suffered under the siege conditions. The working population was forced to receive part of its salary in East Marks, the proportion depending on the volume of trade which the employer carried out in return for western currency; industrial firms predominantly concerned with exporting to the West were thus able to pay their workers mostly in West Marks, whereas businesses dealing in essential commodities like food, transactions normally involving East Marks only, paid out little or nothing of the valuable Western currency. All this, added to the four to one exchange rate in favour of the West Mark, created great disparities in the value of a man's wages, a situation which was a constant source of resentment.

The abolition of the dual currency in West Berlin, though it alleviated most of these problems, unfortunately also created new ones. West Berlin residents who worked in the Soviet Sector or who were employed by concerns under Soviet control, such as the railways, were no longer able to pay for necessities with their East Marks and so had to exchange them into West Marks at the adverse rate of exchange. This was to cause serious trouble a few months later.

Nevertheless, despite such difficulties, the new currency reform was generally welcomed in Berlin as further proof of the Western powers' intention to retain a presence in the city, a valuable morale-booster at this time. Professor Reuter said in a speech to the City Assembly: 'We regard the inclusion of West Berlin in the Western currency area as a recognition of the fact that we in Berlin are a part of the West, and are to be accepted, treated and defended as such.'

Thus the failure of Russian policy in Germany was becoming more apparent every day. The Western embargo was hindering industrial progress in the Soviet Zone. The constitutional discussions for the creation of a West German government were nearing completion. The East Mark was excluded from West Berlin. The success of the airlift operation was becoming ever more evident: on 16 April the combined fleet set out to reach a target of 10,000 tons. In this 'experimental' effort the USAAF alone exceeded the target by 900 tons, and the total freight carried into Berlin on that day actually amounted to 12,994 tons, with 1,398 landings being made at the three airfields. At the same time the Western Alliance had been expanded, to involve the United States into a vast regional defence alliance. The North Atlantic Treaty Organization came into being on 4 April, a final proof to the Soviets of the ineffectuality of much of their policy towards Berlin and the West.

April was perhaps the brightest month for Western Europe and Berlin since the end of the war, as well-supported rumours began circulating in Berlin that the Russians were prepared to lift the Blockade. However, although the Soviet authorities by now found themselves in an untenable position, they still had to find a face-saving solution before they were prepared to raise the siege. Representatives of the four powers at the United Nations began to talk discreetly behind the scenes; the Western Allies were, sensibly enough, as anxious as the Soviets to find a mutually acceptable formula. The main diplomatic objective of the Russians was the reconvening of the Foreign Ministers Conference; they were prepared to lift the Blockade on the day that the date for such a meeting was fixed.

Events in the Far East undoubtedly had a major bearing on the new Soviet attitude towards Europe. In the early months of 1949 the Communists forces in China gained sweeping victories in the civil war, as the Nationalist armies, exhausted by the war with Japan and weakened by corruption which even American arms and money could not counteract, disintegrated before their opponents' disciplined onslaughts. The Kremlin was thus assured that the moral effects of a reverse in Europe would be offset by a Communist victory in China.

Towards the end of April reports began to reach Western capitals that Soviet zone officials were urging a resumption of inter-zonal trade, even at the price of raising the Blockade. Further evidence of a softening of attitude came with the Soviet request for the Reichsbahn summer time-tables to include West Berlin. On 22 April the French Foreign Minister Robert Schuman publicly revealed that for several weeks discussions had been going on at the United Nations headquarters in New York; final agreement on a date for the opening of the

Foreign Ministers Conference was now the only obstacle to a restoration of communications with Berlin. The Western powers reaffirmed that nothing would deflect them from their decision to set up a government in Western Germany and that they would not under any circumstances agree to a Foreign Ministers meeting while Berlin was still under blockade. The Soviet requests were therefore tantamount to an unconditional surrender. For the West, the trade embargo against the eastern zone would become unnecessary once communications were reopened, while participation in another conference committed them to nothing.

The four representatives at the UN finally came to an understanding on 4 May 1949. This was that all restrictions imposed on access to Berlin by the four governments since 1 March 1948 were to be removed by 12 May. The four powers also agreed to reconvene the Conference of Foreign Ministers in Paris on 23 May, when they would discuss matters relating to Germany and Berlin, 'including also the question of the currency of Berlin'.

Moscow accepted these terms without reservation. The British Foreign Minister, Bevin, who arrived in Berlin on 7 May, declared that he had not been so optimistic for the future since 1945. On 8 May, the fourth anniversary of the German capitulation, the Parliamentary Council at Bonn adopted a constitution for the new republic by fifty-three votes to twelve, and the Foundation Law was ratified. The West were clearly ignoring Stalin's request that the creation of a new Republic of West Germany be postponed, and there was a last-minute panic in Berlin provoked by the fear that the Russians would retaliate by maintaining the Blockade. Such fears proved groundless and on 9 May General Chuikov gave the order for 'the removal of all restrictions on communications, trade, and traffic between Berlin and the Western Zones, as well as between the East and West Zones of Germany; the order to take effect from midnight on 12 May 1949'. The Allies drove home their point by making 1,017 landings in Berlin that day, a record for a 'normal' day, bringing in some 6,906 tons of freight. In the 318 days since the beginning of the airlift Allied aircraft had flown in more than one and a half million tons of supplies in nearly 200,000 flights.

At the border with the Soviet zone, an American jeep was the first Allied vehicle to leave Berlin along the autobahn for nearly a year. A few minutes later a British Army convoy, cheered by jubilant Germans, left the checkpoint at the head of a procession of Allied and German vehicles. An American newspaper reporter won the race along the autobahn in the other direction, and was the first person to reach Berlin from the west by road, with a British colleague less than a minute behind. Finally, the vital railway line was reopened by a British military train hauled by a Soviet zone locomotive in the charge of a West German crew.

A footnote to the lifting of the Blockade was the recall of General Clay. Truman had promoted him to General of the Army and he left on 17 May to take up his new duties. One of his last actions there was to address the Berlin Municipal Council, after which he and Mayor Reuter rode through the streets of the city he had helped to save. Everywhere the Berliners lined the streets and cheered him; nowhere were the crowds thicker than in the working-class suburbs, whose populace was seldom in the habit of hailing generals.

The airlift had cost the lives of thirty-nine British and thirty-one US aircrew, as well as nine civilians. In monetary terms it had cost the United States $350 million, Great Britain £17 million and the German people 150 million Deutschmarks. Flights into the city did not stop immediately normal communications were restored, for in the atmosphere of uncertainty that still remained the Allies were determined to build up a stockpile of supplies in case the Russians tried the same move again. Indeed, the *status quo* was really only restored with respect to communications: the Control Commission was not summoned to meet again, nor was the four-power *Kommandatura*, and Soviet affability at checkpoints was not extended to the German civilians who travelled by train in or out of Berlin. Arrogance and discourtesy once again characterized Russian behaviour as these civilians were forced to submit to humiliating searches, their Western newspapers confiscated and their West Marks compulsorily changed into Soviet zone currency. However, although the four-power Foreign Ministers Conference had yet to discuss formally the future of Germany, in reality the Western victory was already won. The West could now confront the Soviets as a united alliance, bound by the ties of a secure treaty. Never again would there be any possibility of dislodging the Western powers from their position in Germany by putting pressure on Berlin.

An exhausted yet exultant Reuter summed up the magnitude of the Western achievement when he said: 'Without the hold, initiative and admirable devotion of all those who created the airlift and co-operated in its development, Berlin could not have withstood the pressure; it would have disappeared into the Soviet zone. The consequences for the whole world would have been incalculable.'

Part Three

Part Three

XII

THE NEW EUROPE
AND THE SCHUMAN PLAN

The Cold War may be defined as the policy of making mischief (on the part of the Soviet Union) by all methods short of war—that is to say, short of war involving the Soviet Union in open hostilities.[1]

THREE SEPARATE political developments influenced the future of Germany in the early months of 1949: the emergence of West Berlin as a distinct entity, the establishment of a West German state and the creation of the North Atlantic Treaty Organization. None of these could have succeeded individually without the contribution of the others and they all occurred within the context of a new movement towards European unity. Their implementation and the success they achieved in their initial stages were largely the result of the ambitions of, and the relationship between, two men, Ernst Reuter, the Mayor of West Berlin, and Konrad Adenauer, the new Chancellor of the Federal Republic of West Germany.

Whereas for Adenauer the days of fame and even notoriety were still to come, Reuter had already reached the peak of his popularity and influence. Symbol of the courageous stand of Berlin under siege, his name had become a household word throughout Western Europe. The main problems confronting him and his city in the immediate post-Blockade period were the security of West Berlin from a renewed Russian threat in the future, the reconstruction of its shattered economy and the status of the city within the new federal structure of West Germany. The new North Atlantic Alliance guaranteed protection in the wider sense simply through the continued presence of military units from France, the United Kingdom and the

[1] Defence in the Cold War (RIIA 1950, p. 12).

United States as part of the garrison of Berlin under the Occupation Statute.[1] However, the question of security also assumed
a more local complexity at this time through the Soviet coun-
ter-creation of the Democratic Republic of Germany (DDR)
at Parkow in 1949, which confronted West Berlin with the
additional problem of how to maintain close relations with
West Germany without provoking a crisis with East Berlin.

The relationship between West Berlin and the Federal
Republic was from the earliest days of 1949 both complex and
ill-defined, affecting both the economic position of the city and
its constitutional status within the new federal state. The main
point at issue was whether West Berlin should be fully incorporated into the Federal Republic as the twelfth *Land* or
whether it would be more politic to defer to the legal fiction of
Four-Power occupation. This was a problem which principally
concerned the three Western governments rather than the
Germans themselves. At this stage East Berlin had not yet been
decreed as the new capital of the Democratic Republic; in
addition the West Berlin authorities had operated throughout
most of the Blockade period on a revised Occupation Statute by
which the Western Allies had allowed them a greater degree of
freedom. However, the Western governments still felt that any
constitutional integration of Berlin into the Federal Republic
would be a violation of the Four-Power agreement as well as
possibly productive of a dangerous response from the Soviet
Union, and hence did not feel able to permit such a drastic
move at this time.

A compromise solution was eventually reached whereby
West Berlin was recognized as a *Land* of the Federal Republic
'in principle', though legally it still remained an occupied
territory. In order to accommodate the requirements of this
compromise, the three Allied commanders in Berlin allowed a
new constitution for the city in which the City Assembly
became the House of Representatives and the *Magistrat* the
Senate, thus bringing the Berlin city government into line with

[1] This guarantee was clearly stated in Article 6 of the Treaty of Washington, which defined armed attack on the contracting parties as including any
attack on their forces of occupation. Also Article 5, inserted at the suggestion
of the Canadians, stated that an attack on one signatory would be regarded
as an attack on all.

the constitutional structure of the *Länder* in the Federal Republic proper. But to prevent any infringement of the Four-Power status the Allied commanders wrote into the new constitution that before any law passed in the Federal Republic could be applied to West Berlin, it had first to be ratified by the city's new House of Representatives. In addition, a West Berliner was not to be automatically regarded as a citizen of the Federal Republic; a passport to this effect could only be obtained after a period of residence in West Germany itself.

The precarious position of West Berlin in the post-war period has to a large extent been caused by the ambiguity inherent in this relationship with the Federal Republic. For economic survival the city is dependent on its ties with Bonn, while for security and defence it is still dependent on the three Western Allies who maintain a military presence there. This presence is not part of their voluntary NATO commitment but rather their legal right under the terms of the Four-Power status agreement.

This relationship between Bonn and West Berlin was far less direct than Reuter had hoped; he had felt from the very beginning that the only way in which West Berlin's future integrity could be assured was through its complete assimilation within the federal structure of the new German Republic. Although the documentary evidence is ambiguous, it seems that Reuter's views were not fully shared by Adenauer. Indeed, in the early days of the new Republic, relations between Bonn and West Berlin were often strained, with the Bonn government showing a distinct reluctance to shoulder the burden of West Berlin. Political commentators have never really agreed on the reasons for this disharmony. An explanation popular amongst those politically opposed to Adenauer is that the Chancellor was simply not interested in pursuing a policy of German reunification; the Socialist Left has always cited the 'Rhenish provincialism' they felt lay behind the attitudes of Adenauer, and also his foreign policy which emphasized the Western alliance at the expense of any initiative towards uniting the two Germanies. However, Adenauer's biographers, especially Paul Weymar, have taken great pains to point out that his public utterances nowhere demonstrated such a prejudice, for example: 'I should at any time prefer a united Germany with the Socialists as the strongest party, to a Federal Republic

separated from the Soviet Zone with the CDU as the strongest
party. In this issue the fatherland and the nation stand above
the party issue, and the statesman begins where the party
politician ends.'[1]

It is indeed true that throughout his political career Adenauer showed a deep-rooted attachment both to his birthplace
in the Rhineland and to his religion as a devout Roman
Catholic. But this alone hardly justifies the suggestion that he
felt a political antipathy towards the Protestant Prussian of the
east. Indeed, the Federal Government all along emphasized
that Bonn was merely a temporary choice as capital and
acknowledged Berlin as Germany's true capital city for the
future. Moreover, Adenauer's success as both politician and
statesman lay in his acceptance of the fundamental rule that
politics is very much 'the art of the possible', and it is therefore
arguable that both he and the Federal Cabinet felt in 1949 that
the prolongation of the direct occupation of Berlin implied an
Allied obligation towards the security and integrity of the city
which the new German government was in no position to
share.

Even this does not fully account for the uneasiness of relations between Bonn and West Berlin in the early years. For
example, it was only with great reluctance, and after considerable prodding from the three Allied High Commissioners,
that Bonn was persuaded to look upon the economic needs of
Berlin as deserving special consideration. The obvious clash of
interests between Erhardt's free economy system[2] and the
Socialist bias of the left-wing-dominated coalition in West
Berlin was only part of the problem. There was also a clash of
personalities between Reuter and Adenauer, for which both
men must share the blame. Reuter tended to treat with scorn
what he considered as a lack of interest by Bonn in the needs of
his people, while Adenauer seems to have regarded Reuter as
something of a challenge to his own authority and position.
The Chancellor and his cabinet disliked the 'special relationship' which West Berlin enjoyed, thanks to its direct access to the
Allied governments, considering it a challenge to the Federal

[1] Paul Weymar, *op. cit.*, p. 502.

[2] *Soziale Markwirtschaft:* the policy of establishing a free economic system
to include social benefits but without imposing rigid controls.

Government's function of representing the German nation to the Western powers.

The economic problems which confronted Reuter at this time are perhaps the easiest to understand since they were by far the most immediate. For despite the lifting of the Blockade and the general easing of tension, the number of unemployed in Berlin increased sharply during the summer months of 1949 to the dangerously high figure of 279,000. It was not until the spring of 1950 that Bonn finally recognized Berlin as an emergency area (*Notstandsgebiet*) of the Federal Republic and increased aid for the city to sixty million marks a month. However, the level of unemployment and the economic climate in general was much worse in the eastern sector, where a serious food shortage resulted in a distinct increase in the number of refugees who flowed into West Berlin: between September and December 1949 more than 170,000 people crossed over. This massive influx all but swamped the already overstretched social relief agencies maintained by the city authorities, who were forced to feed, clothe and shelter these unfortunates, often for months; the necessity for adherence to the rigid priorities laid down by the federal authorities often meant long delays in Berlin before these refugees could become the economic responsibility of the Federal Republic, which further exacerbated the strained relations between West Berlin and Bonn. Reuter was only interested in the immediate local problems confronting his city administration and showed scant sympathy for Adenauer's wider policies towards establishing a secure economic base upon which democracy could flourish in the Federal Republic. Mindful of the failure of the Weimar Republic to ensure Germany's economic prosperity, and thereby creating, in his view, an environment in which democracy could be undermined, Adenauer was convinced that the only way in which his republic could be accepted as an equal in the councils of Western Europe was by the achievement of a viable economy and a parallel political stability. In these terms the problems of West Berlin could hardly be the immediate priority for the federal authorities. The German economy, under the twin benefits of American aid and (in Adenauer's view) Erhardt's system, was beginning to gather momentum; with this as tangible evidence of the good intentions of Germany, by the autumn of 1949

Adenauer was ready to confront the Allied High Commissioners with details of his future policies for their approval, and also to negotiate greater latitude for his government under the revised Occupation Statute. The Chancellor's objective was nothing less than the total 'rehabilitation' of the Federal Republic and its incorporation in the Western power structure; in particular, he wished to ensure that his country should play a significant rôle in any movement towards closer integration in Western Europe. Here again Adenauer could not acknowledge Reuter's priority, which was to see West Berlin fully incorporated into the Federal Republic; Reuter believed that this would remove the political uncertainty concerning the future of his city, which in turn would resolve its economic instability and encourage an influx of free capital and investment to revitalize its sagging industry. What Reuter could not understand and Adenauer appreciated only too well was that such an objective was politically unacceptable since it could only further emphasize the division of Germany and was thus unlikely to be endorsed by the Allied High Commissioners.

Armed with these ambitious designs for the future of the Federal Republic, Adenauer, accompanied by members of his new Cabinet, met the Allied High Commission at their headquarters at the St. Petersburg Hotel, situated on a hill deep in the Rhineland. A centre of worship and pilgrimage since the thirteenth century, when the Cistercians first built a shrine there, this commanding height had always played an important part in the life of the Rhine. By the beginning of the twentieth century the monastery had been replaced by the more materialistic splendour of a luxury hotel, the same hotel where in 1938 Neville Chamberlain waited while Hitler considered the overtures of British appeasement. Subsequently, this historic building had been a convalescent home for Wehrmacht officers and, after the surrender, a British officers' mess, before finally opening its opulent portals to the Allied High Commission.

The ceremony which had accompanied the great occasions held in the St. Petersburg in the past was totally absent from this first formal discussion between the new representatives of the Federal Republic and the Allies. Since the sovereignty of the new German state was incomplete and the task of reconciliation by no means over, Adenauer felt that the first meeting should be as business-like as possible; hence only five members of the Cabinet and his own personal aide attended the meeting. Although there was to be no pomp, the conference would still presumably be subject to the niceties of diplomatic protocol. However, on the arrival of Adenauer and his party these were fortunately brushed aside by the Allied High Commissioners, taking their lead from the French delegate, François-Pousset, who welcomed Adenauer with spontaneous cordiality; thus a potentially uncomfortable moment for all concerned was in the event by-passed by simple kindly sentiment.

The conference began with Adenauer outlining the main objectives of his foreign and domestic policy.[1] He placed great emphasis on a revision of the Ruhr Agreement and the active participation of West Germany in a new movement for European co-operation based on economic integration; although he thus repudiated the concept that the nation state should continue as the basic structure of Western Europe's political organization, Adenauer nevertheless dismissed the possibility of any recognition of the Oder-Niesse territories.

Many meetings followed in the ensuing period, Adenauer invariably travelling to the St. Petersburg as if to do battle. His tough and autocratic personality, stiffened with the self-confidence of a vigorous old age, made subservience difficult for him. He objected strongly not only to the judicial superiority of the High Commissioners, but also to the physical location of their headquarters overlooking his capital at Bonn as well as his own home in the hills of Rhöndorf. The journalistic phrase popular at the time, 'the ghosts of Weimar stalked the corridors of Bonn', was for once an accurate assessment of Adenauer's hopes and fears. For whilst he attempted at each discussion to gain even wider concessions he was well aware that the whole of Europe was watching the development of the Federal Republic with possibly apprehensive interest; hence he vigorously discussed the neo-Nazi revival and, initially at least, re-emphasized his government's firm intention to support the policy of de-militarization. Yet at the same time he took great pains to appear to the German people as a staunch defender of their

[1] The text of this speech had been studied by the Allied High Commission some days previously, although changes in emphasis made by Adenauer in his final draft came as a surprise to them.

rights. Even so, he was accused by Schumacher of being 'the Chancellor of the Allies'.

However, despite the difficulties of his immediate position, Adenauer knew that broadly speaking his policies had the support of the Allied High Commissioners. Although he fought his principal battles with the Allies over the immediate return of Germany to economic and political independence, the Chancellor firmly believed that the best way to ensure that his country should never again embrace the 'nationalist blindness' and 'materialism' of the past was first to seek reconciliation with France and secondly to work increasingly towards a closer integration of the sovereign states of Western Europe, a pair of principles which eventually emerged as the future guidelines for democratic government in the Federal Republic.

In November 1949 the Allied High Commissioners and the Adenauer administration finally reached formal agreement (usually known as the Petersburg Agreement) on the degree of freedom to be enjoyed by the Federal Government and on the general direction of its future policy. Moreover, as a result of the 'political warfare' campaign which Adenauer had waged against the Commissioners, the latter had relaxed their demands for dismantling in many sectors of industry, with a complete relaxation in Berlin. A modest shipbuilding programme had been allowed to start again in Bremen and Hamburg. Even more substantial developments had occurred on the international scene; the Federal Republic had not only become a free and equal partner in the Marshall Plan Organization but would henceforth be able to join many other bodies such as the World Bank, the World Monetary Fund, the International Labour Organization and the World Health Organization. It was furthermore authorized to establish Consular Offices in foreign countries, a major step forward towards normal diplomatic status. Finally, it was formally invited to join the Council of Europe at Strasbourg. Therefore as early as 1949 the Western democracies seem to have recognized that the movement for a united Europe could not really be contemplated without the active co-operation and participation of West Germany.

There have been two major tendencies in this movement towards European unity since the Second World War. In the first instance there has been the so-called 'European Idea', which envisages parliamentary and executive institutions deliberately moving towards international integration and the creation of a European political community. Such a process demands a selfless attitude of supranationalism, and a willingness to surrender sovereign power in certain areas of government to the authority of a wider international control. The other trend has been the move towards unity through intergovernmental co-operation in specific fields and under conditions where the participating governments retain their formal sovereignty and ultimate freedom of action. The creation in 1949 of the Council of Europe by the seventeen signatory nations at Strasbourg was an attempt to reconcile these two approaches to European union, the federal and the functional, on as broad a base as possible.

Many of the organizations which evolved in the period immediately following the creation of the North Atlantic Alliance and the lifting of the Berlin Blockade contained elements of both approaches, but all had a common stimulus in the uncertanties of the Cold War situation. Economic factors in particular played a significant part in reshaping the political contours of Western Europe at this time; the disruption of economic life in post-war Europe was on a scale far beyond the capabilities of individual sovereign powers to restore by their own efforts. Co-ordination of economic planning was thus an imperative; the very success of the Organization for European Economic Co-operation in these early years provided a stimulant for further growth. In addition, the atmosphere of crisis which increasingly prevailed in the post-war period forced nations to approach the problem of their own security from an entirely new standpoint. The Second World War had witnessed an unprecedented expansion of the diplomacy of alliances and as tension began to increase in the late 1940s a shared solution to the problem of security once again became a major objective in the foreign policy of European states. This common preoccupation culminated in the formation of the Atlantic Alliance, whose gradual emergence can be traced back to the Treaty of Dunkirk in 1947 and its later expansion into the Brussels Treaty of 1948. The Dunkirk Treaty envisaged the putative aggressor quite specifically, not as the Soviet Union or any Western power, but as a resurgent Germany.

Germany was indeed the focus of all discussions concerning the security of immediately post-war Europe.

However, as opinion crystallized in the East and West over the future of Germany, the threat to Western Europe began to assume a different identity, an uncertainty about the long-term future security of the whole continent. This change of atmosphere was symbolized by the transition from the Brussels Treaty to the Atlantic Alliance. NATO was a new kind of association, arising from a novel situation in international politics. Hitherto, peacetime alliances between democratic countries had been rare, and the few that had been formed were usually attempts to maintain the *status quo* against possible interference by an opponent. In contrast, the signatories of the North Atlantic Treaty desired to change fundamentally the political framework of Europe. None of the twelve initial member states wished to accept a permanent Russian occupation of Eastern Europe, but nothing short of a massive military attack could have dislodged the Soviet Union from these territories. However, the earnest desire to alter existing political institutions remained, leading to NATO being criticized from two opposing standpoints. On the one hand, some asserted that the mere existence of NATO was enough to preclude any possible revision of the post-war situation through negotiation, whereas the organization's more hawkish members felt that it was not doing enough to effect the desired changes in Europe.

The Atlantic Alliance began well enough, born against a background of Cold War crisis, with the Berlin Blockade a menacing reminder of the dangers of the situation; but with the easing of tension and the lifting of the Blockade the alliance lost some of its cohesion and political will. Many felt that the signing of the Treaties of Washington had in itself brought about the end of the Blockade, in other words, that all Europe needed to do was to present a show of diplomatic strength. However, this unwillingness to accept the reality of a military threat to Europe received a sharp jolt with the outbreak of the Korean War, which provided a fresh stimulus to the movement for European integration.

Yet another approach to the goal of European unity was at this time to be found amongst those who envisaged the creation of a 'European identity'; theirs was a somewhat esoteric movement, which had little popular appeal in the purely electoral sense, but was to a great extent confined to the *élites* of European society, and which postulated that the decline of Europe's political power was basically the result of blind nationalism, manifested particularly in the rivalry that had existed in the past between France and Germany, a rivalry which had in the twentieth century embroiled other nations and dragged them to disaster. This movement, which gained wide support amongst the new political leaders of Western Europe and which first received public acclaim in the famous Zurich speech by Churchill in 1948, was the intelligentsia's reaction against what they saw as the cancer of nationalism. Their consequent desire to create a united federation of Europe made them staunch supporters of the Council of Europe, in which organization they saw the possible embryonic structure for a new Europe.

All such trends had played their part in the creation of NATO and similar organizations, but their objectives came much closer to realization with the publication of what became known as the Schuman Plan. The early moves towards European unity had all been based on somewhat vague declarations of intent; true, the Council of Europe was significant in that it was the first internationally representative institution with parliamentary overtones to be created in Europe, but even this august body could only be seen as a hopeful beginning, since the objections of countries like the United Kingdom concerning the vital area of the surrender of sovereignty had resulted in the creation of a council with little real authority. The novel feature of the Schuman Plan was that it did not consist of empty phrases, but on the contrary a series of concrete and precise proposals. The Plan was announced in a dramatic way to the world when on 9 May 1950 Robert Schuman startled a press conference with the statement that the French government proposed 'to place all Franco-German coal and steel production under a common High Authority in an organization open to the participation of other countries in Europe'. The result of such a measure would be, in Schuman's words: 'the immediate establishment of common bases of industrial production, which is the first step towards European federation and will change the destiny of regions that have long been devoted to the production of war armaments of which they themselves have been the constant victims.'[1]

The importance of the Schuman Plan was twofold. In the first place it represented a major revolution in French foreign policy, a complete departure from the opinion held since the time of Richelieu that the weakness of Germany was the best solution to the security of France. Secondly, the Plan established the ascendancy of the 'functional' approach to European integration over other, more idealistic attitudes; the virtue of this approach was that, although each measure of co-operation would be restricted to a specific area of common economic need, the benefits would be immediate and each government's commitment would be limited to whatever was necessary to achieve a particular objective. Thus Europe could move towards full economic and political union at a pace set by practical possibilities rather than an abstract vision of perfect integration. However, since this philosophy has unfortunately never been adopted to the fullest extent, its strengths and weakness are to a certain extent hypothetical; despite this, the Schuman Plan was a decisive act of faith in the possibility of European union throughout functionalism.

The suddenness of the Schuman Plan, and its drastic reversal of the traditions of French diplomacy, reflected the predicament of France's foreign policy and French politics in general at that time. The French economy, though improving, was still subject to chronic inflation. The International Ruhr Authority, an essential ingredient of the diplomacy which aimed at keeping Germany weak, was showing signs of disintegration. The conflict in Indo-China had escalated into a major confrontation and was proving a severe drain, while the North African colonies showed ominous signs of unrest. To Schuman, the resumption by West Germany of an active rôle in European politics seemed not only inevitable but likely to be immediate, and it was possible that if France persisted in her backward-looking policy the result could be the Anglo-Americans having to make a choice between Germany or France. If the situation continued, Schuman reasoned, the Allies might be more

[1] The text of Schuman's speech is given in Pierre Gerbet's important article, 'La Genèse du Plan Schuman: Des Origines à la Déclaration du 9 Mai' in the *Revue française du science politique*, July/September 1956, pp. 525–53.

impressed by the sturdy impulse towards self-regeneration discernible in Germany than by the obvious frailty of France's parliamentary government and her military weakness abroad. Thus the only alternatives open to him were the pursuit of a narrow neutralism, an unconstructive course, or a fresh approach to the German question. The Schuman Plan thus initiated a new phase in French foreign policy, one which sought to construct a new framework within which German development could proceed along channels that were not only less wearisome for France but which also promised positive benefits to both countries. The logic of this was unassailable; France could not prevent the resurgence of Germany and even to try to hinder it would only weaken her in the long run.

The French Treasury was attracted to the Schuman Plan by the strength of its economic arguments. Europe was experiencing an expansion in steel production but a falling in demand, a situation which cried out for a drastic rationalisation of manufacturing policy. For too long steel production had been planned in terms of markets restricted by national borders, a wasteful division. Only an international market and the free passage of goods to their most rational outlet could make specialization and large-scale production feasible.

Yet a further virtue of the Plan was the comprehensive nature of its proposals, for not only did it give a succinct policy guideline for the future, but also laid down in precise detail the extent of supranational control over the member countries. All this was contained in Schuman's initial announcement since, as he later wrote: 'its planners had, from the very first, a precise picture of the projected system; at the same time they spelled out its objectives, its means and its procedures, with a rigidity that surprised and sometimes shocked those accustomed to greater suppleness in diplomacy.'[1]

The reaction in Bonn to the Schuman proposals was immediate, and positively encouraging in terms of the developing *rapprochement* between the two countries. Adenauer had received details of both the Plan and Schuman's press release on the day they were announced in Paris; for the Chancellor, the main appeal of the Plan was that it envisaged all members being

[1] Reuter, *La Communauté Européenne du Charbon et de l'Acier*, p. 3.

treated as equals, indeed a step forward in Franco-German relations. Another attraction of it for Adenauer was that if the Schuman organization became a reality, the International Ruhr Authority would become obsolete and thus would probably make a silent exit. The Bonn government also recognized the significant contribution that the Schuman Plan would make towards the goal of a European Federation, since a European Coal and Steel Federation was as inconceivable in a political vacuum as a European Army.

While most Germans recognized the value of the Schuman Plan as a constructive attempt to break the deadlock in Franco-German relations by an 'escape into Europe', its economic advantages were not immediately obvious to them. Some cautious politicians even regarded it as a French ruse to maintain a stronghold on German resources after the occupation ended. Yet Schuman held the trump card, as the Germans well knew, and it was quite obvious that he intended to play it. Without French consent the remaining occupation controls over Germany could not be changed or abolished. Schuman, in a move of great finesse, had in fact proposed a scheme which, though it did away with the most irksome remaining aspects of the occupation, at the same time did not completely restore to Germany the sovereignty it had lost; his creation of a supranational authority made it easier for Germany to accept restrictions on her self-determination.

The Schuman Plan also made a tangible contribution to European recovery by providing a new approach to some problems which the OEEC, hitherto the main organization for reconstruction, had done little to solve, in particular the lack of harmonization in national recovery plans and the consequent inability to co-ordinate national investment programmes in a number of different industries, notably steel. The Plan tackled these difficulties in a somewhat more direct way than the OEEC; a straightforward pooling of the heavy industry of Western Europe would ensure not only a more effective division of labour, taking advantage of the larger market, but would also provide stability for investment to shape the future growth of industry in accordance with the needs of the whole area. However, in fairness to the OEEC, the period 1949–50 had been one of its most active periods and hence, in the context of European economic co-operation, the Schuman Plan arose out of a situation of ferment rather than stagnation.

On 20 June 1950 the first conference of the six 'Schuman States' opened in Paris. France, West Germany and Italy were joined by Belgium, Holland and Luxembourg, who had provided a nucleus for the integration of Europe by their wartime creation of Benelux. Italy and the Benelux nations embraced the Plan not only because of what it promised for the future of Europe, but also because they realized what remaining outside it would do to their economies. The West Germans approached this, their first major international conference as a nation of equal status to any other, with the attitude that their full co-operation would be interpreted as a sure sign that their security was safeguarded. Once the West were convinced of this, it could only be a matter of time before all restrictions were lifted and the complete rehabilitation of West Germany would become an established fact. In the event, German hopes in this direction received support from a most unexpected quarter, the Far East. On 25 June 1950, just five days after the conference had convened in Paris, the Communist divisions of North Korea poured across the thirty-eighth parallel to invade South Korea. So began the first major war of the nuclear age, and a conflict which was to influence profoundly the security needs of both Europe and West Germany.

The Korean War, which involved a year of continuous fighting and two more of intermittent skirmishing leading to an armistice negotiation, is relevant to this study only in so far as it illustrates the hardening division between the protagonists of the Cold War, a schism which had an immediate impact on Western Europe. As far back as 1948 the frontiers in the Far East had gradually become as confused as they were in Europe. The thirty-eighth parallel had originally been chosen by the Allies simply to facilitate the surrender of the Japanese forces in Korea, those to the north to submit to the USSR and those in the south to the US forces which arrived in September 1945 from Okinawa. Indeed, the decision made at the Cairo Conference of 1943, and subsequently reaffirmed at Potsdam in 1945, was that Korea in due course should become 'free and independent'. But even by the time the Americans arrived that autumn the Russians had already hardened the line of convenience into a military boundary. The Soviet-American Joint Control Commission, which was established to create a provisional government and to provide interim trusteeship for Korea, quickly became unworkable as each side's attitude degenerated into hostility. The United States enlisted the support of the United Nations, who sent a commission to investigate the problem, but this was not allowed to enter North Korea. Eventually, the Americans arranged elections in the South and created a Republic of South Korea, with a population of some twenty-one million people;[1] the nine million people of the North soon assumed the identity of a new Communist satellite. Throughout 1948 and the following year the two new nations faced each another with increasing hostility across the thirty-eighth parallel, which soon became very much a troubled frontier. In February 1950 the Russians signed a treaty with the new Peoples' Republic of China, followed by a trade agreement in April. Belatedly, the Americans increased their volume of aid to the Nationalist Chinese who by this time were precariously holding on to Formosa and a couple of insignificant offshore islands. Although aid was given to China, the South Koreans seemed to have been considered a doubtful risk by the American State Department. Soviet and Chinese military advisers were busily training the North Koreans and had equipped them with a powerful force of seven assault divisions and one armoured division. By the summer of 1950 their army numbered 140,000 men, many of whom had either been trained in the Soviet Union or had had combat experience in the Chinese Civil War. In response, the Americans had made a half-hearted attempt to improve the South Korean army, which, though strong on paper, had fewer than 500 advisers working with it and was relatively ill-trained and poorly equipped.

The Truman policy of 'containment by force if necessary' was poorly defined, but it seems that there was never an express US intention to respond to a military threat *anywhere* in the world. If necessary, force would be used in Europe, since the creation of NATO certified this resolution, but elsewhere it would only be employed where American investment was

[1] The Republic of South Korea officially came into existence on 15 August 1948.

strong. In South Asia the only country which came into this category was Japan. That the Americans consequently had no real commitment to the integrity of Korea was clearly illustrated in January 1950, when US Secretary of State Dean Acheson defined the line of containment as 'along the Aleutians to Japan and then . . . to the Ryukyus and from the Ryukyus to the Philippine Islands'. Such a line excluded both Formosa and Korea, an error further compounded when, in answer to a question on the need to guarantee these areas against military attack, Dean Acheson stated that it was 'hardly sensible or necessary within the realm of practical relationship'. These comments were construed by both Stalin and his new satellite of North Korea to mean that the United States regarded South Korea as strategically unimportant, an interpretation re-inforced by the American military run-down in that area in 1949; accordingly they decided to launch an all-out invasion of the South. Such a move was in accord with Stalin's personal ambitions, with Russia's traditionally imperialistic Far Eastern foreign policy, and with the requirements of global Communism. As with West Berlin, Stalin's tactics in Korea were to take an initial risk by advancing to the brink, and then to retreat as a counter-threat developed; this policy of 'brinkmanship' was thus in fact a Soviet innovation.

The South Korean Army (ROK) numbered 98,000 men; 60,000 of these were in light combat divisions, of which only four were anywhere near strength. They were lightly armed, possessed no armour at all, and of course lacked the combat experience of their northern adversaries. Despite all the obvious warnings of imminent war, this ill-prepared force was caught completely by surprise when its country was invaded; many units were away enjoying their weekend leave on that Sunday morning. The Communists broke through the defence perimeters with relative ease and, as the South Korean forces together with their American advisers fell back in disarray, the capital of Seoul fell at the end of the fourth day.

The United States' response to this flagrant act of aggression was twofold. They called an emergency meeting of the United Nations Security Council, at the same time ordering their C-in-C Far East, General MacArthur, who had his head-quarters in Tokyo, to supply the ROK army with the necessary munitions and supplies. In the early hours of Monday morning 26 May, the United Nations Security Council called on the invaders to withdraw and asked 'all members to render every assistance to the United Nations in the execution of this resolution'. The reason why this resolution was passed without being vetoed by the Soviet Union was that the latter had been boycotting the Security Council for some months in protest against Nationalist China's continued membership of the Council.

By the end of the month the situation had completely deteriorated in South Korea and, in order to bolster up flagging ROK resistance, Truman, acting on the UN resolution, ordered General MacArthur to despatch naval and air units into the combat zones to counter the Communist invasion. As the US Navy evacuated more than 2,000 American and foreign nationals from the port of Pusan, the first air battles between American and North Korean aircraft were taking place in the skies above, and naval units were bombarding North Korean army units as they marched southwards along the coast roads. But these measures were not enough to restore the situation; the High Command of the ROK appeared to have completely lost control by this time and panic gripped the population, who fled in a mass exodus through the mountains to the southern part of the peninsula.

MacArthur arrived at Pusan on 29 June to co-ordinate the American effort, which now involved ground forces; meanwhile, his carrier-borne strike aircraft escalated the conflict by attacking targets and troop concentrations north of the thirty-eighth parallel. However, it was one thing for the United States to respond with these spectacular gestures to South Korea's appeal for help, but quite another for her to deploy her troops effectively, since by this time ground forces were the only hope of remedying the situation. Total US Army strength was now less than 600,000 men, the lowest since 1932, and already the Pentagon was beginning to regret its over-hasty implementation of massive demobilization, behind what they had believed was the secure nuclear shield. The outbreak of the Korean War brought to an abrupt end a period which strategists have since called 'the age of nuclear innocence', which cherished the belief that nuclear weapons were so destructive that no country would ever again wage war, simply because nuclear retaliation would be so devastating as to completely outweigh any possible political advantage to be gained from going to war. The Korean War, the first limited war of the nuclear age, dispelled these illusions and also made America aware of an entirely new manifestation of the Communist threat. On 27 June 1950 President Truman broadcast to the American people in these words: 'The attack upon Korea makes it plain beyond all doubt that Communism has passed beyond the use of subversion to conquer independent nations and will now use armed invasion and war.'

Unfortunately, as has been stated, the US Army was in no condition to fight that war; the few troops immediately available in the Far East were garrison units from Japan and the Pacific, mostly composed of new recruits with no actual combat experience. The result was predictable; these totally unprepared units arrived in the Pusan perimeter, all that was left to the South Koreans by this stage, only to collapse under the onslaught of the Communists; the hastily-formed US Eighth Army fell back amid scenes of disaster and humiliation, which the many examples of individual heroism could do little to remedy. While US forces thus conceded defeat in Korea it was, however, becoming increasingly evident to the State Department in Washington that the invasion was a calculated probe rather than a fundamental stage in what they saw as the Soviet global strategy. Hence the American and United Nations response had to be such that it would neither encourage nor force the Russians into open participation. This involved the President in considerable domestic difficulties, since he now had to play down the importance of the war to the American people, to limit its significance to a military concept new to the USA, but common in the British imperial experience, that of a police action. However, it was by this time understandably difficult for Americans at home to appreciate the subtle difference even less comprehensible to the battered remnants of the US infantry formations in Korea as they fell back in the face of a massive Communist advance and the full force of the July monsoon.

Thus it was that the Korean conflict was to run its course as a 'limited' war. Although the Americans had a monopoly of nuclear weapons, the constraint placed on their use resulting from a careful consideration of both the strategic consequences and of the political reaction throughout the rest of the world meant that the American and UN contingents had to fight their battles with the weapons and methods of the Second World War. The fact that in Korea the leading Western power did not use its mightiest weapon was a clear hint that the theory of the nuclear deterrent might not always be helpful in practice. For although MacArthur was eventually able, at great cost in American and Commonwealth lives, to stabilize the Pusan perimeter, and indeed to bring about a dramatic reversal in Allied fortunes by his brilliant amphibious landings on the Inchon Peninsula, the lesson of the Korean war very much influenced attitudes in Western Europe, in particular concerning the future of the Federal Republic of Germany.

Finally, the war had a profound effect on other areas of the East, in particular Japan, South-east Asia and Tibet. A draft Japanese peace treaty was prepared by the United States government in October 1950, and in July 1951, before the treaty formally came into force, the Japanese were conceded the right to establish an armed Police Reserve of 75,000 men. The Chinese government accused the Burmese of allowing the Americans to use airfields in Burma, which increased tension along their common frontier. The Vietminh in Indo-China escalated their operations against the French colonial forces to the point of open warfare by the end of 1950. In Malaya, the British campaign against the Communist guerillas took a grave turn for the worse. The Chinese invaded Tibet at about the same time as the UN forces in Korea recrossed the thirty-eighth parallel and advanced northwards. Thus the peoples of the Far East were increasingly forced to take a stand on one side of the Iron Curtain or the other; only Nehru's India could afford the luxury of neutrality, and even this could hardly be called impartial.

XIII

THE ARMED CAMP

The real significance of the North Korean aggression is this evidence that, even at the resultant risk of starting a third world war, Communism is willing to resort to armed aggression, whenever it believes it can win.[1]

THE OUTBREAK of the Korean War completed the transformation of NATO from a multi-guaranty pact into a semi-integrated military organization designed to redress the strategic imbalance on the Continent. In the first year of the alliance, in the absence of the threat of immediate attack, neither the Europeans nor the Americans had seemed prepared to undertake a rearmament effort of the magnitude necessary to put Western forces on a par with those of the Russians. The Europeans were unwilling to jeopardize their economic revival, whilst the United States government was reluctant to foot the bill single-handed. Furthermore, the European signatories had to contend with their electorates; in order to persuade them to accept the possibly provocative commitments of NATO they felt it necessary to assure them that the alliance could actually protect their countries from invasion. But any conventional rearmament at this stage would not only have resulted in an intolerable economic burden, but also have required them, as democracies in a time of peace, to emphasize their military aims at the expense of the advancement of living standards, a step tantamount to political suicide. The answer to the eventual fulfilment of both obligations, modest rearmament and a social welfare programme, was obvious even before the outbreak of the Korean War confirmed it; the inclusion of West Germany in the defence network of NATO. But unfortunately in the early 1950s this was no more acceptable to the European

[1] Secretary of Defence Johnson, in a statement submitted to the Senate Committee on Appropriations in 1951.

members than massive rearmament. This deep-seated aversion to any 'German in uniform' was admirably summed up at the time by Ernest Bevin: 'Germany must naturally be brought back into the family of nations, but giving weapons to German troops is not the right way to achieve that objective.'

This conflict between domestic goals and the demand for rearmament had a profound influence on Western strategy, since as a result NATO tried to achieve a compromise between dependence on the nuclear delivery system of the US Strategic Air Command (SAC) and on conventional defence. It thus attempted to 'raise the outer walls just enough to encourage unimpeded progress in the inner keep';[1] its members felt that adequate 'outer walls' were all they were capable of at that time, but were confident that American nuclear power would always deter an assault on this 'inner keep'. Thus, up to the outbreak of the Korean War and the subsequent conference called by NATO at Lisbon, there was only a gradual build-up of European forces. This Western complacency over the priorities of security must be contrasted with the tremendous weight of armour and conventional forces stationed by the Soviet Union in East Germany. The Russians obviously judged the military situation differently, since under Stalin's guidance the following doctrine was taught: 'Nuclear weapons will never decide the outcome of war. They can only be one of the various factors to be taken into account in fighting a war, for its ultimate outcome depends on which side can physically occupy the others territory, and only the massed fighting men of the Soviet Army suffice for this.'[2] Although this strategic concept was probably partly due to the Russian lack of operational nuclear forces, it was nevertheless undoubtedly more relevant to the circumstances of the European theatre at this time than the NATO compromise.

The outbreak of the Korean War had an immediate effect on Western Europe, since this was the other main area of the world where 'East met West'. Militarily speaking, there was obviously now an urgent need to concentrate forces along the eastern frontier of Western Europe, and here NATO, if only momentarily, was shaken out of its lethargy to look to the

[1] Robert E. Osgoode, *NATO: The Entangling Alliance.*
[2] *Pravda*, May 1949.

pressing needs of security. Many Western politicians paid particular attention to an article which appeared in the *New York Times Magazine* of June 1950. The author, John Foster Dulles, saw the outbreak of the Korean War as the arrival of the 'critical moment', a concept which he had outlined (and which had received wide publicity) at the height of the Berlin Blockade some eighteen months before; it was defined as that point in time when international Communism felt it had exhausted most of its possibilities of gain by indirect aggression: 'It may invalidate the assumption that the Soviet Union would not risk general war for several years to come—the time presumably required for it to develop a large stockpile of atomic weapons. It surely invalidates the assumption that we can continue still for a time to live luxuriously, without converting our economic potential into military reality.'

Amongst the European members of NATO there was by now full recognition of the military necessity for complete rearmament, but the political implications of such a step were enormous, since it would require a total re-appraisal of the European attitude towards West Germany. Although significant progress had been allowed in the rehabilitation of that country, the Korean War put a new and more urgent perspective on the whole question, and the Western powers finally realized that West Germany could no longer be left as a kind of second-class colony, existing in a military and political vacuum. Thus NATO was now confronted with a critical choice; on the one hand it could simply preserve the *status quo* and maintain a significant contingent of occupation forces in Germany, so ensuring that she would remain weak and disarmed. On the other hand, it could acknowledge the fact that now was the ideal time to fully integrate West Germany as a sovereign state into the Western community, which of course would mean not only her resurrection as a political and economic entity, but also as a military power, with her own forces of defence and offence.

The French and the Americans were diametrically opposed over this issue and thus Britain found herself the 'partner of decision'. The official Foreign Office view reflected a fear of renewed German militarism, but at the same time acknowledged the importance to the West of German potential in manpower and industry. However, this official circumspection was considerably shaken by a speech made by Churchill (still the highly volatile leader of the Opposition) to the Council of Europe at Strasbourg in 11 August 1950, in which he called for the creation of a European Army, including a German contingent. Adenauer was at this time in Switzerland, convalescing from pneumonia, and Churchill's pronouncement must have taken him by surprise. However, he was all too aware that such brave words could be no more than a gesture, since Churchill was out of power and the Council of Europe possessed no real legislative authority. Nevertheless, a beginning had been made, in spirit if not in fact. Meanwhile, the war in Korea raged on and the mood of Germany, as Adenauer well knew, grew steadily more pessimistic. What would happen if the 'alert detachment' of the People's Police from East Germany came swarming over the zonal boundary, behind a spearhead of Soviet armour, to 'liberate' Western Germany? Was not the Federal Republic destined to become a second Korea, without even the certainty that the Western powers would defend it with all the means at their disposal? By mid-August Adenauer was back in Bonn and busily negotiating with the Allied High Commissioner for the creation of a special West German paramilitary force as a means of national 'self-protection'. Adenauer envisaged a Defence Force of some 150,000 men which, in his own words, would be 'powerful enough to prevent the possibility of a Korea-type aggression by the Soviet Zone Police'.

The Chancellor was aware that the main supporters of this proposed West German military force were the Americans, since in May of that year at the Foreign Ministers Conference in New York Dean Acheson had stated that the US Congress would only agree to a weighty American contribution to NATO of troops and materials if the Federal Republic assumed a share of the burden commensurate with its means. For this reason, the Secretary of State demanded a measure of German rearmament and the inclusion of the Federal Republic in the NATO defence system as a matter of principle.

Adenauer felt that this American demand was entirely justified, not only in financial terms but also morally, for if American soldiers were prepared to defend Germany, it was obviously the bounden duty of German soldiers to help them—as soon as they were invited to do so. On the other hand, he fully appreciated British and French fears of a resurgence of German militarism and disliked the prospect as much as they; he was not therefore willing to agree to German rearmament unless within the framework of an integrated European defence force. This he considered not only a military necessity but also highly desirable politically, since he was convinced that military co-operation in a European Army, in the same way as economic integration with the Schuman Plan, would sooner or later bring about political unification, the united states of Europe which was his ultimate goal. However, for Adenauer there was one indispensable prerequisite for such integration: a genuinely free and sovereign German partner, enjoying equal rights, released from all tutelage and able to act on its own resolve. During the protracted negotiations over the European Defence Community (EDC) he never yielded an inch from this basic condition.

As has been remarked, initial French reaction to the proposed reconstitution of Germany's armed forces was hostile. Throughout 1950 Schuman watched with increasing alarm the gathering demand for, and publicity over, remilitarisation. However, he reluctantly agreed to proposals which would allow Germany to produce raw materials and steel for armaments, and lent French support to the communiqués of the various international conferences, particularly that of the NATO Ministers in September 1950 which agreed to treat any attack against the Federal Republic or Berlin as an attack upon themselves, and to designate the occupation troops as 'security forces for the protection and defence of the free world including the Federal German Republic and the Western sectors of Berlin'.[1] But in the autumn of 1950 American demands crystallized into a specific suggestion for the raising of two West German divisions by mid-1951. This proposal was totally unacceptable to the French, yet Schuman realized that he dared not procrastinate, since the American sense of urgency might well lead to a bilateral deal with the West Germans; neither could he count on the British supporting his opposition to the plan. Therefore France had to produce an alternative scheme as quickly as

[1] RIIA documents 1949–50, pp. 334–5.

possible, a scheme which would not only gain the support of the coalition government and National Assembly in France, but also satisfy American demands for a German contribution to NATO's task. The only solution to all these conflicting requirements would be some kind of military version of the Schuman Plan.

Therefore, on 24 October 1950, René Pleven, the French Prime Minister, in a major speech to his National Assembly emphasized that 'Germany, though not a party to the Atlantic Pact, benefits from the system of security it gave rise to'. Therefore, he said, 'the French government proposes the creation, for the common defence, of a European Army linked to the political institutions of a united Europe'. Although the National Assembly accepted this proposal, by a slender majority of 348 to 224 votes, there now began a debate which, in the words of Raymond Aron, was 'the greatest ideological-political quarrel that France had probably known since the Dreyfus affair. A quarrel whose most apparent issue was German rearmament, but whose deepest significance affected the very principle of French existence, the national state'.[1]

There were many features of the Pleven Plan which appealed to Adenauer and his colleagues, especially its basic framework of a European union and its provision for the creation of German military contingents within a European army; however, while there was thus little doubt that it would gain majority support in Bonn, its proposals provoked a bitter public debate throughout the Federal Republic. For the Chancellor, the political logic behind the Plan was impeccable, since it would allow West Germany to share in its own defence against possible Communist aggression and also rehabilitate the German soldier, yet at the same time its supranational structure would reassure those fearful of a revived German militarism which might weaken the infant Bonn democracy and increase the influence of the officer corps; the Plan also marked a decisive step toward the 'functional' integration of Europe and reconciliation with France. Finally, it was made clear that the reward for German rearmament would be the end of occupation. Yet such reasonable arguments held little appeal for

[1] Raymond Aron, 'Esquisse historique d'une grande querelle idéologique', in Aron and Lerner's *Querelle de la C.E.D.*, p. 9.

German youth who, oppressed by the chaos and misery of post-war Germany and aware of their collective guilt, now turned against the generations which had brought this calamity on Germany, in a revolt against their teachers, their political leaders and even their parents which crystallized around a deep distrust of the German military legend.

Moreover, most of those fortunate enough to be survivors of that military legend had little desire to serve in the Wehrmacht again; their past experiences on the battlefield, together with the still ubiquitous evidence of the destructiveness of war, had made them acutely aware of the dangers of military adventures. In fact, only one group welcomed the Pleven proposals enthusiastically, the career soldiers and ex-officers whose future livelihood depended on a rehabilitated German army. Veteran associations had been formed as early as 1949 and these now entered the debate over the Pleven Plan with vigour. Predictably, the very enthusiasm of this militarist support for the European Army misfired, since it strengthened fears in both Germany and France that rearmament would only restore the military caste to power.

The lesson of the Korean War had surprisingly little influence on the attitude of those West Germans who opposed rearmament. Instead of concluding from it that West Germany should be rearmed in order to repel a similar invasion by East Germany, a contingency which no German at the time thought improbable, their first reaction was to demand an increase in the occupation forces in Germany and a formal guarantee that they would defend the Federal Republic's eastern borders, More than one cynical commentator, pointing to the Korean invasion, remarked that the West would be unlikely to make the same mistake again, of withdrawing occupation troops too soon. Thus there was a considerable body of opinion that Adenauer had to win over before he could secure popular support for the re-creation of military forces in the Federal Republic.

Nevertheless, the debate over EDC in Germany, although hard-fought, was almost certain to end in eventual ratification, since EDC would lead to the end of occupation, an overwhelmingly desirable objective from Bonn's point of view. In France, no such inevitable outcome could be predicted. In the event, the issue of EDC dragged on for four years before any government came round to presenting the formal proposals before parliament and by that time their rejection was seen as just another move in the 'game of politics' which enervated the Fourth Republic. Despite this, the debate over EDC was of great significance in the history of Franco-German relations since, in the first place, it forced almost every political group in France to define its point of view on the new Germany, and thus hardened attitudes at a time when flexibility was vital. Secondly, the failure of the French government to present the treaty for ratification effectively blocked the return to sovereignty granted by the Bonn Agreements, and so placed upon France alone the responsibility for the prolongation of the occupation. Lastly, the eventual defeat of the EDC treaty in the French Assembly undermined the cause of Franco-German reconciliation within a united Europe by precipitating a revival of nationalism in France and Germany and an attack on those institutions of European integration already established.

Schuman personally felt that the amalgamation of armed forces under a permanent European Command would remove or at least greatly mitigate the threat to France of a rearmed Germany. Instead of the ancient rivalry between the two countries, there would presumably ensure a period of essentially enforced co-operation, leading to an eventual genuine merging of national interests. He saw it as an honest plan for a supranational solution to France's age-old military problem. It was also a realistic plan, in that it took an objective look into the future, to a time when Germany would once more be in a position to influence Europe's political and commercial life by her undoubted economic and demographic superiority. Against such an eventuality the EDC would provide France with the best, if not the only, national safeguard.

The NATO Council of Ministers, whilst showing great interest in the concepts of the Pleven Plan, believed that in practical terms it was unworkable, since the French had postulated the integration of national forces as taking place at the most basic structural level, that of the battalion or its equivalent; in contrast, the Americans advocated the creation of 'combat teams', each of 6,000 men, integrated into European divisions. According to Pleven, the EDC divisions were to be under the authority of a European Minister of Defence, who was in turn responsible to a European Defence Council. Finally, the European Defence Council was to be subject to an 'international political authority', such as a European Parliament. The NATO Council considered this infrastructure as far too complicated, and one which would take far too long to implement, since Communist aggression was then regarded as imminent. A further complication was that two separate military forces would exist within the Atlantic Alliance, the EDC and its participating countries, and members such as the United States, the United Kingdom and Canada, who would only belong to NATO. Moreover, the elaborate system of checks and balances built in, essentially to allay French fears, was not appreciated by the non-European members of NATO. Dean Acheson was heard to remark, 'The French are trying to rearm Germany without arming the Germans.'

Eventual compromise was reached through the findings of a committee created specially by NATO to examine in greater detail the implications of a European defence force. The compromise was called the Spoffard Plan (after the American chairman of the committee) and was based on the American 'combat team' as the national unit, integrated into the general framework of the Pleven Plan. On 27 May 1952 the European Defence Community Treaty was signed in Paris by France, Germany, Holland, Belgium, Luxembourg and Italy; but the process of ratification was to drag on for another two years.

Rearmament in Western Europe now proceeded on two levels, for the Atlantic Alliance had already decided at the Lisbon Conferences to make a massive effort to achieve parity in conventional forces with the Soviet Union. The Korean War was now plainly revealed as a 'conventional' war, and although the Americans still had a monopoly of nuclear weapons, their inability to use them, whilst appreciated by her European allies, also temporarily undermined European confidence in the assumption that American nuclear striking power would always deter the Soviet Union. Hence this first and only serious attempt to create the kind of conventional forces which the military had prescribed for withstanding a Soviet attack in Europe. The United States set the pace for her allies by launching an all-out rearmament programme which would quadruple her defence expenditure within three years. Britain increased the period of National Service from eighteen months to two years, announced plans to form three new divisions, and promised to increase her contingent in West Germany to five divisions by 1953; an ambitious arms programme which would have raised Britain's defence expenditure to the level of twelve per cent of her Gross National Product. France increased her defence budget by thirty per cent and planned to add fifteen new divisions to the forces available to NATO.

As we have seen, it was American fears that Stalin might apply his Far Eastern policy to divided Germany that stimulated the accelerated acceptance of the Federal Republic as a full and equal member of the Western Alliance, and from this moment on the issue of German rearmament dominates international politics. The Western Allies soon became caught up in a paradox of their own making, since they were trying to mobilize German strength against Communist aggression without making Germany strong, and they were to waste the next three years in trying to solve this problem through the device of the European Defence Community. Stalin took advantage of this delay in forming a European army by conducting a relentless campaign against the rearming of Germany. As early as 1950, when the whole issue was still only at the level of politicians' gossip and newspaper speculation, an ominous diplomatic note was addressed to the West from the Kremlin: 'The Soviet Union will not tolerate the recreation of a West German army, since it stands in utter contradiction to the ruling of the Potsdam Conference on the demilitarization of Germany.'

This was followed up by intensive propaganda against the 'Hitlerite Wehrmacht' which was particularly intended to remind the Dutch and French of their recent experiences. In March 1952 the Soviet government handed notes to the three Western powers proposing that all should 'discuss without delay the question of a peace treaty with Germany', and 'examine the question of the conditions favouring the speediest formation of an all-German government expressing the will of the German people'.

The very ambiguity of wording in these statements led the Allies to dismiss them as clumsy attempts to delay the signing of the EDC Treaty, but they have subsequently been seen as a manifestation of Soviet willingness to seek agreement over Berlin, provided that the new German state could exist in a neutral environment. The Western response at the time was a call for free elections throughout Germany, as a prior condition to the singing of a treaty with a new German national government. On 5 March 1953, while both sides were still exchanging notes, Stalin died and the situation changed completely, not least for West Berlin.

The issue of rearmament was one of particular immediacy for that city and its mayor, Ernst Reuter. The Socialist Left (SPD) in the Federal Republic was violently opposed to rearmament and even brought the issue before the Constitutional Court at Karlsrühe, on the grounds that it contravened the Basic Law. Not only was Reuter a member of the SPD and therefore subject to the ties of party loyalty, but he was also heavily dependent on its co-operation for a workable coalition government in Berlin. In addition, he was very much aware of the vulnerability of West Berlin; NATO was still desperately weak, so that any Soviet response to rearmament in West Germany was bound to be felt by Berlin first. Although they hardly expected actual war to break out, the Berliners felt they had good reason to fear that the East German government would take advantage of any opportunity to seize control over the rest of the city.

However, with the death of Stalin, Reuter believed that there was now an opportunity to seek a negotiated settlement of the whole German question. Certainly he was not alone in thinking that henceforth the Soviet Union's attitude towards the West might become more flexible. Stalin's iron determination in the post-war years to make the Soviet Union impregnable in the cause of socialism had meant that he had isolated it from the rest of the world. He had forced Communism on Eastern Europe between 1945–48, not simply out of straightforward imperialist motives, but mainly because the Western Allies had shown such determination not to abandon Germany wholly to Soviet influence that Stalin felt it imperative to safeguard his grip on at least that country's eastern half. Russian foreign policy had thus been a tough but conservative consolidation of the existing position, as the belt of states between Germany and

Russia was developed into a *Cordon Communiste*. Such a cordon also satisfied the requirements of Soviet defensive strategy, since such countries had been the entry point of many past invasions of Russia. Mainly thanks to Stalin, the West now viewed the Soviet Union unsympathetically, as a country where there was harsh suppression of individual freedom and where terror was an important instrument of government, and firmly believed that the Soviet attitude to her one-time allies was now one of implacable hostility. Small wonder that the news of Stalin's death released a flood of speculative journalism in the Western press concerning the policy Russia would follow in the future towards NATO.

There was indeed a shift in Soviet policy, but not a constructive one. Following the predictable intrigues among Stalin's successors, Bulganin eventually emerged as Prime Minister with the ebullient Nikita Khrushchev in the more important post of Secretary-General of the Soviet Communist Party. Their policy was to be, as Krushchev later described it, 'to draw a line under World War II, particularly by accepting the division of Germany as a *fait accompli* which it might be undesirable for either side to try to change'. However, Stalin's brand of chauvinism backed up by threats now simply gave way to Krushchev's repeated endeavours to achieve far too much with far too little, the gap between Soviet objectives and capabilities being bridged by his peculiar variety of rhetoric and bluster. This unhelpful policy furthermore coincided with a period when the world, and particularly the super-powers, was becoming progressively more obsessed by the fear of nuclear war, all the more alarming because the precise form it might take could not be envisaged. The possession of thermonuclear capability by both sides meant that a vast and immensely costly machinery of deterrence had to be erected. At the same time, the security curtain surrounding each camp was made more impenetrable, until the two worlds were practically sealed off from one another.

However, Reuter had principally based his belief in the possibility of a settlement of the German question on what he considered as the imminent likelihood of East Germany collapsing, since Ulbricht had by now become somewhat of a liability to the Communist empire. Many political commenta-

tors since have suggested that Reuter's hopes were well-founded
and that a new régime in the Kremlin might well have given up
East Germany in return for a European settlement, even
though this would have required something of a revolution in
Soviet foreign policy, politically far from easy. In the event,
however, Reuter's expectations of a settlement were shattered,
not by any international failure to reach agreement, but by the
workers' uprising in Berlin in June 1953.

Demands for greater productivity from the working population sparked off the troubles; the citizens of East Berlin were
already overworked and undernourished and in that sweltering
summer the official call for greater effort was the last straw. On
a number of building sites the workers downed tools and
marched in protest to the Government offices. They were
quickly joined by other malcontents, and it was decided to hold
a general strike and protest rallies on the following day, 17
June. The next morning there were 100,000 people on the
streets of East Berlin by eight o'clock. Soviet armour quickly
appeared, clearing the Unter den Linden, Friedrichstrasse and
Potsdamerplatz. Although violence subsequently broke out in
these areas, it was not the tanks which actually suppressed the
rioters but rather the Volkspolizei, East Germans themselves,
who opened fire with machine-guns and automatic weapons.
Clashes between angry demonstrators and the ruthless police
continued throughout the day and many buildings were burnt.
However, the attacks by the demonstrators were purely
gestures and at no point did the rioting show any signs of
becoming a revolution, since it showed no co-ordination and
seemed to have no leaders. By late afternoon, despite growing
casualties amongst the rioters, the Volkspolizei appeared to be
losing control of the situation and a frightened Ulbricht
requested more Soviet help. The tanks reappeared in much
greater strength, accompanied this time by troops, the streets
were quickly cleared, a curfew imposed and by nightfall the
Soviet Army was in complete control. During the next couple
of days the general strike spread to other towns in East Germany and there were outbreaks of violence in Leipzig and
Jena, but without food the people could not hold out for long,
and by 19 June there began a gradual drift back to work.
Ulbricht managed to re-establish control, a series of mass

arrests cowed the population, and within a month the situation was back to normal.

In the ensuing months, whilst both East and West recovered from the shock of this spontaneous violence, a really determined attempt was made to reach some form of settlement. Stalin was dead and there were new men in the Kremlin, and with Eisenhower and Dulles now in power in the USA many Germans looked towards the latter to fulfil his election pledge to 'awe' Russia back behind her frontier. But Russia had already proved, by her demonstration of armoured might in the streets of East Berlin, that she would not be intimidated. Although the West Berlin Senate appealed to the Western governments to seek a settlement through negotiation with Russia, it was already too late. The new Kremlin régime was more heavily committed to Ulbricht than ever, and as Krushchev canvassed support for the recognition of the DDR in the councils of the world, there was now infinitely greater incentive for West Germany to further integrate with Western Europe. Thus all hopes of reunification raised by the death of Stalin had ended by the summer of 1953. Attitudes in the opposing camps hardened and with this came the virtual end of Berlin's major rôle in post-war European politics. Up to this time Reuter had been the anti-pope to Adenauer, but now the voice of Germany was solely the voice of Konrad Adenauer. The West, divided and weak, could not hope to bring about the liberation of Eastern Europe, while Russia, united and strong, would be more determined than ever to hold on to its buffer states.

In September 1953 general elections held in the Federal Republic gave Adenauer and the Christian Democrats a crushing victory over the Socialist Left. The 'economic miracle' was visible proof to the German electorate of their country's new-found status; in addition, Adenauer now enjoyed the complete support and confidence of the West, who wished to encourage German recovery in order to be able to negotiate with Russia from a position of strength. In the same month occurred the death of Reuter; he had united West Berlin and had in his time been the symbol of the central struggle of the Cold War, but although his passing was deeply mourned all his principles and attitudes had already become, literally during the last few months of his life, irrelevant to the new situation in East–West relations.. The years between the June uprising of 1953 and the Hungarian revolt of 1956 witnessed intense diplomatic activity by both sides, in search of common ground over the German question, and although most of this was inconclusive it at least took the pressure off West Berlin and enabled her to concentrate on her own problems of economic and social reconstruction.

The diplomatic game itself got under way in Berlin, where in February 1954 the foreign ministers of the four great powers, Dulles, Eden, Bidault and Molotov, met to discuss the prospects of a European agreement. For once, the Russians seemed in a pliable mood, ostensibly even more so than the West, and realizing that their presence in strength in East Germany had become a liability to themselves as well as providing the West with an incentive to re-arm, they advocated a re-unified and neutral Germany based on some kind of federal structure, in return for which the West was expected to abandon all plans for rearmament and not to allow the new Germany to drift into the Western camp. But the West were in no mood for compromise and rejected this prescription for German neutrality, holding out for Russian withdrawal pure and simple, as laid down in the Eden formula of 'reunification through freedom'. This envisaged free elections throughout a Germany which would be neutral only in the sense that she would be free from Russian interference; pure neutrality was seen by the West as dangerous and utopian. Although both sides ostensibly held fixed views on this question, this meeting should have been an opportunity for them to show that they were capable of at least a measure of flexibility, since some kind of tangible agreement, however limited, was desperately needed; for example, although the Western Allies may well have felt that the Russian demand for a neutral Germany was impracticable, this should not have prevented them from being open-minded about the proposed establishment of a European Security Pact, which could not only have provided the basis for a partial withdrawal of troops from Germany and opened the way to German reunification, but also could have served to limit the extent of German rearmament.

In view of this display of determined intractability, it was hardly surprising that no agreement was reached over the

proposals on the agenda. Since it had been obvious all along
that this would be the outcome, one might ask why the four
powers bothered to hold a conference at all. The answer is that
at this stage in international relations, conferences were no
longer held to settle problems but rather to influence them;
they had become part of the diplomatic charade of the Cold
War. For both sides, the motive for attending such meetings
was to take up positions in the eyes of the world, to register
facts and changes, and to make one's opponents appear
foolish and obstructive, or even to trap them. Consequently, the
suggestion of convening a conference often came from that side
which felt it had temporarily lost the initiative in influencing
and controlling the events which were nominally to be discussed. Hence the Berlin Conference of 1954 was presumably
conducted without any real expectation of agreement. The
Soviet government's aims at this time, as we have seen, were
to prevent the rearmament of Germany and the establishment
of the European Defence Community, two objectives which
were intimately related, since the EDC without German
rearmament would have had no substance, and German
rearmament outside the context of the EDC was still unacceptable to the French. But when Molotov put forward a
draft peace treaty on 1 February, providing for the neutraliza-
tion of Germany and her exclusion from the Western defence
system, he cannot have supposed it would be accepted; he was
merely speaking for the record. Similarly, the Western proposals for the reunification of Germany on the basis of free
elections were previously suspected to be unacceptable to the
Soviet Government, at least since the 1953 East German
uprising.

The destructive cynicism on both sides which caused the
failure of the Berlin talks was particularly unfortunate considering that the international situation was ripe for meaningful negotiation. The European Defence Community had virtually collapsed. France's traumatic defeat at Dien Bien Phu
had led to the emergence of the vigorous government of
Mendès-France and the decision to pull out completely from
Indo-China, although there was by now rebellion in Algeria.
There had been large reductions in the American military
presence in the Far East, and the Korean War was over. Only

in Malaya was there still active warfare between Communism and the West, and there it was already clear that the guerillas were losing in what had never been more than a local action. American reaction to the failure of EDC was one of bitterness, which could well have led to a US withdrawal from Europe. By the summer of 1954 Western European solidarity over mutual security was fast crumbling and in the absence of an overt Soviet threat the justification for NATO and EDC's existence was diminishing in many eyes. Many of the major powers faced internal economic crises which demanded precedence over defence budgets, and so the objectives agreed at the Lisbon Conference faded into history.

The failure of the EDC seriously damaged Franco-German relations. The French Assembly was the only parliament amongst the signatories to the EDC Treaty which had failed to ratify the agreements, essentially because they did not allay French fears of the possible future re-emergence of 'traditional German militarism'.

Consequently in 1953 the French sought to allay their fears of a revived Wehrmacht by trying to persuade the British to participate in the EDC. What France wanted was a British undertaking to station four divisions and a tactical air force on the Continent, envisaging such a military presence as a permanent understudy for the French position *vis-à-vis* Germany, in the event of France's troops being required for service in her troublesome colonies. But Britain remained indifferent to the French overtures.

France then sought monetary aid from the United States, to be used to equip indigenous colonial forces, thus avoiding a possible drain of troops from metropolitan France. In response the Americans, though all in favour of EDC, merely promised to guarantee American forces on the European continent; but this was a formal assurance they had already given, and it in no way satisfied the French demands for finance.

With France's failure to achieve any satisfactory Anglo-American guarantee of her security against a revived German army, her attitude towards EDC became increasingly ambiguous, and as negotiations dragged on throughout 1953, not only did the French government and Assembly become involved in other problems, but the latter in particular became increasingly negative. The Saar issue was resurrected and caused much friction between France and the Federal Republic: the 'Franco-German honeymoon' seemed to be over. Successive French governments were loath to jeopardize their existence in a period of political instability by presenting to the Assembly what had by now become so intractable an issue. When the EDC finally was presented there its demise was brought about by a mere procedural motion; the Communists, Gaullists, and a large number of Socialists and Radicals (Mendès-France's own party) voted against it.

Although the official French fear of a German military revival contributed significantly to this collapse of the EDC, there is good reason to believe that, even had the military problem been solved and British participation guaranteed, the concept would have stood little chance of success. To begin with, from the very inception of the EDC proposals the French government had seemingly deliberately kept the French electorate poorly informed of the nature of their country's proposed commitment and of its obvious advantages to them. This was particularly unfortunate considering the fundamental popular antipathy towards the rearming of Germany which already existed throughout France. Moreover, as French politicians themselves readily admit, the National Assembly has always been a notoriously difficult arena in which to secure a working majority for *any* positive course of action. Add to this the inherent political weaknesses of the Fourth Republic, its diversity of conflicting parties and the frequently wilful opposition for the sake of opposition that was practised, and it is hardly surprising that something like the EDC, which required swift and positive action, failed.

The history of the negotiations over EDC thus shows that the French had no real love for what they had originally proposed; the idea can have represented no more to them than an experiment in supranationalism, a gesture forced on them out of political necessity. It is impossible to avoid the conclusion that France was not genuinely interested in European integration, but was only motivated by the desire to thwart any attempt to resurrect the Wehrmacht; seen in this light, the EDC merely represented the lesser of two evils for the French. However, throughout the long years of negotiation French fears were kept

alive by the fact that the most consistently whole-hearted
advocates of the EDC were the West Germans themselves.

Events outside Europe also influenced French attitudes
towards the EDC. The final stages of the negotiations in spring
1954 coincided with the proposal for a conference between
East and West at Geneva, at which one of the main items up
for discussion would be a ceasefire in French Indo-China.
Hopeful of securing a benevolent response from the Soviet
Union to her efforts to settle the war with Ho Chi Minh, France
was reluctant to irritate Moscow by proceeding further with a
treaty which was anathema to Molotov.

Thus EDC failed. It failed because a French parliament had
shown itself incapable of throwing off the shackles of history
and solving its own problems, and because Britain had been too
lukewarm, Adenauer too enthusiastic, and the Americans too
emphatic in their support; and because the Soviet Union and
Communism elsewhere in the world had succeeded in exerting
significant influence over international affairs. The defeat provoked an immediate wave of anti-French feeling throughout
Western Europe and the United States. The Benelux countries
felt that France had betrayed the cause of European unification, which it had led since the Schuman proposal of May
1950; the cause now ground to a standstill, for both military
and political integration seemed to have been simultaneously
rejected. In Germany the Assembly's vote was interpreted,
correctly enough, as anti-German as well as anti-European;
Adenauer, after sharply criticizing Mendès-France in an inter-
view with the London *Times*, announced in a broadcast that he
intended to negotiate with Britain and the United States
alone.[1] John Foster Dulles, visiting Bonn and London on 16
and 17 September, and ostentatiously ignoring Paris, made it
clear that German rearmament, sovereignty and equality of
rights had to be permitted as soon as possible. Anthony Eden
felt that unless Britain took the initiative by proposing a
positive alternative to EDC which was acceptable to all
parties, not only would German rearmament be conducted

---

[1] *The Times* (London), 4 September 1954. According to Adenauer's
authorized biography, 'This was the greatest and most shattering disappoint-
ment Adenauer had suffered in all his long political career . . . everything he
stood for and had worked for had been ground into dust'.

without limits and without controls, but France would be isolated. In order to make the participation of a West German force in the integrated defence network of Europe acceptable to France, a series of safeguards had to be devised which were effective but not blatant. Eden therefore prepared a revision of the 1948 Brussels Treaty, expanded to include Italy and West Germany in a Western European Union. Militarily, this new organization would have the power to fix the maximum force levels of its members on the recommendation of the NATO military authorities. All Allied forces on the Continent were to be placed under the Supreme Allied Commander in Europe (SACEUR), except those recognized as being more fittingly under national control.

The British commitment was to be maintained on the Continent, four divisions and tactical air units assigned to SACEUR, a radical departure from Britain's traditional foreign policy.[1] As a final assurance to France (for this, in essence, is what the British commitment represented) the United States and Great Britain joined with the six Western European Union countries and Canada in stating that they regarded the North Atlantic Treaty as being of 'indefinite duration'. This extraordinarily rapid implementation of an alternative to EDC threw French politicians into confusion. Many deputies felt that the defeat of EDC had meant the final rejection of German rearmament, yet only five weeks later here they were being asked once again to sanction rearmament and the restoration of sovereignty for the Federal Republic. However, the desirability of a solution to the German problem which did not endanger the integrity of France, which brought Britain into Europe, and which paid at least lip-service to the idea of European unity, spurred Mendès-France, after an autumn of debate, to persuade the majority of the Assembly to ratify the Paris Agreements. These agreements allowed for the termination of occupation statutes in Western Germany, the revision and extension of the WEU Treaty, the admission of the German Federal Republic to NATO and a

---

[1] In the sense that the British commitment would remain for the fifty-year duration of the Brussels Treaty and would not be withdrawn without the consent of the majority of members of the Pact. This annoyed many 'Europeans' who felt that a similar guarantee to the EDC would have ensured its acceptance.

Franco-German agreement of the Saar, which was to have a 'European Statute' within the framework of WEU; at the same time, the Saarlanders were given the right to hold a plebiscite to decide freely whether to accept or reject this last proposal.

In December 1954 the Soviet Union tried a last delaying tactic by proposing a European Security Conference. This was rejected by the West and the Kremlin retaliated by stating that it would in future refuse to discuss German reunification, once the decision to rearm the Federal Republic had been taken. Eden's policy of 'negotiation from strength' had thus failed; he had succeeded in anchoring the Federal Republic to the West, rather than allowing it to 'drift', and had enhanced the security of Western Europe, by enabling NATO to draw on the resources of Germany, but had made the prospect of reunification more remote than ever.

Adenauer felt that Eden's solution was only second-best as far as the objective of European integration was concerned, but he nevertheless conceded that its achievement was considerable. In the spring of 1955 the Federal Assemblies ratified the Paris Agreements, and at twelve noon on 6 May 1955 the Federal Republic emerged as a free and sovereign nation, almost ten years to the day since the capitulation of the Third Reich.

Part Four

XIV

THE BERLIN WALL

THE YEARS which saw the great debate over the European Defence Community and the emergence of the Federal Republic of West Germany as a nation with full sovereignty had been relatively quiet for West Berlin. While Europe concerned itself with the broader issues of continental security, the municipal authorities could proceed with their own programme for social and economic reconstruction in what had temporarily become a backwater of international politics. However, after 1955 events took a different course: by his actions in the ensuing years, Krushchev ensured that Berlin would remain central to all negotiations between the super-powers concerning Europe, and that no agreements over the status of the city could henceforth be reached without reference to broader European issues. For Krushchev, West Berlin symbolized the threat to the Soviet empire in Eastern Europe. Russia had annexed part of German territory, had handed another part over to Poland, and now held a third part in thrall and the German capital in pawn; but West Germany's revival, her impressive economic achievements and successful incorporation into a powerful military alliance, were seen as a danger to these Soviet conquests. Particularly since the enviable prosperity of West Germany was all too easily visible at this time to the impoverished states behind the Iron Curtain, particularly East Germany. West Berlin had finally emerged as the 'shop-window of Western democracy' and the inevitable Soviet response was to demand that Berlin in the future be treated as fundamental to any proposed general agreement on Germany and furthermore that no peace conference on Germany could proceed without some agreement on arms control elsewhere.

However, in Europe in the mid-1950s the trend was in the

opposite direction, since nations on both sides of the Iron Curtain were rearming. The 'two camps' concept of Stalin received a new military impetus at this time with the creation of the Warsaw Pact, which officially came into existence on 14 May 1955 at a ceremony held in the Polish capital. The signatory powers to this new treaty[1] were the Soviet Union, Poland, Czechoslovakia, Hungary, Rumania, Bulgaria and Albania. Delegates from the Peoples' Republic of China and the Democratic Republic of East Germany officially attended merely as observers, although the latter was for all practical purposes already a member of the alliance and eventually signed in January 1956. The official reasons given for the creation of the Pact were West Germany's military and political membership of NATO and the Western powers' refusal to accept the Soviet proposals for a European Security system.

This Soviet claim—that the Warsaw Pact was essentially a defensive organization to counter an acquisitive and expansive Atlantic Alliance—does not bear close examination. In the first place, the Pact was only a ratification of an already well-established military structure in the Eastern bloc. Senior Soviet officers had held positions of high command in the satellite armies since the early 1950s, when these forces had been created as auxiliaries to the Red Army. Many of these armies were by now much bigger than was permitted by the various peace treaties.[2]

Secondly, there were strong political reasons why Stalin's inheritors, Khrushchev and Bulganin, should seek a new formula for controlling their satellite possessions. In Stalin's time these satellites had been tied to the Soviet Union by a complex structure of bilateral treaties, many of which had their origins in the latter years of the Second World War.[3] Such treaties were never more than mere diplomatic fictions, since Stalin's strength of character was such that he exercised an absolute

---

[1] The Warsaw Treaty of Friendship, Co-operation and Mutual Assistance.

[2] For example: Hungary, allowed 65,000 men, possessed 200,000; Rumania, allowed 138,000 men, possessed 275,000; Bulgaria, allowed 65,000 men, possessed 200,000. Czechoslovakia possessed 220,000 and Poland possessed 300,000, both former allies and therefore not restricted. East Germany had built up a paramilitary police force of 150,000 from 1951.

[3] 'Treaties of Friendship, Mutual Assistance and Co-operation.'

personal authority over Eastern Europe. In the last few years of his life, however, Stalin's autocracy coupled with his resistance to change had resulted in stagnation within the Soviet Union and isolation abroad; these satellites had become a tremendous drain on Soviet resources, a wasting asset of a precarious nature, amply demonstrated by the East Berlin uprising of 1953, where Soviet tanks had been necessary to bolster up a collaborating régime. The new Russian leaders desired to transform the relationship between the Soviet Union and the nations of Eastern Europe into something more dynamic. By now, however, the mood of international relations was such that the old-fashioned method of control by coercion might be highly damaging to the new national image the Soviet Union wished to project to the uncommitted nations of the Third World, an area where Khrushchev intended to launch a new diplomatic offensive. Therefore, it was imperative that this new alliance should at least present the appearance of being a partnership, where each signatory's opinion, whether on political or military matters, would be given equal weight.[1]

Alongside this political co-ordination, the Warsaw Pact also effected a much-needed improvement in the Soviet military situation. Stalin's military policy towards Eastern Europe had been remarkably inefficient. To begin with, the appointment of Soviet personnel to the key posts at Command level in the East European national armies[2] limited the career prospects of native-born soldiers and hence sapped morale; also, the enforced use of Soviet military codes and regulations caused resentment. Moreover, these armies served no strategic purpose, other than that of police force; even if they had been given a more important rôle, their obsolete Soviet equipment would have made it difficult for them to discharge it adequately. These factors, together with the atmosphere of distrust engendered by the frequent Stalinist purges of the respective

[1] Article 3 of the Warsaw Treaty stated that the signatories would: 'Consult one another on all important international moves affecting this common interest.' While the function of political consideration was underlined in Article 6 of the Treaty which stated that a Political Consultative Committee would be established for 'the purpose of consultation among the Parties, and for examination of questions which may arise in the operation of the Treaty'.

[2] The best example was the appointment of Marshal Rokossovski to the post of Minister of Defence in Poland in 1949.

national officer corps, meant that the Soviet Union had created military organizations which had neither purpose nor self-respect. But now, as a result of Stalin's death, Soviet defence policy had been redefined in the light of the military require-ments of a nuclear environment. The ground forces of Russia herself had been improved by new weapons systems and better transport and mobility, and Krushchev realized that the Soviet bloc forces could no longer be left out of this modernizing process, since their rôle in the advent of war would now not only be that of police force but also as an integral part of those mobile units envisaged as advancing rapidly westwards to destroy NATO forces and occupy NATO territory. As well as this offensive function, East European forces would also play an important part in the defence of the Soviet Union's open western frontier, by manning the 'buffer zone' between that frontier and the West. But the Eastern bloc armies had to be reorganized, re-equipped, cut down to realistic strengths and provided with the necessary mobility before they could provide anything like realistic support to the Soviet Army; the Warsaw Pact was created by Khrushchev and Bulganin to implement this massive military reform.

For NATO also, the membership of West Germany and the formation of a West German military contribution created problems. The Federal Republic joined NATO at a time when the latter was in the throes of one of its successive reappraisals of function. The Americans believed that in West Germany they had gained an important new advocate, since the deep-rooted anti-Communist sentiments of both American and West German society, and their total commitment to a capitalist free enterprise system, resulted in Bonn and Washington having a single outlook on many issues affecting national security, in particular their common conviction that the Soviet Union was a dangerous enemy with whom no profitable negotiation was possible. In return, Adenauer and his colleagues in Bonn at first showed every readiness to fall in with the wishes of Dulles and Acheson in Washington; this was in part due to the grati-tude the West Germans felt for the support of the United States during the previous decade, particularly in the debate over rearmament. However, within eighteen months the first signs of disharmony began to appear, concerning aspects of

NATO strategy. The European members of NATO were already finding the programme of rearmament, as originally agreed at Lisbon in 1952, an intolerable strain on their economies, and they saw the development of tactical nuclear weapons as a way out of their predicament. For their part Britain and the United States also envisaged a stockpile of tactical nuclear warheads as an adequate military substitute for large conventional ground forces. This led to a demand that the European partners, together now with West Germany, should 'specialize' in conventional defence while the United States, and to a lesser extent Great Britain, should concentrate their energies on nuclear weapons. Thus massive retaliation still remained the basic operational strategy for Europe, but with substantial local defence as its partner, to meet immediate needs of deterrence. However, any decrease in American conventional strength tended to deepen Bonn's sense of insecurity and provoke new tension within NATO over American credibility. The basic problem was to reconcile the forward defence of West Germany's eastern boundaries with a strategy which would not involve massive destruction of that territory in the event of war. This difficulty was soon exacerbated by the development of thermo-nuclear warheads by both superpowers, which had a shattering effect on European, and in particular West German, morale, if only because they were that much closer to the Soviet Union and her strategic bomber force. So, as NATO strategy began to move away from the somewhat simplistic illusion of 'massive retaliation' towards a 'new look' strategy based upon tactical nuclear weapons and conventional specialization, the gulf between the Americans and the European partners began to assume significant proportions.

In essence, this 'new look' strategy was an attempt to reconcile three different concepts. First, the quick 'knockout punch' by airborne delivery of atomic war-heads into the industrial and administrative heart of the Soviet Union. Secondly, the countering of any invasion by Russia's vastly superior land forces through the use on the battle front (that is, West German territory) of the new atomic missiles and shells. And finally, the idea of containment without conflict, by deploying sufficient strength on the ground to provide an effective deterrent to

aggression. But the European partners, especially Bonn, became
only too aware that this strategy was an attempt to reconcile
three incompatibles, and although Anglo-American intoxica-
tion with atomic power made things look more hopeful,[1] all
illusions were shattered by the explosion of the H-bomb, which
made obsolete all current notions of warfare, as it had been
conceived and conducted from the time of Napoleon and
Clausewitz to that of Hitler and Churchill. The hydrogen
bomb was thus more of a handicap than a help to the policy of
containment, and so the 'new look' strategy in effect became
out of date as soon as it appeared. It was in fact an 'old look'
refurbished, the expression of an over-optimistic desire for
stability, at a time when conditions were highly unfavourable
to the fulfilment of that desire. For although possession of a
thermo-nuclear weapon reduces the likelihood of full-scale
war, it increases the possibilities of limited war pursued by
widespread local aggression. The aggressor can exploit any-
number of conventional techniques and make a great deal of
headway, capitalising on his opponent's understandable hesi-
tancy over employing nuclear retaliation.

As a result of this 'new look' strategy, large numbers of
tactical nuclear weapons were shipped into Europe under what
was called the 'double key system'. The principle behind this
was that the consent of both the United States and the nation
on whose soil the weapons were based was required before they
could be used. However, much resentment was caused in West
Germany because, although many such weapons were deployed
in her territory, she was barred as yet from having any say in
their use. Moreover, the definition of 'tactical nuclear weapons'
was ambiguous; for the Supreme Allied Commander Europe
controlled weapons of a range and destructiveness indis-
tinguishable from those in the arsenal of Strategic Air Command. Thus the former could only be called 'tactical' in the
sense that they were stationed in Europe and not in the United
States, and were controlled by SACEUR rather than the
Commanding General of the Strategic Air Command.

Conventional weapons, which formed the arsenal of the new
Bundeswehr and the armies of the other European partners,

[1] See British White Paper on Defence, 1957, for the influence of atomic
weapons on British defence priorities.

were demoted to a minor rôle in this strategic concept, their function being to deal with minor incursions or to act as a screen to determine the strength and direction of a Soviet force. Such an arrangement was obviously unsatisfactory to those members of NATO and a new formula was needed to establish the relationship of such conventional forces to a nuclear environment, if only to compensate for West Germany's sense of being exposed to Soviet pressures.

In September 1956 the NATO Council approved a directive for its future military plans, based on the concept of 'forward defence' and taking into account the continued rise in Soviet capabilities and the various types of new weapons available for the defence of Europe. This was in essence a five-year plan,[1] which aimed to create thirty combat-ready divisions, which were designated the 'shield', deployed within the context of a planned nuclear retaliation in the event of war, to be carried out by the units which comprised the 'sword', the US Strategic Air Command, RAF Bomber Command with its V-Bombers, and those American and British naval units capable of contributing to a long-range bombing offensive of the Soviet Union. The 'sword' was envisaged as the main deterrent to Soviet aggression against NATO territory.

A major problem was still unsolved, however: that of convincing the non-nuclear NATO members of the viability of their contributions to the 'shield'. It was apparent in Paris and Bonn, particularly by this stage, that thirty divisions by themselves would be incapable of denying any territory to the Soviet Union. At the same time, if the massive retaliation, or even the later concepts of graduated response, of the 'sword' were mobilized, the devastation resulting from this would be so immense that the Russians would hardly be concerned with the cost of a military confrontation between conventional ground forces. Thus for the Europeans the value of the 'shield' as a deterrent did not lie in its direct denial capability, but rather the extent to which its weakness would strengthen the willingness of the Western nuclear powers to mobilize the full force of their nuclear 'sword'. In fact, the Europeans were more interested in the national composition of the ground elements than in any comparison of strength, since in their view the deployment

[1] SHAPE Concept of Minimum Forces Strategy (MC 70).

of British and American troops on the frontier with East Germany would give the Russians notice that any violations of the sovereignty of the Federal Republic would precipitate immediate involvement of Western nuclear nations. The assumption of the Europeans was that the 'shield' must contain forces that would take the ultimate decision on strategic retaliation. But there were signs that the Americans in particular were loath to commit substantial ground forces to European defence. In 1956, when Admiral Radford, Chairman of the US Joint Chiefs of Staff, was reported to be considering a plan[1] for the reduction of American ground troops in Europe to token strength, and their replacement by increased reliance on nuclear weapons, Bonn's resultant sense of insecurity led to a tension which has since never really been resolved.

While the NATO countries were thus still trying to resolve their differences, the situation in the West was radically altered by the launching of the first man-made satellite, the Russian *Sputnik*. The implications for European security and Atlantic solidarity of this Soviet 'first' in the space-race were enormous. For the United States immediately assumed that she had now lost the two advantages which hitherto she had believed she would enjoy in the event of war with Russia: geographical inaccessibility and a vast preponderance in military potential. Accordingly, the initial reaction in the United States was to greatly over-emphasize the Soviet capacity to deploy operational strategic missiles.[2]

The European members of NATO viewed these developments with increasing alarm. In the first place, it was now obvious to them that the United States was as vulnerable as they were to a Soviet surprise attack, and that in an extreme situation Western Europe would be left defenceless. At the same time, their security would be equally jeopardized if all-out war was not precipitated deliberately, but broke out by accident, leading to a Soviet first strike or simultaneous first strikes by both super-powers. Now that the United States had lost the

[1] A document known as JSDP 60, which proposed a reduction of the American armed forces by 800,000 men.

[2] For example, in Congressional Hearings 1959, Secretary of Defence McElroy admitted that by 1961 the Soviets might have an ICBM ratio of 3:1, or some six hundred ICBMs targeted on the USA.

power of 'absolute deterrence', Europe was well aware that Moscow would in the future exploit its missile superiority, not only in diplomacy but also in military aggression of such limited nature that an American threat of massive retaliation would not be feasible or might safely be suspected as a bluff.

Hence, from this time on, Europe and the major powers became more than ever preoccupied with the threat of thermonuclear war, and there was general recognition that in a crisis great advantage lay with the side that struck first. In the period following 1957 each side felt itself particularly vulnerable to such first strikes and so an even more elaborate and costly structure of deterrence than before was erected by each protagonist, in an ever-accelerating arms race. As a further insurance against surprise aggression, the stringent international security curtain existing since the early 1950s was now made even tighter.

In a still weak and now even more demoralized Europe, fresh attention was focused on the German question, where there appeared to have been few changes. The situation the Soviet government had inherited from Stalin still obtained: partition of the country, Soviet armies in the eastern part, loyal satellite leaders in power, and non-recognition by the West of what was rapidly emerging as economically the most advanced 'people's democracy'; Khrushchev's various initiatives involving diplomatic relations with Bonn and trade with West Germany had not been entirely successful. Moscow therefore found that Germany was still what she had been twenty years before— both a desirable ally and a dreaded enemy, both a promise and a threat. The Russians had also come to consider the DDR in a special light: expansionist and aggressive, although contained by Moscow, it was envisaged as the 'shock troop' of the Socialist camp in Europe.

Khrushchev, far less cunning and more outspoken than Stalin, was however committed to exactly the same course, a Communist take-over in West Germany as a necessary preliminary to unification: 'What does the reunification of Germany mean under present conditions of existence of the two German states? On what basis could it be accomplished? The advocates of working class interests cannot even think of making the workers and peasants of the German Democratic Republic,

who have set up a workers' and peasants' state and are successfully building Socialism, lose all their gains through reunification and agree to live as before in capitalist bondage.'[1]
The same message was being promulgated in Bonn, where the
Soviet Ambassador told a group of German political leaders
that among the Soviet conditions for reunification were the
following: 'major industry would have to be nationalized . . .
the power of "monopoly capital" would have to be broken and
the working class [i.e. the Communist Party] would have to
assume political dominance.'[2] Thus the creation of a strong
pro-Western power in Central Europe was still seen by the
Kremlin as a major threat, and it was to neutralise this that
Khrushchev embarked upon a new diplomatic offensive, which
was to last from 1957 to 1963.

At first Soviet proposals embodied the twin concepts of
neutrality and disengagement. Neutrality was envisaged as the
successor of the demilitarization prescribed by Stalin at Potsdam in 1945; it was also a concept which benefited from the
surviving residue of post-war fears and thus aimed at engaging
the support of those in the West who still saw in the Bundeswehr the threat of revived German militarism. In 1957 Moscow
produced its first positive proposal, a plan to create a neutral
belt of states stretching from the far north of Europe through
the heart of the continent, involving both Germanies, and
southwards to the Mediterranean. This belt would consist of
three distinct geographical entities. In the north a nuclear-free
zone would be created in the Baltic, thus making it a 'sea of
peace'. More controversial was the Soviet proposal for Central
Europe; called the Rapacki Plan, after the Polish Foreign
Minister, it envisaged a neutral and nuclear-free zone em-
bracing Poland, Czechoslovakia and East and West Germany.
In Southern Europe a Balkan Pact was suggested, on similar
lines. At first the West took some interest in this Soviet blue-
print for Europe and were inclined to accept their invitation to
hold a summit conference to discuss it, particularly since the
Rapacki Plan was projected as the first stage of a far-reaching
scheme for disarmament in Central Europe. But eventually the
entire proposal was rejected as an effort to consolidate Soviet

[1] Speech in Leipzig, 7 March 1959, reported in *Pravda*, 27 March 1959.
[2] *New York Times*, 14 March 1960.

ALLIANCE EUROPE: NATO and WARSAW PACT

NATO   WARSAW PACT |||||| Mutual assistance treaty with Soviet Union

★ Treaties on stationing of Soviet troops

ICELAND

ATLANTIC OCEAN

SWEDEN

NORWAY

FINLAND

UNITED KINGDOM

IRELAND

DENMARK

BALTIC SEA

BERLIN

SOVIET UNION

NETHERLANDS

BELGIUM

West East

GERMANY ★

POLAND ★

LUX.

CZECHOSLOVAKIA ★

FRANCE

SWITZ.

AUSTRIA

HUNGARY

★

RUMANIA ★

ITALY

YUGOSLAVIA

BLACK SEA

PORTUGAL

SPAIN

BULGARIA

ALBANIA

MEDITERRANEAN SEA

MALTA

GREECE

TURKEY

CYPRUS

0 100   500 miles

dominance of Central and Eastern Europe. The central weakness of the plan was obvious: its creation of a no-man's-land in Central Europe, which would, like every previous demilitarized zone in history, sooner or later fall under the authority of its strongest neighbour.

However, Khrushchev was still determined to reach a solution to the German problem, so in 1958 he put pressure upon what he still regarded as the weak link of the Atlantic Alliance —the Western presence in Berlin. A victory over Berlin at this time would not only mean increased prestige for the entire Socialist camp but would also force the Western powers to accept the German Democratic Republic as no longer a mere Soviet satellite, to be accorded second-class status under the terms of the Hallstein doctrine,[1] but as an equal nation. Such a victory would also result in the humiliation of Bonn and, by implication, NATO. Finally, it would be a triumph for the Khrushchev brand of 'peaceful co-existence', which involved paying lip-service to the *status quo* with the West while the Soviet 'system of society' exploited the nationalist awakening and social unrest in the world at large.

The Berlin crisis which culminated in the building of the Wall in 1961 can be said to have begun on 10 November 1958, with the first of Krushchev's ultimatums concerning the city. He proposed that Berlin be reconstituted as a free city, in other words that all foreign troops be withdrawn, and stated in no uncertain terms that unless a settlement of the German question were negotiated within six months, Moscow would proceed with its own peace treaty with the DDR. The implications of this Soviet declaration were immediately apparent to the West: the superiority of the paramilitary forces of the DDR over the police forces of West Berlin would inevitably result in a merger of the two parts of the city. That Moscow ever seriously believed such a proposal would be accepted in the West can only be explained by their over-emphasis on the discord they believed was rife within NATO. For a short while their optimism was not unfounded. In his last few months as American Secretary of State Dulles was attracted to some parts of the Soviet plan, and suggested in press conferences that East Germany might be allowed a share of control over the access to

[1] See Chapter XV, p. 221.

West Berlin, and, even worse from Bonn's point of view, that the reunification of the two Germanies need not necessarily take place according to the hitherto-agreed Western formula of free elections as a first step. This attitude provoked a further outbreak of German-American tension, which even the personal visit of Dulles to Bonn in April 1959 did not completely resolve, and lingering fears of an American inclination to 'sell out' West Berlin to the Russians persisted in Adenauer's mind.

Britain also showed a positive reaction to the Soviet proposals. The British Prime Minister, Harold Macmillan, claimed to detect a genuine relaxation in international tension, and interpreted many domestic trends in the Soviet Union, towards material prosperity and internal stability, as something of a middle-class revolution under Communist labels and hence favourable for the West. He saw Khrushchev as a man honestly searching for peaceful solutions to outstanding problems and therefore deserving of at least a hearing. For this purpose in February 1959 he visited Moscow for ten days. Although Macmillan freely admitted in his memoirs that on most points at issue little agreement was reached, at least on the question of disengagement and Germany's rearmament there were signs of compromise. The final communiqué proposed further discussions towards establishing security in Central Europe by the limitation of arms both conventional and nuclear, on condition that a mutually acceptable and effective system of inspection could be set up.

Bonn was highly suspicious of this British optimism; Adenauer believed that Macmillan was by implication halfway towards recognizing the German Democratic Republic. In Moscow, Khrushchev was confident that he had at least caused a split in Western solidarity.

Events soon proved both Adenauer's fears and Khrushchev's confidence equally unfounded. The subsequent conference of foreign ministers of the great powers, together with diplomatic representatives of the two Germanies, failed dismally, despite a summer of negotiation in Geneva. The West linked their proposals on Germany to an overall European security system, in order to overcome what they regarded as the central difficulty: military withdrawal while two hostile states, representing the respective political and military investments of each bloc, still faced one another in central Europe. Their suggestions failed because it would have been impossible to erect any European security system without incorporating East Germany, which they had already refused to do. The Soviet counter-proposal of a non-aggression treaty between NATO and the Warsaw Pact also foundered on this Western refusal to recognize East Germany. Thus not only had the West doomed the Geneva meeting to failure but had further compromised their position over Berlin by allowing East German representatives into the negotiations. The West's dilemma was obvious: a solution of the Berlin question could now only be reached in terms of a *de facto* recognition of the East German régime.

In the autumn of 1959 Khrushchev visited the United States. Dulles was dead and his newly-appointed successor, Christian A. Herter, had not had time to master his new office, a fact which did not go unnoticed by Khrushchev in this, the next round of his diplomatic offensive. While Khrushchev talked with Eisenhower at Camp David, the prospect of a deal between the super-powers caused much anxiety in Paris and Bonn. In the event, no specific promises on Berlin were made by either side, but the atmosphere of goodwill resulted in the decision to hold a summer meeting the following year. That spring Khrushchev made further preparations for the summit by paying a prolonged visit to France; the new French leader De Gaulle was as yet an unknown quantity in his calculations. Neither German states had been invited to the summit, which suited Adenauer since it implied that the West did not wish to make any further gestures which might be interpreted as partial recognition of the German Democratic Republic. Khrushchev also felt that Adenauer's absence would be an advantage, since he regarded the German Chancellor as the main obstacle to a settlement of the Berlin question in Russia's favour.

In Paris Khrushchev indefatigably played on the traditional French fear of Germany; his constant theme, in speeches delivered both in the capital and throughout the provinces, was the devastation and atrocities that both France and Russia had suffered at the hands of the German invader. He appealed to that body of French opinion which saw the only means of insuring against a future German threat as being a close alliance with the Soviet Union. In a speech in Paris on 23 March, Khrushchev said: 'I believe that the German revenge-seekers are a bigger threat to France than to any other country ... Now that militarism is being revived in Western Germany one must prevent a repetition of the errors of the past.'[1] Although Khrushchev failed to win over De Gaulle, who stood firm on the Western pre-conditions for Berlin—respect for the *status quo* and free elections—he nevertheless left for home convinced that a large proportion of French public opinion had been won over to his views.

Such preparations by Khrushchev for the forthcoming talks made it imperative for the Western powers to work out a common policy on Berlin. De Gaulle's firmness allied with Adenauer's influence and Washington's disinclination now to yield the West's position determined the eventual policy: no substantial concessions to the Khrushchev proposals. Since the Berlin question was the main subject on the agenda, the summit was thus doomed before it began. The mood of pessimism throughout the foreign offices of the West communicated itself to the Western press, which was speculating on the possible results of the failure of the talks long before the leaders ever met in Vienna. A breakdown of negotiations would be a particularly hard blow for Khrushchev, who had not only initiated the conference but had also staked much of his own and his party's prestige on its successful outcome. The Russian leader's position within the Kremlin was at this time precarious and in particular opposition from the armed forces was becoming increasingly strong. They resented his interference in matters of strategic doctrine, and his emphasis on minimum deterrence meant that in a conflict situation the Soviet armed forces now had but a single option—nuclear war. Therefore, Khrushchev needed a positive agreement on Berlin at the summit talks if only to safeguard his own position at home and prove that his particular tactics were superior to any other 'Communist Course' and the best way of dealing with 'imperialists' such as the United States of America.

Khrushchev's difficulties within the Kremlin clearly dic-

[1] Khrushchev in France, 23 March and 3 April, 1960—Speeches, Interviews, TV Addresses, Report to Moscow Meeting, Soviet Booklet No. 71, London, May 1960, p. 13.

tated his behaviour over the U-2 Incident, which occurred just
before the conference: an American high-altitude intelligence
aircraft, the U-2, was shot down over Soviet territory and its
pilot, Gary Powers, was subjected to the panoply of a Kremlin
show trial. Khrushchev's tactics became clear when he demanded a full apology from Eisenhower; even if the Berlin
question was not to be resolved in Russia's favour, at least the
public discomfiture of an American president would be some
compensation for the Soviet leadership. However, the Western
reaction, particularly in the news media, was to support the
Americans and play down the whole incident by putting it into
its proper context, the normal processes of Cold War intelligence activities. Widespread espionage was conducted by both
sides, as an important contribution to national security during
the arms race. In the West there had been a major operation in
1959 to suppress the activities of a prolific Soviet spy system,
both in the United States and in Europe.[1] As far as the West
were concerned, there was no basic difference between Soviet
espionage agencies operating on the ground and US Intelligence overflights of the Soviet Union, except that the latter was
probably more productive and certainly more cost-effective.

With the subsequent failure of the summit conference owing
to deliberate sabotage by Khrushchev, Soviet foreign policy
took on a new direction and emphasis. At first it was a difference in style rather than substance, a change in terminology,
which nevertheless created the impression of a real war being
planned. Khrushchev chose as his arena the United Nations,
where his violent tirades seemed to herald a return to the hard-
line days of Stalin. This post-summit trend in Soviet policy
certainly produced side-effects, which were not all in accordance with Moscow's plans. Khrushchev had expected that his
diplomatic offensive against the United States would result in
renewed support and influence for Russia among the nations of
the Third World. However, except in Cuba and the Congo,

[1] More than 450 spies had been arrested in West Germany in the period
1952–60. In addition there are grounds for speculating that Washington,
recalling how, in 1941, the Japanese Government had resorted to negotiations
to cover the surprise attack on Pearl Harbour, ordered this particular U-2
mission at this particular time to determine whether the Russians were
making preparations for a similar surprise in connection with the summit
meeting.

such benefits were not forthcoming, probably because his sabre-rattling threats of missile attack now perplexed those governments who had originally expressed confidence in Khrushchev's peaceful intentions.

The atmosphere of tension, and crises such as the U-2 affair, sapped the morale of the people of West Berlin; in their eyes, the Western powers had demonstrated that under the threat of nuclear war not only could they not devise any positive alternative to the *status quo* in the city, but that they did not even consider it feasible to hold Berlin indefinitely against mounting Soviet pressure. In East Germany, Ulbricht was becoming restive and the West Berliners were fully aware that the continued refusal of either side to force a showdown over Berlin might well leave the field clear for the East German leader to act independently. His own régime was still desperately weak, which fact alone might tempt him into some rash action. The plight of Ulbricht's government, and its unpopularity amongst the East Germans, was fully appreciated by Khrushchev, and many of his actions in the autumn of 1960 and the following spring were conditioned as much by this circumstance as by the need to mollify the Kremlin. For Khrushchev, the only way in which East Germany could avoid a repetition of the 1953 uprising was by securing control over both parts of Berlin. This assertion was supported by the serious political difficulties experienced by the satellite, the shabbiest of all Communist enterprises in Eastern Europe. As long as a free West Berlin existed as a shop window for the material benefits of Western capitalist society and as long as the city provided so convenient an escape route for the East German, then the consolidation of Communism in East Germany remained in doubt. The sheer loss in manpower through West Berlin was partly the motivation behind Khrushchev's urgent demands in 1961 for an end to the anomalous situation in Berlin. Authoritative sources in Bonn estimated that in the ten years of the Ulbricht régime more than four million East Germans had made their way to the West via West Berlin—almost a quarter of the total population. What was even more significant was the nature of these refugees: most were young and many came from the élite professions of teaching, medicine and technology. Although the initial time-limit set by Khrushchev in June 1959 for a negotiated settlement of the German question had long since come and gone, it was still his declared aim to stabilize East Germany by making Berlin its capital by any means short of war or the risk of war; but he was fast running out of options.

On 4 June 1961 Khrushchev met the new US President, John F. Kennedy, at Vienna and presented him with what might be termed an *aide-mémoire* on the question of a peace treaty for Germany. This document contained three main proposals: the first suggested that the Germans should be given six months to agree on a method of reunification, and if they then had still failed to reach a settlement, then the four powers should sign separate peace treaties with the two German states; secondly, West Berlin should become a free city and completely demilitarized; finally, all questions of access to Berlin should be decided through direct negotiations with the German Democratic Republic. Khrushchev emphasized in subsequent speeches that the Soviet Union would sign a separate peace treaty with the East Germans if the Western governments refused an all-German treaty: 'The Soviet Union and all other peace-loving countries will do all that they can so that it is signed by the end of the year.'[1]

Here the Kremlin reverted to the setting of a time-limit over Berlin. The previous one had been allowed to be exceeded because of the proximity of the summit conference, but now that the meetings had occurred and international differences over Berlin were seen to be as wide as ever, the Russians felt that the only way in which they could make the West modify their position was by the use of threat.

The Kennedy response was immediate and dramatic. In a speech on 25 July 1961 he said: 'I have said that West Berlin is militarily untenable. And so was Bastogne. And so in fact was Stalingrad. Any dangerous spot is tenable if men—brave men—will make it so.' This was a somewhat unrealistic statement, since Berlin was and still is militarily completely untenable; the only effective defence of the city is the threat of thermo-nuclear war, since it could never be held by conventional ground forces. Nevertheless, Kennedy placed a new emphasis on such conventional forces by increasing the overall strength of US combat divisions by 200,000 men and allocating a further

[1] *Document on Germany*, p. 672.

$2,000 million for conventional weapons and civil defence. An additional 40,000 men were flown in as reinforcements to the US Seventh Army in Germany, while at the same time both Britain and France brought some of their units up to combat strength. The West Germans responded by delaying the release date for many of the conscripts in the Bundeswehr.

Kennedy's speeches and the overt military preparations of that summer had an important influence on American domestic politics. By increasing the draft, calling up reserve formations, and above all by focusing attention on Civil Defence, Kennedy brought home to the American people the seriousness of the crisis. And while Khrushchev increased Soviet military strength in East Germany to counter the NATO build-up, the significance of the American moves was obvious: Kennedy was determined to hold on to West Berlin, even if it meant war.

By August 1961 the atmosphere in Central Europe was electric, and there was a marked increase in the number of refugees who fled from the East into Berlin. At the same time a number of significant initiatives came from the West aimed at de-escalating the crisis. To the dismay of Adenauer and Bonn, influential voices in the American Senate, particularly Senators Mansfield and Fulbright, called for Western recognition of the German Democratic Republic. Another popular proposal at the time was that the United Nations Organization be moved from New York to the Charlottenburg. However, such suggestions were soon made irrelevant by Ulbricht's ensuing actions: whether he was backed by the Russians or not has never been established, but he began a new campaign of intimidation against the *Grenzgänger* (Western citizens who worked in East Berlin) and raised tension to crisis pitch. Rumours began to circulate in West Berlin and the Federal Republic that Ulbricht was planning to close the frontiers and a supposedly secret meeting of the Warsaw Pact powers in Moscow in early August seemed to lend substance to such speculation. By now, an average of 1,500 people a day were crossing into West Berlin; meanwhile, Western Intelligence plotted the movement of Soviet units around the city itself.

In the early hours of Sunday, 13 August, squads of East German workers erected makeshift wire barriers and fences along the line of demarcation across the city, while at the same time the underground railway and municipal train services which operated across the sectors came to a halt. The first stage of the isolation of West Berlin had been completed.

The construction of the Berlin Wall was very much a logical development in post-war European politics. The Berlin crisis was hourly increasing the risks of a head-on clash between the super-powers, and West Berlin's open invitation to refugees only exacerbated the situation. The only other means of preventing the movement of refugees would be to organize a vast network of police and troops around the eastern approaches to the city; however, such a cordon would be inefficient and in any case could only be operated for short periods. The construction of a barrier and the control of crossing-points represented the most logical solution to the problem, at the same time demonstrating Khrushchev's desire to separate the two crises, the abnormal circumstances of Berlin from the question of a divided Germany. The closure of the frontier was felt in Moscow to increase the chances of Western recognition of the Democratic Republic.

The governments of the West have since been criticized at home for not reacting immediately to stop the Wall being built; it certainly caught them by surprise, being a development which had apparently never been contemplated even by the experts on crisis management. It was a flagrant breach of the Four-Power Status on Berlin because although thirteen crossing points were left open to allow Allied forces to move in East Berlin, in practical terms it meant that East Berlin was finally integrated, by unilateral action, into the German Democratic Republic. But the use of actual force would be dangerous and Khrushchev, in common with the Western leaders, knew very well that he could make no moves against West Berlin without incurring the counter-threat of thermo-nuclear war; for the very same reason, however, he was free to do whatever he wished over East Berlin. The Soviet leader was at great pains to emphasise that the building of the Wall did not in any way threaten the integrity of the Western presence, either through pressure on access routes or by a direct threat to West Berlin, but was rather a punitive move against East Berlin. Nevertheless morale was badly shaken in West Berlin and Bonn, and the usual gossip circulated to the effect that the West had in fact

long known about the plan.[1] The people of Berlin and West
Germany hence felt that the Allied commitment to protect
them had been seriously undermined; a feeling which fortunately soon passed. Positive military action would have been
foolhardy anyway, simply because the Communists had such
overwhelming superiority in local armed forces; even if the
West had moved in and torn up the barriers, the East Germans
would then have erected them inside their own territory,
which would have involved the West in a violation of sovereignty if they had attempted to pull the obstacles down a second
time.

It must be stressed that the Soviet stake in this dispute was
much greater than that of the Western powers, being nothing
less than her own credibility in the eyes of the German Democratic Republic. The survival of the Ulbricht régime was
dependent on the presence of Russian armed forces and if the
Kremlin had shown that it would allow the Western powers to
determine how they should use this force, the result might well
have been the East German population displaying open
resistance to their government. Hence, any Western demand
for the demolition of the wire obstacles, even at this early stage,
would have provoked a challenge to the East German régime,
which would thus have greatly increased the risk of conflict.
The Soviet Union had allowed the closure of the city in circumstances that were the most favourable possible to the West,
and any counter-move by the West, no matter how local or how
limited, could well have resulted in a threat to their own access
routes, a situation which would have left the West with no
option but to escalate the confrontation.

At first there was no great interference in the movement of
West Berliners across the new frontier; this did not occur until
23 August, when the wire was replaced by the permanent
ugliness of a wall and there was a gradual reduction in the
number of access points. Many commentators have pointed out
this time-lag between the initial appearance of the wire and the
eventual construction of the Wall and suggested that if the

[1] Speculation was based on the fact that the three Allied garrison commanders had been summoned to Koriev's HQ on the day before, and also
that the East German military units which had covered the construction of
the fence had been unarmed—there is no evidence to substantiate the latter.

West had made a move against the former then the Communists would have thought twice about building the latter. Although it does seem that the total acquiescence of the Western authorities to the initial barrier might well have encouraged Ulbricht to turn the wire into concrete and impose further restrictions on movement, the facts of the case were that the Soviet Union held all the cards, unless the West wished to invoke the threat of nuclear retaliation. Even a carefully-limited Western resistance ran the risk of a Soviet 'over-response' and the Wall was simply not worth that risk.

Into the autumn of 1961 the initiative remained with the Soviet Union and East Germany. Ulbricht, behind the closed frontiers of his state, could now really concentrate on the massive programmes of social and economic reconstruction. For Khrushchev, the very fact that Russia could prolong the situation indefinitely in a way which had not been possible in 1949 meant that the Berlin crisis could be used to further other objectives on an international level. Particularly valuable diplomatically was the fact that the crisis could now be linked with the arms race and the recent Soviet explosion of a fifty-megaton nuclear device.

The Western response to these mounting pressures was mainly symbolic; there was little concrete they could do until Soviet intentions became clearly defined. A US armoured regiment moved along the autobahn from Helmstedt to West Berlin, General Clay was dispatched to Berlin as Kennedy's ambassador extraordinary and the three Western powers instituted daily flag patrols into the eastern sector of Berlin. In response, the Soviets introduced what were later known as 'salami tactics'; searchlights were beamed on to incoming civilian flights at Tempelhof, whilst Soviet Army helicopters hovered over the French airfield at Tegel and interfered with the free movement of the Caravelles. Refugees were still finding ways to cross the Wall, but the flow was now cut to a mere trickle; although the crossing points were reduced to just four to stop this traffic, tension was still high and there were frequent gun-battles between the Volkspolizei and the West Berlin police, who gave covering fire to refugees crossing.

The Western governments were still trying to find a way out of their dilemma when the Soviet Union quietly shelved its time-limit and hinted that a partial recognition of the German Democratic Republic would suffice. Unfortunately, there could now be no return to the days of 1949, when private deals were possible behind closed doors at the United Nations; any positive move by the West would perforce involve some kind of recognition of East Germany, which would be a contravention of the Paris Agreements of 1954 and thus only possible if the Federal Republic changed its attitude.

However, during the ensuing months the West Germans and the people of West Berlin gradually came to terms with the Wall. There were still frequent incidents, but the movement of refugees practically stopped, since the possibilities of crossing the Wall, either under or over it, were exhausted and only the foolhardy would risk death by crucifixion on the wire entanglements that festooned it. West Berlin's morale was supposedly reinforced by the presence of General Clay in the city (although what he was supposed to do there and what exactly were his terms of reference is difficult to discover) and the visit of the American Vice-President, Lyndon B. Johnson. Eventually the President himself came to the city, gazed across the Wall and declared to an enthusiastic crowd: 'Ich bin ein Berliner!'— a comment which, though clearly unrehearsed, showed a natural grasp of crowd psychology.

Despite this utterance the Wall remained. The Kennedy administration had not backed down under pressure, but neither had it pushed forward; a deadlock ensued. Nevertheless, the United States had permitted a subtle change in status: West Berlin was still protected, but the future of East Berlin had now been unilaterally determined by the construction of the Wall. To a certain extent this was a setback for Western policy: Berlin could no longer serve as the symbol of the quest for a united Germany, since its eastern sector had been irretrievably lost. Both the United States and the Soviet Union, tense over Berlin, now rearmed and headed toward a more dangerous confrontation.

XV

EUROPE IN SEARCH OF SECURITY

IN THE summer of 1962 world attention was drawn away from Berlin towards the rapidly-evolving clash of interests between the super-powers in the Caribbean. The ensuing Cuban missile crisis had an important influence on later events in Europe. The ostensible Soviet aim was to deploy medium-range ballistic missiles on Cuban territory to compensate for their inferiority in long-range strategic delivery systems, and also to counter the US deployment of Thor missiles in Turkey. The Kremlin thus allowed the Berlin situation to mark time while it tested American resolve in the Caribbean. However, the Cuban affair turned out to be far more than merely a probe, but rather the most daring adventure of the Khrushchev régime, and one which produced the world's first nuclear confrontation. For the first time the two major nuclear powers faced each other directly on an issue exclusively concerning nuclear weapons. This has not been the case in previous Cold War crises such as Korea, Indo-China, the Formosan Straits, Lebanon or Laos, in all of which the Soviet Union had been only indirectly involved. It had not even been so over NATO, the division of Germany, or Berlin itself; both sides had referred to the nuclear deterrent but it had not been the central issue.

Secretary of Defence McNamara has stated his belief that the Cuban missile crisis and Soviet objectives in Berlin were directly related. The missiles represented 'the trump card', he said, 'which Mr. Khrushchev intended to play in the next round of negotiations on the status of Berlin'.[1] Success in Cuba could have allowed the Russians bold moves over Berlin. Cuba

[1] US Congress House Committee on Armed Services, *Hearings on Military Posture*, 88th Congress, 1st Session, 1963, p. 300.

and Berlin were inter-related in another sense, because the former was the first example of the implementation of the new NATO doctrine of 'flexible response', involving the whole gamut of US arms from naval blockade to strategic missiles; however, the same flexibility was lacking on the Soviet side, since there was no attempt to counter the American moves by tampering with the access routes into Berlin.

US firmness had succeeded in checking a seriously provocative Soviet move; by a carefully-judged response the United States had skilfully outmanoeuvred the Soviet Union in that most dangerous of games, nuclear diplomacy. But apart from the obvious skill which the Kennedy administration had displayed during the crisis, it was clear that the United States also had an inherent military advantage: by October 1962 the 'missile gap' had been exploded as a myth—the United States now possessed a clear lead in strategic long-range missiles (ICBMs) and an overwhelming superiority in long-range bombers. The Russians had gambled and lost. In less than two years the Kennedy administration had managed to restore American prestige at home and in Europe, and had at the same time confirmed the viability of the strategy of nuclear deterrence when the stakes were high. The repercussions of this Soviet failure were felt all the way back to Berlin, where the situation had de-escalated to such an extent by October 1962 that this date may be taken as the effective termination of the crisis which Khrushchev had originally provoked in November 1958.

In particular, the Cuban victory was taken by McNamara as a clear endorsement of the doctrine of 'flexible response'; yet when he attempted to incorporate this into NATO strategy he met with strong opposition from the Europeans. This dispute, more political than military in its implications, was provoked by the emergence of the new Paris–Bonn axis, with De Gaulle backing West Germany in its firm stand. Indeed, Berlin was at this time only one of the issues over which France increasingly diverged from the views of Washington and London. The two current preoccupations of French foreign policy were concern over mounting Soviet pressure and a sensitivity to German reactions. De Gaulle's awareness of the latter was shown not only by his firm support of Bonn but also by the concession he offered to Russia of acceptance of the Oder–Niesse line. This move was completely misinterpreted by the Western press as practically French recognition of the German Democratic Republic. However, De Gaulle, far from offering immediate recognition, obviously intended merely to suggest that an eventual reunified Germany should retain the present frontiers of the two separate states. De Gaulle seemingly envisaged a Franco-German alignment as becoming the dominant feature of European politics. However, also uppermost in his thoughts throughout was an awareness of the dangers of not keeping Germany within the Western alliance. De Gaulle, by showing a more sympathetic response to the problems of Bonn than either Washington or London, succeeded in arousing Franco-German suspicions of the intentions of the United States and Britain concerning Europe.

The situation was exacerbated by the fact that the rapport which had existed between Eisenhower and Adenauer had disappeared with the advent of the Kennedy administration. There was little common ground between the young and dynamic President, surrounded by a galaxy of talent (which the press labelled 'the Kennedy whizz-kids'), and the elderly Chancellor with his staid entourage. Relations between Bonn and Washington were particularly strained because of Adenauer's constant fear that at some stage the United States might be prepared to sacrifice West German interests for the sake of a reconciliation with the Soviet Union. The above-mentioned lack of communication was probably responsible for this, since as a result Adenauer tended to over-emphasize the importance of a détente in Kennedy's list of priorities.

Finally, Washington itself was displeased by the inconsistency of a situation whereby West Germany carried on considerable trade with East Germany, yet refused to allow the Allies to deal with the Soviet satellite. West Germany's attitude was that contact at the relatively humble level of trade in no way implied political recognition, but was merely of mutual convenience, whereas similar commercial intercourse between East Germany and the Allies would be inadvisable because of its broader implications. The dilemma was that, although trade and cultural exchanges were the only way the two Germanies could move closer to an understanding, by implication such moves were bound to result in a weakening of the German case against Allied contact with East Germany.[1]

It was against this background of political retrenchment that the great NATO debates of the 1960s took place, with the challenge by De Gaulle to Kennedy's grand design for an Atlantic partnership reaching its logical conclusion in France's eventual withdrawal from NATO.

The central problem was the control of nuclear weapons. This has been a subject of contention between the USA and Europe ever since the advent of the missile age finally made nonsense of the simple policy of massive strategic retaliation against aggression in Europe. This nuclear debate has been further complicated by factors such as the revived economic strength and potential political strength of Western Europe, with the resultant danger that the nuclear weapons programme of Britain and France might be imitated by the Federal Republic, and the problem of the credibility of any American response to a serious attack on Europe in the light of the growing vulnerability of her own population.

Out of these debates, which took place at both official and unofficial levels, emerged three possible courses of action for NATO. The first has been called the 'multinational approach' and emphasized the sovereignty of the nations within the Alliance, recognizing that, although there is a standby international command system for certain forces, the principal nations of NATO are not prepared to delegate major decisions

[1] The Hallstein Doctrine was pronounced by Adenauer on 22 September 1955 when he returned from Moscow. He had agreed to exchange ambassadors with the Soviet Union, which also had an embassy in the DDR. So that a precedent should not be created, it was stated that the Federal Republic would: 'Regard the establishment of diplomatic relations with the "German Democratic Republic" by third countries with which it has official ties as an unfriendly act, calculated to deepen the division of Germany.'

In practice, this meant that Bonn would break off relations with those who acted in this way. It was also deemed to preclude establishing relations with the states which had already recognised the DDR. The whole doctrine is based on the principle, acknowledged by the Western powers in the London Agreements of 1954, that West Germany is the sole representative of Germany as a whole.

The 'author', Professor Hallstein, was at the time a senior official at the Foreign Office in Bonn; he was later to rise to high office in the European Economic Community.

of policy, let alone of peace and war, to one other or to a central command system.

The second solution arose from the successful development of the European Economic Community and its encouragement by the Kennedy administration. The intention here was to create an analogous relationship in the strategic field to the growing transatlantic economic partnership, which would result in an alliance between blocs of roughly equal strength and influence. It would necessitate the development of a European strategic nuclear force under the control of an authority evolved within the Community itself. Although necessarily this would have inferior nuclear capability to that of the USA it would have sufficient importance in both US and Soviet eyes to enable Europe to develop its own strategic conceptions and to co-ordinate its military resources with those of the Americans on the basis of right rather than concession.

This concept of a European force has never found much favour except amongst the dogmatic advocates of European federalism. The idea was pushed out of the realms of practical politics by the exclusion of Britain, a thermo-nuclear power, from the EEC. Even had this not occurred, it was felt by many experts that an EEC expanded to include Britain and several of her EFTA partners would probably become far too unwieldy to undertake functions such as crisis diplomacy or nuclear command and control. In addition, the notion of the 'twin pillars' of a European-American partnership did not appeal to the West Germans as much as the third alternative—the development of a multilateral force.

The multilateral solution suggested the creation, within the framework of an alliance of sovereign states, of a new force owned, operated and controlled jointly by the nuclear and non-nuclear powers.

None of these alternatives has yet been entirely dismissed; with the entry of Britain into the Europe Economic Community there is speculation about the possibilities of reviving the idea of the European force, to meet the long-term needs of European security. However, it has hitherto been the multilateral solution which has been most exhaustively explored by governments. This is curious, since it was the one proposal which least met the requirements of the Europeans concerning nuclear control, nor did it satisfy their stipulations on security. From the very beginning France expressed lack of interest in the proposal, the British were lukewarm, and though some of the other European powers toyed with it, only in West Germany was there any significant debate and any real gesture of support.

However, it was the Americans who really put their weight behind the multilateral force,[1] as the means to restore the cohesion of NATO. Nevertheless, Kennedy's support for the concept was always qualified by the formidable condition that the European partners should meet their agreed goals in conventional forces before 'we look to the possibility of eventually establishing a NATO seaborne missile force which would be genuinely multilateral in ownership and control'.[2] This American initiative went a long way towards compensating the West Germans for the abandonment of the strategy of massive retaliation,[3] by allowing them some say in the use of nuclear forces.

By the autumn of 1962 the United States had devised a plan for a multilateral force, which was announced, for her allies' consideration, just before the December meeting of the NATO ministers in Paris. The nuclear force was to consist partly of Polaris submarines, partly of mobile land-based medium-range missiles. However, at this stage an entirely new factor entered the discussions on the Multilateral Force (MLF) and caused much confusion later on. In December 1962 Macmillan and Kennedy met at Nassau to discuss future British requirements of nuclear weapons after the cancellation of the Skybolt project. Kennedy's intention was to pursue both the multinational and

[1] The concept had in fact something of a mixed ancestry. It was launched after studies conducted at SHAPE during the eighteen months following the December 1957 meeting of NATO heads of government, but it received little active response from the British and French Governments. The United States began a second, more detailed study of a 'NATO deterrent' in April 1960 and an offer was formally made by Christian Herter, the outgoing Secretary of State, at the NATO ministerial meeting in December 1960, again with little positive European response. President Kennedy established an informal commission of inquiry under Dean Acheson. The idea dropped out of sight for about eighteen months and reappeared in 1961.

[2] Kennedy's speech in Ottawa, 17 May 1961.

[3] It had in reality been abandoned years earlier—but this was not officially acknowledged until McNamara's speech to the NATO Council in Athens in April 1962.

multilateral approach in order to see which would prove the more acceptable. Macmillan, however, was convinced he was discussing a purely multinational project, which would mean the assignment of British V-Bombers and the new Polaris missile submarines to a NATO nuclear force targetted in accordance with NATO plans.[1] Thus the British view was that the future organization of NATO should be based on a closer commitment of existing national forces, whereas the Americans envisaged an entirely new force, jointly planned, financed, owned and controlled by the NATO participants, and in which the non-nuclear allies would have a say by virtue of their financial contribution.

The multinational solution suffered a heavy blow when, less than three weeks after the Nassau discussion, President De Gaulle rejected the American offer of Polaris submarines and made it clear that France would proceed with her own national nuclear programme and exclude Britain from the EEC also. At the same time Macmillan, under pressure to defend the Nassau agreements in the House of Commons, strove to emphasize the continuing national command of British nuclear forces. In European eyes, this robbed the British nuclear contribution to NATO of much of its significance.

Despite all these setbacks, by February 1963 a new multilaterally-owned and -controlled nuclear force had become a prime objective of American foreign policy. US determination was primarily a reaction to what they considered as undesirable trends in West German foreign policy. The Franco-German Pact, signed in January 1963, profoundly alarmed the United States, for it offered the prospect of eventual Franco-German nuclear co-operation. No time, it was argued in Washington, must be lost in offering the West Germans an alternative solution.

The West Germans proved to be the only European partner who showed any real enthusiasm for the multilateral force. Greece and Turkey agreed in principle to participate, although they seemed more concerned with watching each other, whilst Italy showed some interest in the initial stages. Britain became increasingly tepid in her attitude as time went on, while the

[1] Communique of the Nassau Conference (para. 6). In para. 8 this was called a 'multilateral force'.

Benelux nations tried to steer a middle path between German enthusiasm and British lack of interest.

The situation arose in part because the defence ministries of Europe were sceptical of the project, whilst the foreign offices, afraid of the political consequences of non-participation, were advocating membership. Despite the voices of dissent, the plan progressed from preliminary negotiation to the stage where the size and composition of the Multilateral Force was agreed upon. Initially it was to consist of twenty-five surface warships, each carrying eight A3 Polaris missiles.[1] Each ship was to be manned by crews drawn from at least three nations and no single power could contribute more than forty per cent of the total force. Finally, it was decided that the degree of command exercised by each member nation was to be fixed in proportion to its commitment.

In monetary terms the West Germans were to be the largest of the European contributors, paying almost seventy per cent of the continent's share; this represented forty per cent of the total cost, the same as the US contribution, while the six other nations together provided the remaining twenty per cent. The timetable for implementation was that each nation should sign the MLF treaty before the end of 1964 and then ratify it during 1965. Thus, if all went according to plan, France would be politically isolated and the West Germans securely anchored to an American alliance.

Throughout the long-drawn-out negotiations the Americans had tended to concentrate on the technical problems while side-stepping the issue of how the force would be controlled. This procrastination was quite unrealistic, since the political difficulties would have to be faced sooner or later. In the remaining months of 1964 French opposition became more vociferous, and the West Germans found themselves caught between the conflicting views of their closest allies.

For the Americans, MLF seemed to solve the question of nuclear control, and would also appease the ambitions of Western Europe and consolidate American leadership of NATO. Yet the whole scheme aroused considerable disquiet in Europe, not so much because it would give the West Germans access to

[1] Polaris A3 IRBMs, with a range of 2,500 miles and a warhead in the upper kiloton yield.

nuclear weapons, but because of the implicit threat of a Bonn–
Washington axis which might, under certain circumstances,
operate against the interests of other European nations.

The Multilateral Force was also criticized by academic
strategists and defence experts, who considered the concept
totally irrelevant to the needs of European security, on both
military and political grounds. In military terms, the Americans envisaged MLF as a counter-balance to the Soviet
medium-range missiles, and also a force which could work in
conjunction with Strategic Air Command to obliterate Russian
industrial targets in the event of war. The first rôle could be
criticized on the grounds that MLF, as conceived, was simply
too small to act as a deterrent against Soviet MRBMs. In
addition, it would be difficult to justify the presence within
NATO of two nuclear forces, in both of which the Americans
had the final say. Strategic Air Command would perform the
main offensive rôle, and the contribution of MLF here could
only be marginal, granting the Europeans little access to
American strategic planning. Thus the main criticism from the
military standpoint (which had considerable influence on the
eventual demise of the scheme) was that, if joint planning was
confined to MLF, it was inadequate, and if it was extended to
cover all strategic nuclear forces, then MLF was unnecessary.

Politically, MLF was seen by the Americans as a means to
prevent nuclear proliferation by providing a framework which
would allow the NATO allies to abandon their national nuclear
programmes. This was immediately made ineffective by the
refusal of the British and French either to abandon their
respective programmes or to agree to a realistic integration of
their nuclear forces into an all-European one. An equally
important political intention of MLF was to give the West
Germans equal status in nuclear terms. Although from the
strategic point of view it was imperative that West Germany
enjoy equality in the Atlantic alliance, considering that most
of the other allies at this time did not have the resources to
achieve nuclear capability, to give the West Germans atomic
bombs hardly seemed the most sensible way to ensure such
equality. There was probably no particular desire by the West
Germans for nuclear weapons, but rather a fear of being left out
of a possible 'nuclear directorate' of France and Britain, which

suggests they were mainly interested in equality in the political
sense. Even Franz Josef Strauss, the German Minister of
Defence, did not ask for actual control over nuclear weapons,
but merely a greater say in the location of the missiles and warheads already stockpiled in West Germany. Bonn was well
aware of both the nuclear renunciation clauses in the Paris
Agreements and the political risks, at home and abroad,
involved in a German rearmament up to nuclear potential.
Thus was created a vicious circle of the kind which has so often
bedevilled NATO's operations. The United States put forward
a proposal, based on her assumption of what Germany wanted,
which the Germans in turn felt obliged to accept because they
did not want to thwart American wishes. In other words, what
was originally intended as a device to tie the Federal Republic
to NATO and the United States to Europe eventually became
an end in itself.

It is a matter of debate whether MLF grew up as a response
to German nuclear desires, or whether it initially stimulated
them; in any case the problem in the event became very much
an international one, of controlling a nuclear force in which the
Federal Republic was the major shareholder. Nevertheless, of
all the prospective partners, the MLF was of most vital interest
for the West German government. Ever since 1962 doubt had
been accumulating in Bonn about US policy. The McNamara
strategy of 'flexible response', announced without any prior
consultation, seemed hardly suitable for the security requirements of an exposed country like West Germany. The increasing
emphasis on arms control had made the German government apprehensive that the United States might, in order to
meet her own security requirements, be forced to make arrangements with the Soviet Union which would conflict with West
German interests.

So, in West German eyes, the Multilateral Force offered the
means to bind US military power even more closely to Europe,
while at the same time ensuring a stronger West German voice
in Washington. Hence the German attitude to MLF underwent a significant transition, from intelligent interest to something akin to a demand.

Internal politics in West Germany also affected the debate
on MLF. Ever since leaving the Defence Ministry, Franz

Joseph Strauss had advocated a form of German Gaullism which envisaged a reorientation of German policy away from the Atlantic affiliations and more towards a Franco-German partnership. As a result, the Christian Democratic leadership in West Germany attacked MLF as the symbol of 'Atlanticism'.

The failure to establish the Multilateral Force as a positive contribution to European security was symptomatic of the discord which bedevilled NATO in the mid-1960s. As early as 1958 De Gaulle had pointed out this fundamental weakness of the organization; his suggestion of a Directorate[1] was an attempt to overcome this. For if NATO were to retain any vitality, it needed a common foreign policy, or at least a range of divergence, not just in European terms, but a world-wide approach which would by its very nature bear upon the issues of European security. In the absence of this, any attempt to devise a common military understanding was doomed to futility. As long as NATO could not even agree on a common trade policy with the Communist bloc, it would be impossible to persuade its members to relinquish their freedom of action over matters affecting their very survival. De Gaulle's pronouncements struck at the very heart of NATO's problems, and were borne out by the fact that the extent of international co-operation practised in the mid-1960s fell woefully short of the requirements of security.

By 1965 France's view was that NATO had ceased to have any real significance in the free world's defence structure, so French military contributions to NATO were withdrawn and NATO command and logistical networks were ordered to leave French territory. Although in political terms France has remained a loyal member of the Alliance, the loss of French combat units and the denial of French territory had an adverse affect on NATO's cohesion and so undermined Western European security. The French contribution consisted of about 65,000 men and the II Corps of two armoured divisions, and their withdrawal seriously diminished the quantity of ground forces of the 'shield' available to SACEUR to meet any conventional threat.

[1] A scheme whereby the British, Americans and French would assume the role of senior partners of NATO; it was cold-shouldered by the USA and Britain.

However, France had long maintained that troops should be deployed in forward positions only in order to identify aggression and to measure the minimum level of every attack 'having the characteristics of such aggression as would bring the nuclear defence strategy into play';[1] a concept of reconnaissance in force with immediate recourse to nuclear weapons which was completely out of tune with NATO doctrine. In addition, much of the equipment of the French units and the level of training of their personnel left a great deal to be desired by NATO standards.[2] They could never have been really considered as genuine reserves for SACEUR, since it had always been evident that the French would never have allowed the NATO High Command unfettered control over them. Being thus less available than the contributions of other nations, it was probable that they would only have been committed to joint military action in time of war, and even then in such a way as to allow France complete freedom of action in situations where her interests were particularly at stake.

Considering this, the loss of the air forces and the missile systems of France was arguably far more serious than that of the combat divisions, since the French interceptors and strike aircraft were up-to-date supersonic machines which had hitherto made a valuable contribution to Europe's air defence.

One of the major problems which has since confronted NATO is the 'reabsorption' of the French forces into the alliance's military structure in the event of a major crisis. Although the death of De Gaulle and the emergence of a more amenable régime has meant that the French military have become more disposed towards co-operation and joint planning, the special position of the French defence units has made it difficult to draw up a coherent NATO strategy for an emergency situation. The loss of French land and air space has been particularly damaging, since it has meant that NATO supply bases, headquarters and administrative units have had to be moved out. They have since been relocated either in the United Kingdom, which is simply too far back, or in the Low Countries

[1] General Ailleret in the *Revue de Défense Nationale* (translated in *Survival*, November–December 1964).

[2] General Steinkoff, writing in *Europa Archiv*, 10, viii, 66 (reprinted in *Survival*, November 1966).

and West Germany, which is too far forward and also necessitating the use of airfields in areas with the additional hazard of high population density.

The removal of NATO military headquarters from France proved tremendously expensive and caused considerable disruption of communications. Belgium has become the host country for SHAPE, whilst AFCENT and the headquarters complex of LANDCENT and AIRCENT have moved from Fontainebleau to Brunsuum and Hendrik in the Netherlands, an important step towards closer NATO integration, since the three headquarters are now combined into one, under a single commander. At the same time the resignation of the French commander of AFCENT has enabled this key post to be given to a senior officer from the German Federal Republic, whose share of High Command appointments has hitherto been felt to be smaller than its contributions to NATO deserves. Although, with SHAPE south of Brussels, the three major military headquarters are admittedly within a hundred miles of each other, they are in a crowded part of Europe and much further foreward than is really desirable.

Despite French defiance, in 1967 NATO officially adopted the doctrine of 'flexible response' by a resolution in council. However, it must be stressed that it is by no means exactly identical with the doctrine originally put forward by McNamara in 1963. The new European version involves a two-tier strategy: initially, it envisages the use of the combat forces provided by the member governments to contain minor incursion without resort to nuclear weapons; secondly, in the case of a major attack, the enemy advance would be delayed with 'shield' forces until a decision can be taken by the partners whether to initiate the use of nuclear weapons. The NATO ministers have at last agreed in advance on principles for the initial deployment of such weapons; this should cut down the time required to decide whether to 'go nuclear'. However, there are still areas of disagreement over the current policy and so at the present time NATO is involved in yet another reappraisal of its function. The problem is that, for 'flexible response' to be viable, it is essential that there should first be sufficient ground forces available. Experts stress that the present force levels are probably inadequate for full implementation, and not only is there little chance of more reinforcements, but a distinct possibility of further substantial withdrawals in the near future. The gap between strategy and capabilities is already wide and a continuation of present trends might result in a sapping of alliance morale. Hence NATO's major priority is now to effect a workable compromise between the political desirability of 'forward defence' and the official strategy of 'flexible response'. Any changes made in the deployment of ground forces might well meet with the disapproval of the West Germans, since they would inevitably affect the integrity of 'forward defence'. For example, a strategy which envisaged holding a Soviet advance on the Rhine, though militarily sound, would be politically unacceptable. There is little prospect at present of the French rejoining NATO and resuming their full military commitments; they are no nearer to being able to accept either 'forward defence' or 'flexible response', and are still holding fast to their concept of the 'trip-wire' followed by an immediate recourse to nuclear weapons. But if there should be a substantial reduction of US forces, and the Europeans followed suit, this 'trip-wire' strategy would become the only viable one; it is arguable that Europe as a whole might find this more acceptable than 'flexible response'. However, it is doubtful whether Americans would be prepared to accept the 'trip-wire', since its feasibility would depend entirely upon US support and it would involve a greater risk of nuclear confrontation.

There have been two major reasons why the Europeans have had difficulty in reconciling themselves to the doctrine of 'flexible response'. In the first place, they are well aware that 'European NATO' has been in retreat since 1956, when the development of long-range missiles with thermo-nuclear warheads introduced the prospect of a global confrontation between the super-powers and made the European theatre less important to US strategic planners, in the sense that it no longer represented the only area where conflict with the Soviet Union was possible. This decline of Western Europe in US priorities has created a mistrust of American credibility. Secondly, there has been much misunderstanding of the implications of 'flexible response', many considering that it envisages the use of conventional forces only. In fact the concept provides for a response appropriate to the level of aggression;

the deterrent power of nuclear weapons in an extreme situation is still very much part of its strategy. The conventional forces would be used in the initial stages of the conflict, when the threat of nuclear retaliation would be an over-reaction; the 'flexibility' comes in when, a conventional confrontation having failed, the nuclear deterrent is used to escalate the response, conditional upon the approval of the politicians. So the true objective of 'flexible response' is to create a structure of deterrence which utilizes the full spectrum of available military forces and weapons.

When this revized strategy was announced, the NATO forces had for some time been equipped and trained in accordance with the concept of 'massive retaliation'. This gave maximum priority to nuclear delivery systems, conventional forces receiving scant consideration; the resultant lack of effective conventional capability was most noticeable amongst the air forces. In fact NATO strategy might well have foundered on this issue of inadequate air power, had it not been for two circumstances which helped to redress the balance. There was at that time a coincidental re-equipment of the United States Air Forces in Europe with the Macdonnell F4 Phantom, a high-performance aircraft which fortunately could perform a number of differing rôles. Also, there was the 'spin-off' from the war in Vietnam. The large-scale orthodox ground combat that this entailed had transformed research and development of conventional weapons in the United States, not only in terms of technical improvements but also of new tactics, an area of study which had lain fallow since Korea for the United States, and 1945 for the Western Europeans. The latter have benefited in recent years not only from this US research but also the battlefield testing of these improved weapons and their associated electronic devices. Also, the combat experience of American aircrews has been of great value in the training of the air forces of the European partners.

However, although it can be claimed with some justification that the conventional forces presently available are probably better equipped and better trained than ever before in the history of NATO, there are still simply not enough of them, hardly sufficient to deter even a surprise attack. Warsaw Pact manoeuvres are frequently held in the central and western areas of East Germany, often quite close to the frontier, and were there to be a further force reduction and an increase of the prevailing apathy within NATO, the possibility of the Russians using a large-scale exercise as cover for a quick incursion with limited objectives into the Federal Republic should cause great concern to the NATO commanders.

Against this background of an alliance whose strategy is in disarray, the search for European security has progressed into its most recent phase, the attempt to reach agreement through negotiation. In the last twelve months the Soviet Union has endeavoured to initiate a debate on security by calling for a European security conference. To understand the implications of this move and its relationship both to agreement over Berlin and the strategic arms limitations talks at present taking place between the super-powers, it is necessary briefly to recapitulate on Europe's search for lasting security since the end of the Second World War. As that war came to its violent conclusion in spring 1945, the inconsistencies inherent in co-operation between the West and the Soviet Union became manifest, proving that unity was only possible in the context of a common goal, defeating Nazi Germany. Although the United Nations had been created, the Allies had not worked out a realistic scheme for a permanent peace settlement in Europe. As we have seen, the hardening of attitudes finally led to hostility, as both East and West came to recognize the importance of Germany in terms of control over Europe. In 1949 a military dimension was added to the conflict over Germany, and by 1956 it had emerged as the most intractable cause of the schism between the two halves of Europe. On the Western side NATO, the symbol of the free world's unity of purpose in the face of Soviet expansionism was created; whether the Communist threat was accurately perceived is questionable, but at the time it seemed real enough, the West's strong reaction to it owing a great deal to the lessons learnt from the failures of the 1930s. In response, the Soviet Union firmly consolidated her position in Eastern Europe, to meet her enduring need for a *cordon sanitaire*.

The central problem of peace-making remained as what to do with a defeated Germany. Not only had Germany twice been the major enemy in the lifetimes of those who were called upon to deal with her, but all the major Allies had occupying armies on her territory, ready to dispute it between them. In the very broadest sense the war-time allies had and still have a common aim, to ensure that Germany can never again endanger world peace by dominating Central Europe. Initially, however, the Allies had widely differing ideas on how to achieve this and although time has mellowed them, attitudes have not changed to any fundamental extent; the French and the Russians, for obvious reasons, still take the hardest line, the Americans have always been more inclined to 'dust the bully boy off' than to 'shake him down', whilst Britain has always appreciated the need to involve the Americans in Europe as a defence against both German revanchism and Russian expansionism. The problem was made more complex because the zones of occupation followed no particular logic; they gave no guide as to the eventual shape of a German state or states, whether or not the zones should be permanent, and the uneasy status of Berlin only made things worse.

We have seen that the aim of Soviet foreign policy in the post-war period was initially to exact the maximum reparations and to compensate Poland with East German territory for the loss of her eastern provinces. This successfully achieved, the Russians went on to establish a Communist polity in Germany's Soviet-occupied zone, both for its own sake and against the day when free elections might be held in a reunited Germany. In the wider strategic context East Germany was seen as part of the buffer zone of dependent states which would insulate the Soviet Union against the 'capitalist onslaughts' that Stalin expected; in addition, ever since the immediate post-war period Russia has used the territories she thus acquired to support her claim to a dominant rôle in the management of European affairs.

Neither side's policies took much account of the susceptibilities of their opponents; for example, although the West might protest that the Soviet fear of invasion was unfounded, for them it was real. Likewise, although Western demands for democratic constitutions in the liberated areas could well be construed as an attack on Communism, they did stem from a genuine concern for freedom and prosperity. In addition, there was never in the early years any determined attempt to discover how such differences might be overcome. The machinery to implement a settlement was there, as were the principles on which it might be based, but the desire was lacking. Europe was cast into the mould of Potsdam and the clearer it became that there was no common understanding on Europe, the more important the strategic confusion created by the dismemberment of Germany became.

On the military side, the United States' commitment became no less vital after the Soviet Union broke her monopoly of nuclear weapons, and the Korean war tended to support the theory that Soviet expansionism would take a military form. Hence the principles of forward planning and the prior commitment of resources embodied in the NATO agreements came to be accepted as basic requirements for preparedness in the atomic age. With the prospect of nuclear war becoming more likely to involve directly the territory of the super-powers, there grew up an appreciation of the need to possess conventional resources to deal with non-nuclear aggression. In the Eastern bloc the Warsaw Pact has never performed the same diplomatic functions as NATO, but its military potential, particularly in conventional terms, is one which NATO has vainly tried to equal. The Western allies have had to provide forces not only to deter the Warsaw Pact but also to protect NATO territory should deterrence fail; one of their basic problems has been the wide geographical spread of NATO, which has inevitably resulted in differing notions about security among the partners—West Germany's priorities are obviously not those of Italy or Belgium.

After the Cuban crisis of October 1962 there was a relaxation of international tension which lasted until the summer of 1968, when Soviet and Warsaw Pact forces invaded Czechoslovakia. This period saw a sharper distinction between the attitudes of the two major power blocs, and within the blocs the relationships between respective allies were clarified. The dependent nations welcomed the comparative calm of the post-Cuba period, taking it as a justification for reducing military expenditure. Somewhat perversely, the Europeans felt that, as Soviet power grew *vis-à-vis* the United States, this would allay Russian fears of aggression and diminish the importance to her of her Eastern European redoubt. The Soviet Union encouraged the hope that improvements in cultural and economic relations between East and West would lead on to agreement over wider political issues; accordingly, the Kremlin revived the proposals for a European Security Conference which had originally been put forward in the Molotov era (1954–56). East European nations such as Rumania reacted favourably, if only because such a conference might well relax Soviet pressure on them. West Europeans hoped that the military blocs might thereby establish a system of mutual guarantees, which would lead to a saving of men and money and some dismantling of the apparatus of deterrence.

In January 1965 the Consultative Committee of the Warsaw Pact officially called for a European Security Conference, a request repeated in March the following year by Leonid Brezhnev, at the Communist Party Congress in Moscow. The Soviet Union put forward four proposals which it felt could serve as a basis for negotiation: an atom-free zone in Central Europe, a freeze on the development of nuclear weapons by Europeans, a treaty of non-aggression between NATO and the Warsaw Pact, and a German settlement based on international recognition of the *status quo* of two Germanies. On this German question the Russians quite explicitly demanded guarantees of the inviolability of existing frontiers in Europe, particularly the Oder–Niesse line, and also international *de jure* recognition of the German Democratic Republic. The Kremlin also reiterated its suggestion that West Berlin should become a separate political entity and that the Federal Republic should renounce the Hallstein Doctrine and its claim that only Bonn could speak for the whole of Germany.

The Soviet diplomatic offensive gained strength during the succeeding years, applying particular pressure to the members of NATO, which was as usual split by internal dissension. However, the chance of these overtures being taken seriously in the West was disastrously undermined by the Warsaw Pact invasion of Czechoslovakia in 1968. Czechoslovakia has always had particular significance for the West, since previous Czech crises in 1938 and 1948 had had drastic repercussions on the rest of Europe. The episode had no major effect on the military balance in Europe, other than provoking a revision of troop deployments; however, it invalidated the assumption that the Soviet Union was seriously prepared to regularize her relationship with the countries of Eastern Europe to one of greater tolerance. The invasion thus confirmed the suspicions of those NATO members who had doubted Soviet sincerity in calling for a European Security Conference, claiming that the Communist initiatives were aimed at fomenting discord within NATO under cover of an attempt to de-escalate international tension.

Since 1968 the Soviet Union has made great efforts to rehabilitate herself in the eyes of the West, and it now seems that the Czechoslovak incident has not materially affected the campaign for normalising the West's relations with the Eastern bloc, although it may have set it back some years. The long-standing German question, with its crucial implications for the European strategy of the West, has to some extent exercised a mesmerism over NATO; this is where the major Allied forces and the Bundeswehr are concentrated, and where the most difficult military problems are thought most likely to arise. However, it can be argued that other areas, either because less well-policed, such as Norway and the northern flank, or because now inherently more volatile, such as south-east Europe, are soon likely to hold greater potential for military confrontation. The same is true of the eastern basin of the Mediterranean, where Cyprus remains a likely source of dispute between Turkey and Greece, while the latter is still formally at war with Albania; in this region the Soviet Union has developed an effective intervention capability, along with an extensive interest in the affairs of the Arab world. In addition, the various territorial and ethnic disputes existing between the Soviet Union and Yugoslavia, Rumania, Bulgaria and Hungary are of intrinsic international importance, in so far as the tension they might generate could spread to Europe and affect the exposed Western position in Berlin.

In response to Soviet initiatives, the NATO position on a European Security Conference and Mutual and Balanced Force Reductions (MBFR) was defined initially at the Council of Ministers meeting at Reykjavik in 1968, and again in Brussels in 1969. With regard to force reductions, the NATO position had not really altered:[1] any proposed disarmament should be

[1] See the NATO Council Communiqué, February 1969, published in *The Times*, 21 February 1969.

compatible with the vital security interests of the Alliance and should not operate to the military disadvantage of either side, having regard to the differences arising from geographical and other considerations; reductions should be balanced in scope and phased according to a mutually agreed timetable, including both stationed and indigenous forces as well as their weapon systems in the area concerned; finally, there must be adequate verification and control arrangements to ensure the observance of any agreement.

Despite the apparent unaminity of NATO statements, Western governments, like their Eastern counterparts, have held differing opinions about the idea of a European Security Conference. Nevertheless, generally speaking the Western approach is to stress the desirability of a permanent body to deal specifically with the problems of European security. There is an undeniable need to institutionalise the arms balance in Central Europe, to parallel in a more restricted context the institutionalized balance of nuclear weapons amongst the super-powers arising from the Strategic Arms Limitation Talks. The United Nations is of little value in this respect, since it is now much too large and too non-European in composition to function satisfactorily as an organization of permanent contact for Europe; besides, it is nowadays preoccupied with colonialism and the Third World and is more concerned to sustain a balance and a dialogue between the developed and the under-developed world than between European nations.

In June 1971 the NATO Council of Ministers met in Lisbon and agreed to respond in a positive manner to the Soviet initiatives by sending Signor Brosio, one-time secretary-general of NATO, to Moscow to discuss a possible agenda for a security conference. Three factors undoubtedly influenced the new attitudes in Western Europe. Hitherto US enthusiasm for such a conference had been lukewarm, but when President Nixon came under pressure[1] in the Senate to reduce the number of American combat units stationed in Europe, their attitude changed to active support. In addition, the President is still technically committed to an eventual policy of an all-volunteer army, which would mean a smaller force and fewer troops available for overseas service; hence it would be convenient if

[1] Let by Senator Mansfield, leader of the Democratic Party majority.

the Russians could be persuaded to pull a couple of divisions out of Europe whilst NATO still possessed some bargaining power. Secondly, the apparent success of the *Ostpolitik* policy of Chancellor Brandt, which has led to the Bahr agreement on a non-aggression pact between West Germany and the Soviet Union,[1] has produced an atmosphere more conducive to dialogue between East and West. Finally, the events of the summer of 1971 held out real prospects of an agreement on the Berlin question.

The Soviet advocacy of planned troop reductions and a European security conference stems from the fact that their military hierarchy are now probably more approachable over such questions than at any time in the past thirty years. The new generation of senior officers, which has taken over control from the veterans of the Second World War, has reached the top, thanks to its proven ability to manage large armies in peacetime and it is as much concerned as its Western counterparts to avoid overstretching resources. So, provided the proposed cuts are not so drastic as to affect their own positions, such men are likely to be more flexible and probably more influential than their predecessors.

However, there are two other, diametrically-opposed, explanations of the Soviet moves. The optimists believe that at last Russia is really interested in a quieter Europe and will rely less on garrisons and more on such devices as economic subsidies to keep her grip on Eastern Europe; they cite as evidence the signs that the Soviet Union is feeling the economic strain of spending nine per cent of her gross national product on defence. The pessimists on the other hand maintain there is no proof that the Russians are ready for a settlement in Europe, and see their proposals as being nothing more than diplomatic manoeuvring designed to precipitate an American withdrawal and to make public opinion in the West even more reluctant to spend money on defence than it is now; they also stress that from a military standpoint mutual troop reductions cannot conceivably tilt the military balance against the Russians and that in fact the reverse is more likely to be the case.

Although any plan for troop reductions in Europe that would combine undiminished security with smaller defence budgets

[1] The text of this agreement is contained in Appendix A.

would be a desirable objective for all concerned, there is little
value in speculating on this without first defining the criteria
for such reductions. In the first place, the word 'balanced' is
misleading, since as has been stated a man-for-man reduction
would favour the Russians; they have far more troops in the
field than NATO, plus overwhelming superiority in armour.[1]
In such a comparison geography is also on the side of the Soviet
Union; for her the European theatre extends from the Urals
westwards, an area where hitherto she has possessed the
capability to mobilize seventy divisions within thirty days.
Moreover, it is an area in which communications have been
revolutionized by air transport, which would suggest that even
if Soviet units were pulled back into Russia under an international agreement they would lose little of their effectiveness.
This situation must be compared with that of the West, where
American, and possibly British, units would have to be ferried
from their homelands into Europe at a time of crisis. The
Warsaw Pact possesses one final and decisive advantage over
NATO: it is an organization with a highly centralized chain of
command and standardized weapons, ordnance and organization, and hence could absorb reinforcements in a period of
crisis far more easily than the diverse and nationalist structures
of the Western armies. It would seem therefore that the West
cannot afford to negotiate reductions on a man-to-man basis;
they must keep their ground forces intact and offer something
else in exchange for Russian troop withdrawals. The only
feasible gesture is a weapons run-down; it has been suggested
that NATO might dispense with two of its seven thousand
tactical nuclear warheads and a couple of aircraft carriers, in
return for four Soviet armoured divisions. But this is an un-
reasonable rate of exchange which would hardly impress the
Soviet Union. Thus the military aspect of any European
security agreement would present knotty problems. However,
whatever the extent of agreement, the West would still be
obliged to maintain its troop levels, since a security conference
would only deal with arms control, not disarmament, and so a
risk of conflict would still remain. 'Flexible response' at present
is only just viable, and any further troop reductions would

[1] The Soviet Army in Europe numbers 900,000 men, whereas NATO has
580,000 men and only one-third of the armour.

weaken NATO'S bargaining position and require the alliance
to look for other strategies.

Any discussion of the military aspect of force level reduction
would be meaningless without some concerted attempt to relax
those political tensions which might lead to war in the first place.
A major contribution to this relaxation was the signing in
Moscow on 12 August 1970 of a non-aggression pact between
the Federal Republic and the Soviet Union. In a television
address to the German people, broadcast from Moscow, the
German Chancellor, Willy Brandt, tried to forestall some of the
inevitable criticism from his own people by emphasizing that
'nothing is lost with this treaty that was not gambled away long
ago.'[1] Brandt's statement was correct in a literal sense, for the
Federal Republic, by declaring that it had no territorial claim
against anyone and would not assert such claims in the future,
was simply accepting the consequences of Germany's defeat in
the Second World War. But the situation was not as simple as
Brandt would have his electorate believe; his action was to have
dangerous implications for his fragile coalition government.
However, his emphasis that ratification would be dependent on
a four-power agreement over Berlin created an atmosphere
conducive to negotiations on the outstanding problems of
European security. NATO in turn emphasized that the goodwill of the Soviet Union in the matter of balanced force reductions would be measured by her willingness to come to terms
over Berlin. In consequence, diplomatic manoeuvring amongst
the four powers increased during the summer of 1971, to culminate in the twenty-second Formal Session on Berlin on
25 June. The agenda dealt with the question of free access, the
legal position of the city and whether the Bundesrat had a legal
right to meet in Berlin. However, the subsequent agreement[2]
has not altered the *status quo* to any great extent, since it is
mainly concerned with local arrangements for the Western
presence in West Berlin. Indeed, it is doubtful whether any
four-power agreement on Berlin could ensure lasting stability,
since the situation is governed by two intractable factors; the
geographical vulnerability of the Western position in Berlin,
and the steadfast American determination to go to the brink if

[1] The text of this treaty is contained in Appendix B.
[2] See Appendix C for the communiqué on the Berlin Settlement.

necessary, should the Russians, or the East Germans with Russian backing, ever test the Western determination to defend West Berlin. No one can be sure that a such trial will not occur at some time in the future, and the recent agreements have in no way radically diminished the likelihood.

Nevertheless, the Russian sseem to have passed the test of integrity demanded by NATO, and the chances are that at some time in the near future a European Security Conference will take place. As a postscript it is relevant to note that alone of NATO members Britain is somewhat less than enthusiastic about the Soviet overtures. The thesis of the British Foreign Office is that talks on European security would increase the pressures on the US government to reduce its force levels in Europe and at the same time strengthen the hand of those in Britain who are hostile to NATO and cannot see why British forces should be committed to the defence of Berlin and the Federal Republic; moreover, talks on mutual and balanced force reduction in particular would be long drawn-out and might provoke a kind of emotional disarmament, in the belief that summoning a conference is synonymous with the achievement of security. The British believe that the final outcome is bound to be failure, which might result in a hunt for scapegoats by the left wing, their obvious target being the United States and West Germany; indeed, NATO itself could be split asunder by the breakdown of such a security conference. At present, however, the Foreign Office accepts that such a conference will inevitably occur and sees its own task as minimizing its importance and ensuring that it should not be convened before a Berlin settlement is reached and the West German treaties with Poland and the Soviet Union ratified. It remains to be seen whether this gloomy but undeniably realistic prognosis of the British Foreign Office will be borne out by events.

XVI

CONCLUSION

SINCE 1945 Berlin has been the symbol of the unreconciled partition of Germany and of Europe. But the division of Germany, a situation which has been the rule rather than the exception in that country's history, has in the same period coincided with a high degree of stability in both German states and in the overall European balance of power. So although Berlin still offers the most tangible evidence of the schism between East and West in Europe, there are grounds for hope in the skill both sides have shown in handling successive Berlin crises, in the sheer resourcefulness they have devoted to preventing conflict from flaring up into actual hostilities.

After the serious crises of the early 1960s, the city's rôle in the East–West confrontation underwent a significant change. On the Western side there was a decline in the crusading zeal that had characterized the 1950s, in favour of a more pragmatic approach, a willingness to accept the Wall as a starting point for negotiation, which tended to reduce the political sensitivity of Berlin. In turn, whilst the basic objective of the Soviet Union's European policy has remained the stabilizing of her power in East and Central Europe, she has nevertheless seemed more inclined to recognize the Western position in Berlin.

In September 1971, after seventeen months of intricate negotiations, involving the four powers responsible for Germany, the two German states and the North Atlantic and Warsaw Pact alliances, agreement was finally reached on Berlin. This was the first major East–West agreement in Europe since the Austrian State Treaty in 1955; in an age of 'crisis management' it is refreshing to realize that old-fashioned diplomacy can still produce results.

The Berlin Agreement is merely the result of one out of a

whole group of talks, each mutually dependent on the other, which are taking place between the Soviet Union and the major Western powers; others include the Strategic Arms Limitation Talks (SALT), the *Ostpolitik* of Bonn, and the projected European Security Conference.

Of these, the Berlin settlement has particular importance in that it implies a recognition of the frontiers between the protagonists, and is therefore not only a contribution towards the settlement of the Cold War, but also the closest Europe can ever expect to come to a peace treaty to end the Second World War. A successful conclusion to all these diplomatic initiatives, especially Berlin, could result in Europe moving away from the quasi-military confrontation of the Cold War towards a political situation which would permit more emphasis on the interdependence of industrial societies with mutual interests. Thus Europe as one could seek solutions to such universal threats to its society as pollution of the environment, urban proliferation and the misuses of technology. But for a New Order in Europe to become reality the many difficulties involved in each of these diplomatic overtures must be resolved; a failure in only one could well result in Europe reverting to the age of the 'armed camp'.

For the Berlin Agreements to work, two conditions must be met: firstly, the people of West Berlin must have confidence in the settlement and, secondly, the international climate in Europe must be favourable. This not only demands a continuing *détente* between the super-powers, but also positive progress in Bonn's *Ostpolitik*; this in turn requires that the German Democratic Republic be allowed to assume a meaningful rôle in Central Europe. If the Agreement is successful, it will establish, at least for some time to come, a *modus vivendi* for one of the most sensitive areas in Europe since the Second World War. Even those parts of the Agreements already in existence prove it to be the longest and most detailed of all quadripartite pacts on Berlin; this fact alone demonstrates the wide variations existing in the evaluation of the Berlin situation by each of the four powers, as well as the determination of the Western governments not to repeat the mistakes of the past—the loopholes which existed in earlier agreements have been closed, allowing no room for misinterpretation in the future.

The Agreements[1] deal with four main topics: the legal status of Berlin, the relations between West Berlin and the Federal Republic, the freedom of movement of West Berliners, and communications between West Berlin and West Germany.

The four powers did not in fact agree on the legal status of West Berlin, because the Western governments believe that Berlin should be considered as a whole, whereas the Soviet position is that, since East Berlin is already an integral part of the DDR, the only problem concerns West Berlin. However, deadlock was avoided by both sides agreeing to disagree. Even so, there was progress, in another direction, when the four governments gave a specific undertaking to 'mutually respect their individual and joint rights and responsibilities, which remain unchanged'. This is in effect a confirmation of the right of the three Western powers to retain a presence in Berlin, precisely the right which the Soviet Union has contested in the past.[2]

Concerning the ties between West Berlin and West Germany, the Western governments here took great care to secure as precise an agreement as possible without causing too obvious a loss of face for the Soviet Union. In this section of the settlement the Federal Republic gains major concessions, notably concerning the application of federal laws, the presence of federal authorities and the sessions of committees of the Bundesrat and Bundestag in Berlin. Here the main objective for the Soviet Union was to secure confirmation from the Western powers that West Berlin does not form part of the constitutional framework of the Federal Republic. So the Federal President and all Federal authorities and institutions, including the courts, are precluded from performing 'constitutional or official acts' which might imply the exercise of direct powers over West Berlin. In exchange, the Soviet Union has agreed to less visible, but far more important, ties of an economic, legal and financial nature. Finally, no mention is made of the participation of Berlin deputies in the Bundestag, Bundesrat and the Federal Assembly. Therefore it is possible for the Mayor of Berlin, in his

[1] For full text of Agreements, see Appendix C.
[2] The continuing validity of the 'wartime and post-war agreements and decisions of the Four Powers' is also confirmed. This should be compared with the note of 22 November 1958, in which the Soviet Union stated that she considered the 1944 London Protocols as being no longer in force.

capacity as President in rotation of the Bundesrat, to act in the absence of the Federal President as head of state.

In addition, the Agreements have increased the West Berliner's freedom of movement into the Eastern Sector and have made this journey safer. They have also confirmed the present arrangement whereby the Federal Republic will protect the interests of West Berliners abroad and represent West Berlin in international organizations and conferences, provided that these do not involve issues of status and security.

Fortunately, the agreements on access to Berlin are particularly precise. The vagueness of the arrangements concerning access made between 1945 and 1949, which have remained in force ever since, has allowed the German Democratic Republic, with the tacit support of the Soviet Union, to persistently disrupt traffic along the Berlin approach routes. Significantly, the Soviet Union has now curbed the sovereign rights over access routes which she originally ceded to the DDR in 1955, and has once again assumed overall responsibility for transit traffic. Though many of the technical details are still to be worked out, it is already agreed that normal customs procedures will be applied on the access routes.[1] For civilians travelling by public transport and private car, control procedure will be limited to identification, and the Agreements at last specify that 'procedures applied to such travellers shall not involve delay'.

If the Agreements are observed in practice, a notable improvement in West Berlin's circumstances can be expected. However, much will depend on the reaction of its citizens; in the past they have been particularly susceptible to fears of being 'abandoned' by the Western powers. The clarification of those areas of doubt which have for so long affected the economic and social stability of the city should now ensure a greater equilibrium in the future. The practical intervention of Federal agencies in city affairs has been increased, but at the cost of the symbolic Allied presence. Although this development will assist the normal day-to-day life of Berlin, should there be an increase in tension and a return to crisis, it is imperative that there should still be the opportunity for a demon-

[1] This means that goods will be sealed before departure and scrutiny will only extend to seals and relevant documents.

stration of unity with the Western powers and the Federal
Republic. Thus the Agreements, although stabilising the
arrangements for access and encouraging renewed confidence
in the future economic prosperity of West Berlin, do not offer
any solution to the major problem of establishing a new status
for the city. Much will therefore depend on the goodwill of the
German Democratic Republic.

There is nothing in the Agreements to suggest that the
DDR's political aims have radically changed,[1] but perhaps
some of the reasons why it has sought to obstruct access to
Berlin in the past have been removed. Certainly the international position of the DDR has improved as a result of the
Agreements; to its *de facto* control of access routes has now been
added a legal acknowledgement of its administrative competence. It has passed the test of stability for a communist
régime, through the smooth transfer of power from the veteran
Walter Ulbricht to Erich Honecker. Its Communist Party
(SED) has been in power for twenty-three years, longer than
any German government since the fall of the monarchy in 1918.
Since the building of the Wall in 1961, the DDR has been more
stable than most other states of the Eastern bloc; indeed, there
has been no significant unrest since 1953.

In its policy towards East Germany, the Bonn government
has made a reservation which is politically vital in terms of its
present domestic position and its future foreign policy: it has
refused to accord the DDR complete recognition, maintaining
that intra-German relations are of a special nature and not the
same as those with foreign countries. On the success of this
policy will depend both the further progress of intra-German
negotiations and the continuation of the *détente* in Europe. If the
DDR is prepared to accept the distinction and still sign satisfactory agreements with the Federal Republic, Bonn in turn
will cease opposing East German contacts with other countries
and agree to its membership of the United Nations. To date, the
Federal Republic has been successful in convincing many
governments to delay recognition of the DDR until the two

[1] There are significant differences between the German text of the
Agreements published in the DDR, and that published in West Germany;
for example, the former speaks of 'links' rather than 'ties' between West
Berlin and the Federal Republic.

Germanies have reached an agreement. But Chancellor Brandt is running out of time, and his precarious domestic position is a further hindrance. Of the twenty-three states that now accord East Berlin full recognition, more than half are non-communist, and popular pressure in favour of recognition is mounting in NATO countries such as France, Britain, the Netherlands and Denmark. Although Brandt's policy of *Ostpolitik* in relation to East Germany professedly aims at establishing a working relationship to halt the increasing divergence between the development of East and West German society and political structures since 1945, the Communists do not necessarily see Bonn's overtures in quite the same light. They could well conclude that Brandt's government also hopes through this working relationship to appeal to the rapidly-expanding East German middle class and the moderate faction of the SED, thus promoting political pluralism in East Germany—in Communist eyes tantamount to subversion. A further problem is that the idea of the German nation still retains considerable political potential, the more so since Brandt himself has revived the vision of a single Germany,[1] and so the lack of a national basis will remain the greatest weakness of the DDR for as long as the concept of the nation state exists as the prime determinant of political attitudes in Europe. Thus it is evident that Bonn's policy towards East Germany runs a risk of perpetuating the partition that it seeks to eliminate.

In some ways the Berlin Agreements also demonstrate the failure of East Germany's foreign policy. She has clearly been rebuffed by the Soviet Union, who has firmly taken away the capacity she formerly possessed to make trouble. The major miscalculation by the DDR was to imagine that she could demand international recognition, as part of a general acceptance of the post-war map of Europe, without herself recognizing the status of West Berlin as evolved since the War. A further error was to regard control over access to Berlin as an essential attribute of her sovereignty, instead of seeing that broader perspectives would open up if the Berlin blockage were removed. These mistakes are considered by the West to be a

[1] The SED discovered to its dismay that when it recently polled workers on this question, seventy-one per cent of them considered Germany rather than the DDR as their fatherland.

result of the hard-line policy of Ulbricht; perhaps the new régime will see things in a different light.

So, in terms of an overall European *détente*, the Agreements represent not a final solution but merely a temporary arrangement. However, both the Western governments and the Soviet Union were well aware that at the present moment the only realistic agreement is a limited one; although this has inevitably produced limited results, it is arguable that a wider objective would have produced no results at all. In the long run, both the effectiveness of the Agreements as they stand and hopes for future progress will depend on continuing this *détente* in Europe. There is no evidence in the Agreements to suggest a complete change of heart among the Eastern bloc. Indeed, many Western commentators believe that the Communists still have the same objectives concerning Berlin, and have merely changed the methods by which they hope to achieve these objectives. For East Germany, Cold War confrontations are neither outmoded nor inexpedient; she undeniably has an interest in prolonging tension—she has provoked it often enough in the past—and her obstructive potential remains considerable. Success and progress would seem to depend on the willingness of the DDR to play a positive rôle in intra-German negotiations, and acceptance by the West of an East German contribution to the forthcoming talks on European security. A new pattern of East–West relations in Europe could scarcely be sustained unless the DDR is allowed to participate in its development, from which it may well gain a clearer perception of its interests than that which isolation has bred.

The way is now open for negotiations on mutual and balanced force reductions between the Warsaw Pact and NATO. But it is questionable whether talks on troop reductions are feasible without the direct involvement of East Germany, whose army is considered the most efficient in the Eastern Bloc, and whether a security conference without the participation of that member of the Warsaw Pact which feels itself most insecure is likely to produce a safer Europe. Whether the moment is opportune for the reduction of military defences in Europe is debatable, but the Berlin Agreements have ensured one positive result, the emergence of the German Democratic Republic as a full participant in the politics of Europe.

BAHR AGREEMENT

I

The Federal Republic of Germany and the Union of Soviet Socialist Republics consider it an important objective of their policies to maintain international peace and achieve détente.

They affirm their endeavour to further the normalization of the situation in Europe and in doing so to proceed from the actual situation existing in this region and the development of peaceful relations on this basis among all European States.

2

In their mutual relations as well as in matters of ensuring European and international security, the Federal Republic of Germany and the Union of Soviet Socialist Republics shall be guided by the purposes and principles embodied in the statutes of the United Nations.

Accordingly, they will settle their disputes exclusively by peaceful means and undertake to refrain from the threat or use of force in any matters affecting security in Europe or internationally as well as in their mutual relations pursuant to Article 2 of the statutes of the United Nations.

3

The Federal Republic of Germany and the Soviet Union share the realization that peace in Europe can be maintained only if no one disturbs the present frontiers.

They undertake to respect without restriction the territorial integrity of all States in Europe within their present frontiers.

They declare they have no territorial claims against anybody, nor will assert such claims in the future.

They regard today and shall in future regard the frontiers of all States in Europe as inviolable such as they are on the date of signature of this agreement, including the Oder-Neisse Line, which forms the western frontier of the People's Republic of Poland, and the frontier between the Federal Republic of Germany and the German Democratic Republic.

4

The agreement between the Federal Republic of Germany and the Union of Soviet Socialist Republics shall not affect the bilateral or multilateral treaties and agreements previously concluded by the two sides.

5

Agreement exists between the Government of the Federal Republic of Germany and the Government of the Union of Soviet Socialist Republics that the agreement on . . . (the official designation of the agreement to be inserted) to be concluded by them and corresponding agreements (treaties) of the Federal Republic of Germany with other socialist countries, in particular the agreements (treaties) with the German Democratic Republic (see 6), the People's Republic of Poland and the Czechoslovak Socialist Republic (see 8) form a homogeneous whole.

6

The Government of the Federal Republic of Germany declares its preparedness to conclude an agreement with the Government of the German Democratic Republic that shall have the same binding force, usual between States, as other agreements the Federal Republic of Germany and the German Democratic Republic conclude with third countries. Accordingly, it will frame its relations with the German Democratic Republic on the basis of full equality of status, non-discrimination, respect for the independence and autonomy of both States in matters concerning their internal competency within their respective frontiers.

The Government of the Federal Republic of Germany proceeds on the premise that the relations of the German Democratic Republic and the Federal Republic of Germany with third States will develop on this basis, in accordance with which neither of the two States can represent the other abroad or act on its behalf.

7

The Government of the Federal Republic of Germany and the Government of the Union of Soviet Socialist Republics declare their preparedness, in the course of the détente in Europe and in the interest of the improvement of the relations among the European countries, in particular the Federal Republic of Germany and the German Democratic Republic, to take steps resulting from their appropriate status to support the accession of the Federal Republic of Germany and the German Democratic Republic to the Organization of the United Nations and its specialized agencies.

8

Agreement exists between the Government of the Federal Repub-
lic of Germany and the Government of the Union of Soviet Socialist
Republics that the issues connected with the invalidation of the
Munich Agreement are to be settled in negotiations between the
Federal Republic of Germany and the Czechoslovak Socialist
Republic in a form acceptable to both sides.

9

The Government of the Federal Republic of Germany and the
Government of the Union of Soviet Socialist Republics, in the
interest of both sides and the strengthening of peace in Europe, will
continue to develop the economic, scientific, technological, cultural
and other relations between the Federal Republic of Germany and
the Union of Soviet Socialist Republics.

10

The Government of the Federal Republic of Germany and the
Government of the Union of Soviet Socialist Republics welcome the
plan of a conference on matters concerning the strengthening of
security and cooperation in Europe and will do everything that
depends on them for its preparation and successful prosecution.

TREATY BETWEEN THE FEDERAL REPUBLIC OF GERMANY AND THE UNION OF SOVIET SOCIALIST REPUBLICS, 1970

The High Contracting Parties

Anxious to contribute to strengthening peace and security in Europe and the world,

Convinced that peaceful co-operation among States on the basis of the purposes and principles of the Charter of the United Nations complies with the ardent desire of nations and the general interests of international peace,

Appreciating the fact that the agreed measures previously implemented by them, in particular the conclusion of the Agreement of 13 September 1955 on the Establishment of Diplomatic Relations, have created favourable conditions for new important steps destined to develop further and to strengthen their mutual relations,

Desiring to lend expression, in the form of a treaty, to their determination to improve and extend co-operation between them, including economic relations as well as scientific, technological and cultural contacts, in the interest of both States,

Have agreed as follows:

Article 1

The Federal Republic of Germany and the Union of Soviet Socialist Republics consider it an important objective of their policies to maintain international peace and achieve détente.

They affirm their endeavour to further the normalization of the situation in Europe and the development of peaceful relations among all European States, and in so doing proceed from the actual situation existing in this region.

Article 2

The Federal Republic of Germany and the Union of Soviet Socialist Republics shall in their mutual relations as well as in matters of ensuring European and international security be guided by the purposes and principles embodied in the Charter of the United Nations. Accordingly they shall settle their disputes exclusively by peaceful means and undertake to refrain from the threat or use of force, pursuant to Article 2 of the Charter of the United Nations, in any matters affecting security in Europe or international security, as well as in their mutual relations.

Article 3

In accordance with the foregoing purposes and principles the Federal Republic of Germany and the Union of Soviet Socialist Republics share the realization that peace can only be maintained in Europe if nobody disturbs the present frontiers.

— They undertake to respect without restriction the territorial integrity of all States in Europe within their present frontiers;
— they declare that they have no territorial claims against anybody nor will assert such claims in the future;
— they regard today and shall in future regard the frontiers of all States in Europe as inviolable such as they are on the date of signature of the present Treaty, including the Oder-Neisse line which forms the western frontier of the People's Republic of Poland and the frontier between the Federal Republic of Germany and the German Democratic Republic.

Article 4

The present Treaty between the Federal Republic of Germany and the Union of Soviet Socialist Republics shall not affect any bilateral or multilateral treaties or arrangements previously concluded by them.

Article 5

The present Treaty is subject to ratification and shall enter into force on the date of exchange of the instruments of ratification which shall take place in Bonn.

Done at Moscow on 12 August 1970 in two originals, each in the German and Russian languages, both texts being equally authentic.

For the Federal Republic of Germany	For the Union of Soviet Socialist Republics
Willy Brandt *Walter Scheel*	*Alexei N. Kosygin* *Andrei A. Gromyko*

Letter on German Unity

On the occasion of the signing of the Treaty, the Federal Government handed over in the Soviet Foreign Ministry the following letter:

Dear Mr. Minister

In connection with today's signature of the Treaty between the Federal Republic of Germany and the Union of Soviet Socialist Republics the Government of the Federal Republic of Germany has the honour to state that this Treaty does not conflict with the political objective of the Federal Republic of Germany to work for a state of peace in Europe in which the German nation will recover its unity in free self-determination.

I assure you, Mr. Minister, of my highest esteem.

Walter Scheel

QUADRIPARTITE AGREEMENT ON BERLIN, 1971

The Governments of the United States of America, the French Republic, the Union of Soviet Socialist Republics, and the United Kingdom of Great Britain and Northern Ireland, represented by their Ambassadors, who held a series of meetings in the building formerly occupied by the Allied Control Council in the American Sector of Berlin,

Acting on the basis of their quadripartite rights and responsibilities, and of the corresponding wartime and postwar agreements and decisions of the Four Powers, which are not affected,

Taking into account the existing situation in the relevant area,

Guided by the desire to contribute to practical improvements of the situation,

Without prejudice to their legal positions,

Have agreed on the following:

PART I

General Provisions

1. The four Governments will strive to promote the elimination of tension and the prevention of complications in the relevant area.
2. The four Governments, taking into account their obligations under the Charter of the United Nations, agree that there shall be no use or threat of force in the area and that disputes shall be settled solely by peaceful means.
3. The four Governments will mutually respect their individual and joint rights and responsibilities, which remain unchanged.
4. The four Governments agree that, irrespective of the differences in legal views, the situation which has developed in the area, and as it is defined in this Agreement as well as in the other agreements referred to in this Agreement, shall not be changed unilaterally.

PART II

Provisions Relating to the Western Sectors of Berlin

A. The Government of the Union of Soviet Socialist Republics declares that transit traffic by road, rail and waterways through the territory of the German Democratic Republic of civilian persons and goods between the Western Sectors of Berlin and the Federal Republic of Germany will be unimpeded; that such traffic will be facilitated so as to take place in the most simple and expeditious manner; and that it will receive preferential treatment.

Detailed arrangements concerning this civilian traffic, as set forth in Annex I, will be agreed by the competent German authorities.

B. The Governments of the French Republic, the United Kingdom and the United States of America declare that the ties between the Western Sectors of Berlin and the Federal Republic of Germany will be maintained and developed, taking into account that these Sectors continue not to be a constituent part of the Federal Republic of Germany and not to be governed by it.

Detailed arrangements concerning the relationship between the Western Sectors of Berlin and the Federal Republic of Germany are set forth in Annex II.

C. The Government of the Union of Soviet Socialist Republics declares that communications between the Western Sectors of Berlin and areas bordering on these Sectors and those areas of the German Democratic Republic which do not border on these Sectors will be improved. Permanent residents of the Western Sectors of Berlin will be able to travel to and visit such areas for compassionate, family, religious, cultural or commercial reasons, or as tourists, under conditions comparable to those applying to other persons entering these areas.

The problems of the small enclaves, including Steinstücken, and of other small areas may be solved by exchange of territory.

Detailed arrangements concerning travel, communications and the exchange of territory, as set forth in Annex III, will be agreed by the competent German authorities.

D. Representation abroad of the interests of the Western Sectors of Berlin and consular activities of the Union of Soviet Socialist Republics in the Western Sectors of Berlin can be exercised as set forth in Annex IV.

PART III

Final Provisions

This Quadripartite Agreement will enter into force on the date specified in a Final Quadripartite Protocol to be concluded when the measures envisaged in Part II of this Quadripartite Agreement and in its Annexes have been agreed.

DONE at the building formerly occupied by the Allied Control Council in the American Sector of Berlin, this 3rd day of September, 1971, in four originals, each in the English, French and Russian languages, all texts being equally authentic.

For the Government of the French Republic:

Jean Sauvagnargues

For the Government of the Union of Soviet Socialist Republics:

Piotr Abrasimov

For the Government of the United Kingdom
of Great Britain and Northern Ireland:

R. W. Jackling

For the Government of the United States of America:

Kenneth Rush

ANNEX I

Communication from the Government of the Union of Soviet Socialist Republics to the Governments of the French Republic, the United Kingdom and the United States of America

The Government of the Union of Soviet Socialist Republics, with reference to Part II A of the Quadripartite Agreement of this date and after consultation and agreement with the Government of the German Democratic Republic, has the honour to inform the Governments of the French Republic, the United Kingdom and the United States of America that:

1. Transit traffic by road, rail and waterways through the territory of the German Democratic Republic of civilian persons and goods between the Western Sectors of Berlin and the Federal Republic of Germany will be facilitated and unimpeded. It will receive the most simple, expeditious and preferential treatment provided by international practice.
2. Accordingly,
   (a) Conveyances sealed before departure may be used for the

transport of civilian goods by road, rail and waterways between the Western Sectors of Berlin and the Federal Republic of Germany. Inspection procedures will be limited to the inspection of seals and accompanying documents.

(b) With regard to conveyances which cannot be sealed, such as open trucks, inspection procedures will be limited to the inspection of accompanying documents. In special cases where there is sufficient reason to suspect that unsealed conveyances contain either material intended for dissemination along the designated routes or persons or material put on board along these routes, the content of unsealed conveyances may be inspected. Procedures for dealing with such cases will be agreed by the competent German authorities.

(c) Through trains and buses may be used for travel between the Western Sectors of Berlin and the Federal Republic of Germany. Inspection procedures will not include any formalities other than identification of persons.

(d) Persons identified as through travellers using individual vehicles between the Western Sectors of Berlin and the Federal Republic of Germany on routes designated for through traffic will be able to proceed to their destinations without paying individual tolls and fees for the use of the transit routes. Procedures applied for such travellers shall not involve delay.

The travellers, their vehicles and personal baggage will not be subject to search, detention or exclusion from use of the designated routes, except in special cases, as may be agreed by the competent German authorities, where there is sufficient reason to suspect that misuse of the transit routes is intended for purposes not related to direct travel to and from the Western Sectors of Berlin and contrary to generally applicable regulations concerning public order.

(e) Appropriate compensation for fees and tolls and for other costs related to traffic on the communication routes between the Western Sectors of Berlin and the Federal Republic of Germany, including the maintenance of adequate routes, facilities and installations used for such traffic, may be made in the form of an annual lump sum paid to the German Democratic Republic by the Federal Republic of Germany.

3. Arrangements implementing and supplementing the provisions of Paragraphs 1 and 2 above will be agreed by the competent German authorities.

ANNEX II

Communication from the Governments of the French Republic, the United Kingdom and the United States of America to the Government of the Union of Soviet Socialist Republics

The Governments of the French Republic, the United Kingdom and the United States of America, with reference to Part II B of the Quadripartite Agreement of this date and after consultation with the Government of the Federal Republic of Germany, have the honour to inform the Government of the Union of Soviet Socialist Republics that:

1. They declare, in the exercise of their rights and responsibilities, that the ties between the Western Sectors of Berlin and the Federal Republic of Germany will be maintained and developed, taking into account that these Sectors continue not to be a constituent part of the Federal Republic of Germany and not to be governed by it. The provisions of the Basic Law of the Federal Republic of Germany and of the Constitution operative in the Western Sectors of Berlin which contradict the above have been suspended and continue not to be in effect.

2. The Federal President, the Federal Government, the Bundesversammlung, the Bundesrat and the Bundestag, including their Committees and Fraktionen, as well as other state bodies of the Federal Republic of Germany will not perform in the Western Sectors of Berlin constitutional or official acts which contradict the provisions of Paragraph 1.

3. The Government of the Federal Republic of Germany will be represented in the Western Sectors of Berlin to the authorities of the three Governments and to the Senat by a permanent liaison agency.

ANNEX III

Communication from the Government of the Union of Soviet Socialist Republics to the Governments of the French Republic, the United Kingdom and the United States of America

The Government of the Union of Soviet Socialist Republics, with reference to Part II C of the Quadripartite Agreement of this date and after consultation and agreement with the Government of the German Democratic Republic, has the honour to inform the Governments of the French Republic, the United Kingdom and the United States of America that:

1. Communications between the Western Sectors of Berlin and areas bordering on these Sectors and those areas of the German Democratic Republic which do not border on these Sectors will be improved.
2. Permanent residents of the Western Sectors of Berlin will be able to travel to and visit such areas for compassionate, family, religious, cultural or commercial reasons, or as tourists, under conditions comparable to those applying to other persons entering these areas. In order to facilitate visits and travel, as described above, by permanent residents of the Western Sector of Berlin, additional crossing points will be opened.
3. The problems of the small enclaves, including Steinstücken, and of other small areas may be solved by exchange of territory.
4. Telephonic, telegraphic, transport and other external communications of the Western Sectors of Berlin will be expanded.
5. Arrangements implementing and supplementing the provisions of Paragraphs 1 to 4 above will be agreed by the competent German authorities.

ANNEX IV

A. Communication from the Governments of the French Republic, the United Kingdom and the United States of America to the Government of the Union of Soviet Socialist Republics

The Governments of the French Republic, the United Kingdom and the United States of America, with reference to Part II D of the Quadripartite Agreement of this date and after consultation with the Government of the Federal Republic of Germany, have the honour to inform the Government of the Union of Soviet Socialist Republics that:

1. The Governments of the French Republic, the United Kingdom and the United States of America maintain their rights and responsibilities relating to the representation abroad of the interests of the Western Sectors of Berlin and their permanent residents, including those rights and responsibilities concerning matters of security and status, both in international organizations and in relations with other countries.
2. Without prejudice to the above and provided that matters of security and status are not affected, they have agreed that:
   (a) The Federal Republic of Germany may perform consular services for permanent residents of the Western Sectors of Berlin.

(b) In accordance with established procedures, international agreements and arrangements entered into by the Federal Republic of Germany may be extended to the Western Sectors of Berlin provided that the extension of such agreements and arrangements is specified in each case.

(c) The Federal Republic of Germany may represent the interests of the Western Sectors of Berlin in international organizations and international conferences.

(d) Permanent residents of the Western Sectors of Berlin may participate jointly with participants from the Federal Republic of Germany in international exchanges and exhibitions. Meetings of international organizations and international conferences as well as exhibitions with international participation may be held in the Western Sectors of Berlin. Invitations will be issued by the Senat or jointly by the Federal Republic of Germany and the Senat.

3. The three Governments authorize the establishment of a Consulate General of the USSR in the Western Sectors of Berlin accredited to the appropriate authorities of the three Governments in accordance with the usual procedures applied in those Sectors, for the purpose of performing consular services, subject to provisions set forth in a separate document of this date.

B. Communication from the Government of the Union of Soviet Socialist Republics to the Governments of the French Republic, the United Kingdom and the United States of America

The Government of the Union of Soviet Socialist Republics, with reference to Part II D of the Quadripartite Agreement of this date and to the communication of the Governments of the French Republic, the United Kingdom and the United States of America with regard to the representation abroad of the interests of the Western Sectors of Berlin and their permanent residents, has the honour to inform the Governments of the French Republic, the United Kingdom and the United States of America that:

1. The Government of the Union of Soviet Socialist Republics takes note of the fact that the three Governments maintain their rights and responsibilities relating to the representation abroad of the interests of the Western Sectors of Berlin and their permanent residents, including those rights and responsibilities concerning matters of security and status, both in international organizations and in relations with other countries.

2. Provided that matters of security and status are not affected, for its part it will raise no objection to:

   (a) The performance by the Federal Republic of Germany of consular services for permanent residents of the Western Sectors of Berlin.

   (b) In accordance with established procedures, the extension to the Western Sectors of Berlin of international agreements and arrangements entered into by the Federal Republic of Germany provided that the extension of such agreements and arrangements is specified in each case.

   (c) The representation of the interests of the Western Sectors of Berlin by the Federal Republic of Germany in international organizations and international conferences.

   (d) The participation jointly with participants from the Federal Republic of Germany of permanent residents of the Western Sectors of Berlin in international exchanges and exhibitions, or the holding in those Sectors of meetings of international organizations and international conferences as well as exhibitions with international participation, taking into account that invitations will be issued by the Senat or jointly by the Federal Republic of Germany and the Senat.

3. The Government of the Union of Soviet Socialist Republics takes note of the fact that the three Governments have given their consent to the establishment of a Consulate General of the USSR in the Western Sectors of Berlin. It will be accredited to the appropriate authorities of the three Governments, for purposes and subject to provisions described in their communication and as set forth in a separate document of this date.

Final Quadripartite Protocol

The Governments of the Union of Soviet Socialist Republics, the United Kingdom of Great Britain and Northern Ireland, the United States of America and the French Republic,

Having in mind Part III of the Quadripartite Agreement of September 3, 1971, and taking note with satisfaction of the fact that the agreements and arrangements mentioned below have been concluded,

Have agreed on the following:

1. The four Governments, by virtue of this Protocol, bring into force the Quadripartite Agreement, which, like this Protocol, does not affect quadripartite agreements or decisions previously concluded or reached.

2. The four Governments proceed on the basis that the following agreements and arrangements concluded between the competent German authorities (list of agreements and arrangements) shall enter into force simultaneously with the Quadripartite Agreement.

3. The Quadripartite Agreement and the consequent agreements and arrangements of the competent German authorities referred to in this Protocol settle important issues examined in the course of the negotiations and shall remain in force together.

4. In the event of a difficulty in the application of the Quadripartite Agreement or any of the above-mentioned agreements or arrangements which any of the four Governments consider serious, or in the event of non-implementation of any part thereof, that Government will have the right to draw the attention of the other three Governments to the provisions of the Quadripartite Agreement and this Protocol and to conduct the requisite quadripartite consultations in order to ensure the observance of the commitments undertaken and to bring the situation into conformity with the Quadripartite Agreement and this Protocol.

5. This Protocol enters into force on the date of signature.

DONE at the building formerly occupied by the Allied Control Council in the American Sector of Berlin this .... day of ...., 1971, in four originals each in the English, French and Russian languages, all texts being equally authentic.

For the Government of the French Republic

For the Government of the Union of Soviet
Socialist Republics

For the Government of the United Kingdom
of Great Britain and Northern Ireland

For the Government of the United States
of America

Note of the Three Ambassadors
to the Soviet Ambassador

The Ambassadors of the French Republic, the United Kingdom of Great Britain and Northern Ireland and the United States of America have the honour, with reference to the statements contained in Annex II of the Quadripartite Agreement to be signed on this date concerning the relationship between the Federal Republic of Germany and the Western Sectors of Berlin, to inform the Ambassador of the Union of Soviet Socialist Republics of their intention to send to the Chancellor of the Federal Republic of Germany immediately following signature of the Quadripartite Agreement a letter containing clarifications and interpretations which represent the understanding of their Governments of the statements contained in Annex II of the Quadripartite Agreement. A copy of the letter to be sent to the Chancellor of the Federal Republic of Germany is attached to this Note.

(Formal close)

Soviet Reply Note

The Ambassador of the Union of Soviet Socialist Republics has the honour to acknowledge receipt of the Note of the Ambassadors of the French Republic, the United Kingdom of Great Britain and Northern Ireland and the United States of America, dated September 3, 1971, and takes note of the communication of the three Ambassadors.

(Formal close)

Letter of the Three Ambassadors to the Federal Chancellor

Concerning Interpretation of Annex II

His Excellency
The Chancellor of the
Federal Republic of Germany

Your Excellency:

With reference to the Quadripartite Agreement signed on September 3, 1971, our Governments wish by this letter to inform the Government of the Federal Republic of Germany of the following clarifications and interpretations of the statements contained in Annex II, which was the subject of consultation with the Government of the Federal Republic of Germany during the quadripartite negotiations.

These clarifications and interpretations represent the understanding of our Governments of this part of the Quadripartite Agreement, as follows:

(a) The Phrase in Paragraph 2 of Annex II of the Quadripartite

Agreement which reads: '. . . will not perform in the Western Sectors of Berlin constitutional or official acts which contradict the provisions of Paragraph 1' shall be interpreted to mean acts in exercise of direct state authority over the Western Sectors of Berlin.

(b) Meetings of the Bundesversammlung will not take place and plenary sessions of the Bundesrat and the Bundestag will continue not to take place in the Western Sectors of Berlin. Single committees of the Bundesrat and the Bundestag may meet in the Western Sectors of Berlin in connection with maintaining and developing the ties between those Sectors and the Federal Republic of Germany. In the case of Fraktionen, meetings will not be held simultaneously.

(c) The liaison agency of the Federal Government in the Western Sectors of Berlin includes departments charged with liaison functions in their respective fields.

(d) Established procedures concerning the applicability to the Western Sectors of Berlin of legislation of the Federal Republic of Germany shall remain unchanged.

(e) The term 'state bodies' in Paragraph 2 of Annex II shall be interpreted to mean: the Federal President, the Federal Chancellor, the Federal Cabinet, the Federal Ministers and Ministries, and the branch offices of those Ministries, the Bundesrat and the Bundestag and all Federal courts.

(Formal close)

For the Government of the French Republic:

Jean Sauvagnargues

For the Government of the United Kingdom of Great Britain and Northern Ireland:

R. W. Jackling

For the Government of the United States of America:

Kenneth Rush

AGREED MINUTE I

Agreed Minute I

It is understood that permanent residents of the Western Sectors of Berlin shall, in order to receive at appropriate Soviet offices visas for entry into the Union of Soviet Socialist Republics, present:

(a) A passport stamped 'issued in accordance with the Quadripartite Agreement of September 3, 1971'.

(b) An identity card or other appropriately drawn up document confirming that the person requesting the visa is a permanent resident of the Western Sectors of Berlin and containing the bearer's full address and a personal photograph.

During his stay in the Union of Soviet Socialist Republics, a permanent resident of the Western Sectors of Berlin who has received a visa in this way may carry both documents or either of them as he chooses. The visa issued by a Soviet office will serve as the basis for entry into the Union of Soviet Socialist Republics, and the passport or identity card will serve as the basis for consular services in accordance with the Quadripartite Agreement during the stay of that person in the territory of the Union of Soviet Socialist Republics.

The above-mentioned stamp will appear in all passports used by permanent residents of the Western Sectors of Berlin for journeys to such countries as may require it.

Agreed Minute II

Provision is hereby made for the establishment of a Consulate General of the USSR in the Western Sectors of Berlin. It is understood that the details concerning this Consulate General will include the following:

The Consulate General will be accredited to the appropriate authorities of the three Governments in accordance with the usual procedures applying in those Sectors.

Applicable Allied and German legislation and regulations will apply to the Consulate General. The activities of the Consulate General will be of a consular character and will not include political functions or any matters related to quadripartite rights or responsibilities.

The three Governments are willing to authorize an increase in Soviet commercial activities in the Western Sectors of Berlin as described below. It is understood that pertinent Allied and German legislation and regulations will apply to these activities. This authorization will be extended indefinitely, subject to compliance with the provisions outlined herein. Adequate provision for consultation will be made. This increase will include establishment of an 'Office of Foreign Trade Associations in the Western Sectors of Berlin', with commercial status authorized to buy and sell on behalf of foreign trade associations of the Union of Soviet Socialist Republics. Soyuzpushnina, Prodintorg and Novoexport may each establish a bonded warehouse in the Western Sectors of Berlin to provide storage and display for their goods. The activities of the Intourist office in the British Sector of Berlin may be expanded to include the sale of tickets and vouchers for travel and tours in the Union of Soviet Socialist Republics and other countries. An office of Aeroflot may be established for the sale of passenger tickets and air freight services.

The assignment of personnel to the Consulate General and to permitted Soviet commercial organizations will be subject to agreement with the appropriate authorities of the three Governments. The number of such personnel will not exceed twenty Soviet nationals in the Consulate General; twenty in the office of the Soviet Foreign Trade Associations; one each in the bonded warehouses; six in the Intourist office; and five in the Aeroflot office. The personnel of the Soviet Consulate General and of permitted Soviet commercial organizations and their dependents may reside in the Western Sectors of Berlin upon individual authorization.

The property of the Union of Soviet Socialist Republics at Lietzenburgerstrasse 11 and at Am Sandwerder 1 may be used for purposes to be agreed between appropriate representatives of the three Governments and of the Government of the Union of Soviet Socialist Republics.

Details of implementation of the measures above and a time schedule for carrying them out will be agreed between the four Ambassadors in the period between the signature of the Quadripartite Agreement and the signature of the Final Quadripartite Protocol envisaged in that Agreement.

Letter of the Three Ambassadors to the Federal Chancellor

His Excellency
The Chancellor
of the Federal Republic of Germany,
Bonn

Your Excellency:

We have the honour by means of this letter to convey to the Government of the Federal Republic of Germany the text of the Quadripartite Agreement signed this day in Berlin. The Quadripartite Agreement was concluded by the Four Powers in the exercise of their rights and responsibilities with respect to Berlin.

We note that, pursuant to the terms of the Agreement and of the Final Quadripartite Protocol which ultimately will bring it into force, the text of which has been agreed, these rights and responsibilities are not affected and remain unchanged. Our Governments will continue, as heretofore, to exercise supreme authority in the Western Sectors of Berlin, within the framework of the Four Power responsibility which we share for Berlin as a whole.

In accordance with Part II (A) of the Quadripartite Agreement, arrangements implementing and supplementing the provisions relating to civilian traffic will be agreed by the competent German authorities. Part III of the Quadripartite Agreement provides that the Agreement will enter into force on a date to be specified in a Final Quadripartite Protocol which will be concluded when the arrangements envisaged between the competent German authorities have been agreed. It is the request of our Governments that the envisaged negotiations now take place between authorities of the Federal Republic of Germany, also acting on behalf of the Senat, and authorities of the German Democratic Republic.

Part II (B) and (D) and Annexes II and IV of the Quadripartite Agreement relate to the relationship between the Western Sectors of Berlin and the Federal Republic. In this connection, the following are recalled inter alia:

—the communications of the three Western Military Governors to the Parliamentary Council of 2 March, 22 April and 12 May, 1949,
—the letter of the three High Commissioners to the Federal Chancellor concerning the exercise of the reserved Allied rights relating to Berlin of 26 May 1952 in the version of the letter X of 23 October 1954,
—the Aide Memoire of the three Governments of 18 April 1967 concerning the decision of the Federal Constitutional Court of 20 January 1966 in the Niekisch case.

Our Governments take this occasion to state, in exercise of the rights and responsibilities relating to Berlin, which they retained in Article 2 of the Convention on Relations between the Three Powers and the Federal Republic of Germany of 26 May 1952 as amended October 23, 1954, that Part II (B) and (D) and Annexes II and IV of the Quadripartite Agreement concerning the relationship between the Federal Republic of Germany and the Western Sectors of Berlin accord with the position in the above mentioned documents, which remains unchanged.

With regard to the existing ties between the Federal Republic and the Western Sectors of Berlin, it is the firm intention of our Governments that, as stated in Part II (B) (1) of the Quadripartite Agreement, these ties will be maintained and developed in accordance with the letter from the three High Commissioners to the Federal Chancellor on the exercise of the reserved rights relating to Berlin of 26 May 1952, in the version of letter X of October 23, 1954, and with pertinent decisions of the Allied Kommandatura of Berlin.

(Formal close)

A SELECT BIBLIOGRAPHY

ACHESON, DEAN, *Power and Diplomacy*. Cambridge, Mass., and London 1958

ARON, RAYMOND, *On War; Atomic Weapons and Global Diplomacy*. London 1958

BRANT, STEFAN, *The East German Rising*. London 1958

BUCHAN, ALASTAIR, *N.A.T.O. in the 1960s*. London and New York 1960

BUCHAN, ALASTAIR and WINDSOR, PHILIP, *Arms and Stability in Europe*. London 1963

CALVOCORESSI, PETER, *World Politics since 1945*. London 1968

CHUIKOV, VASSILI, *The End of the Third Reich*. London 1967

CLAY, LUCIUS, *Decision in Germany*. New York 1950

DULLES, ELEANOR, *Berlin*. North Carolina 1967

FONTAINE, ANDRÉ, *A History of the Cold War*. London 1970

FORSTER, THOMAS, *The East German Army*. London 1967

GARTHOFF, RAYMOND, *Soviet Military Policy*. London 1966

HALLE, LOUIS, *The Cold War as History*. London 1967

HAYTER, WILLIAM, SIR, *Russia and the World*. London 1970

HEALEY, DENIS, *A Neutral Belt in Europe*. Dorking 1958

HUNTER, R., *Security in Europe*. London 1969

I.I.S.S., 'Military Balance 1971'. London 1972

KISSINGER, HENRY, *Nuclear Weapons and Foreign Policy*. New York and London 1967

LIDDELL HART, B. H., *History of the Second World War*. London 1970

NETTLE, J. P., *The Eastern Zone and Soviet Foreign Policy in Germany 1945–50*. London 1951

OSGOOD, ROBERT, *Limited War: The Challenge to American Strategy* Chicago and Cambridge 1957

— *NATO, the Entangling Alliance*. Chicago and London 1962

RICHARDSON, JAMES, *Germany and the Atlantic Alliance*. Harvard 1966

RYAN, CORNELIUS, *The Last Battle*. London 1966

SPAAK, HENRI, *Why NATO?* London 1959

TOLAND, JOHN, *The Last Hundred Days*. London 1968

WEYMAR, PAUL, *Konrad Adenauer*. London 1952

WILLIS, FRANK, *France, Germany and the New Europe*. Stamford 1968

WINDSOR, PHILIP, *City on Leave*. London 1965

INDEX OF PROPER NAMES

SUBJECT INDEX

Soviet Union—*contd.*
military strategy, 3, 11–12, 172, 197–8, 234, 239–40, 243; navy, 25, 55; relations with West, 48, 54, 69–70, 74–5, 82, 141–2, 180; sector of occupation, Berlin, 61–3, 78; zone of occupation, Germany, 56, 70, 138–9, 140, 143
Spoffard Plan, 179
Sputnik, 202
SS (*Schutzstaffel*), 9, 14, 23, 30, 61
Steel production: German, 70, 130; European, 163
Strategic Arms Limitati on Talks (Salt), 238, 244
Supreme Allied Commander, Europe (SACEUR), 190, 200, 228–229
Supreme Headquarters Allied Expeditionary Force (SHAEF), 13
Supreme Headquarters Allied Powers Europe (SHAPE), 223, 230

Tanks: Josef Stalin (Russian), 33; Panzer (German), 10; T34 (Russian), 10, 33
Teheran conference (1943), 13, 22, 42
Truman Doctrine, 79–80

Ukrainian campaign (1944), 11
United Kingdom: Conservative Party, 80; Commonwealth, 58–9; defence policy, 6–7, 18, 180; domestic affairs, 58, 72; foreign policy, 47–8, 58–9, 80, 137, 173–4, 189–90, 242; Labour administration (1945–51), 48, 58, 72; sector of occupation, Berlin, 78, 83–4; zone of occupation, Germany, 41, 64–5, 71
United Nations Organization (UNO), 52, 57, 94, 144–5, 210–211, 213, 233, 238; Charter of, 131; declaration of, 54; interven-tion in Korea, 166; Security Council, 167–8
United Nations Relief and Rehabilitation Agency (UNRRA), 54, 66
United States of America: air force, 5, 119; army, 168–9; domestic affairs, 52, 169, 213; foreign aid, 71–2, 79, 80–2; foreign policy, 39–40, 41, 51–4, 57, 131–2, 166–7, 174–175, 180, 187, 202, 220, 231, 238–9; military government, Germany, 40; military strategy, 7, 38, 43; navy, 168; 'New Left', 52–3; sector of occupation, Berlin, 78, 83–84; Senate, 80–1, 82, 131; State Department, 38, 43, 81, 169; Strategic Air Command, 172, 200, 201, 226; zone of occupation, Germany, 60, 65, 71
U–2 Incident, 209–10

Vandenberg Declaration (1948), 131–2
Versailles Treaty (1919), 47, 48–9
Volkspolizei (East German police), 183, 217
Volkssturm (German Home Guard), 30

Warsaw Pact (1955), 196–8, 232–3, 235–6, 240
Warsaw Uprising (1944), 22–5
Washington conference (1949), 131, 152, 160
Wehrmacht, 3, 8–9, 12, 14, 21–2, 26, 30
Weimar Republic, 124, 134, 155, 157
Western European Union (WEU), 190
Western Union (1948), 131

Yalta conference (1944), 40, 47, 56–57, 70
Yugoslavia, 6, 26; Resistance, 6, 26